Visualising Small Traumas
Contemporary Portuguese Comics at
the Intersection of Everyday Trauma

**STUDIES IN
EUROPEAN COMICS
AND GRAPHIC NOVELS**

Editorial board

Hugo Frey, Editor in Chief (University of Chichester)
Jan Baetens (KU Leuven)
Bart Beaty (University of Calgary)
Christopher Pizzino (University of Georgia)
Ann Miller (University of Leicester)

Visualising Small Traumas

Contemporary Portuguese Comics at the Intersection of Everyday Trauma

Pedro Moura

LEUVEN UNIVERSITY PRESS

© 2022 by Leuven University Press / Presses Universitaires de Louvain / Universitaire Pers Leuven
Minderbroedersstraat 4, B-3000 Leuven (Belgium)

All rights reserved. Except in those cases expressly determined by law, no part of this publication may be multiplied, saved in an automated data file or made public in any way whatsoever without the express prior written consent of the publishers.

ISBN 978 94 6270 303 2
e-ISBN 978 94 6166 419 8
D/2022/1869/6
https://doi.org/10.11116/9789461664198
NUR: 617

Layout: Frederik Danko
Cover design: Johan Van Looveren
Cover illustration: Marco Mendes, "Fontinha," originally published in *Buraco* issue 4 (2012), n. p.

Every effort has been made to contact all holders of the copyright to the visual material contained in this publication. Any copyrightholders who believe that illustrations have been reproduced without their knowledge are asked to contact the publisher.

During the completion of this book, João Paulo Cotrim, to whom I refer as a key figure in the Portuguese comics scene, sadly passed away.
I would like to humbly dedicate this work to this friend, who opened many doors, on many occasions.

"There is no quotidian life in contemporary societies of control that does not presuppose a form of microterror."

José Gil

Contents

Acknowledgments	9
Introduction: Going small to widen the scope	11
1. The semi-peripheral role of the Portuguese comics scene	23
2. A short history of trauma	71
3. Marco Mendes and the ever-temporary rebuilding of the self	93
4. Miguel Rocha and working through the acting out of history	119
5. Minor comics and atomised responses to small traumas	165
Conclusion	215
References	223

Acknowledgments

Any project such as this one can not be completed without the support and sometimes sacrifice of others. This was no exception. It demanded patience, abnegation, and a disinterested helping hand from too many people around me.

My first thanks goes, with unending admiration, to Jan Baetens, who has gone way beyond the call of duty and human levels of patience to put up with my project. His was the first book that made me realise, decades ago, that one could think about comics intellectually and engage with them in serious academic research. I hold the copy of the 1998 *Formes et politique de la bande dessinée* as the centrepiece of my library. His was an invisible hand helping in my Master's degree in Lisbon, back in 2007. And, finally officially, throughout the PhD project, his guidance and careful readings and lessons have been invaluable. I hope I don't do him a disservice to consider myself as his pupil for life.

The readability of the book you hold in your hands is only possible thanks to the keen eye and the unfathomable display of generosity of Ann Miller. English still has mysteries to me, and I am glad I had her as my guide. The fact that she is also one of the most internationally renowned, celebrated comics scholars just makes her encouragement a wonderful honour.

Do not doubt that if faults remain, and they do, they are but my own.

I would like to thank the artists that I have mentioned, quoted from and studied, many of which have helped in providing me with information, high resolution images or sending me additional material. Without their work, how could I have written this?

People whom I have come across during this path have been paramount in stimulating me to try aiming for the best I can do. The Comic Studies community is incredibly diverse and altruistic with their time and knowledge. The Comix Scholars List has always been, even if with bumps, a safe and fun haven to exchange ideas and discover new dimensions in an often incredibly cordial environment.

Mihaela Precup was a very strong influence on my budding scholarship, as we have met in a moment of my academic infancy. Her generosity and openness towards her own work put me in contact with a broader world of research and questioning. Miriam Sampaio is an outstanding artist whose life ethics and passion for knowledge were a revolution for me. If I am a little more familiar with what "trauma" may mean, it's thanks to her.

Fernanda Gil Costa, from FLUL, was paramount in my integration within the world of the Lisbon University, and a vivid dialogue with other disciplinary routes. I would also like to thank Ângela Fernandes for her helping guidance in the last leg of the path in Lisbon. The team from Leuven University Press, whose patience I have taxed immensely (a recurrent theme) deserve a big thank you for making the waters calmer for me. Some of the information I have used on the contemporary state of comics in Portugal was provisioned liberally by Nuno Pereira de Sousa, Marcos Farrajota, and Mário Freitas, all of them extremely active agents of the comics scene in Portugal, in very different roles and capacities.

Just talking in person to Pascal Lefèvre, Hugo Frey, Gert Meesters, Maaheen Ahmed, Simon Grennan, and Conceição Pereira has always been an eye-opener and a lesson in itself. Throughout my little career within the world of comics, I have met many of the people that I admired for years, and I am continually baffled by their incredible kindness and humbleness when sharing their thoughts with an overtly anxious person such as myself. I will always be in debt to Geraldes Lino, who was always available for yet another phone call with complicated questions and always ready with the right answer. His passing still hurts. More or less informal talks with people like Domingos Isabelinho, Sara Figueiredo Costa, Renaud Chavanne, Ilan Manouach, Rik Spanjers and the wonderful David Kunzle have provided me with incredible stepping stones.

The time I have spent in Leuven was not only fruitful in terms of academic work, but also in other dimensions. Sharing an office with Júlio Landim was engaging, and resulted in great talks, as well as outstanding food experiences.

There are not enough words to express the gratitude I have for the Peeters family. While I was in Leuven and Kessel-Lo, they opened their doors to a complete stranger who happened to study comics. This was not only an incredible act of kindness, but also the providing of a marvelous, soothing and fun environment for the awkwardness of staying, for a while, away from home. To discover, in fact, a second home. For the ceiling, great talks and wine, and for helping me cross and be able to say "Bondgenotenlaan", a big *dankjewel* to Patrick, Chris, Charlotte and Beetle.

Benoît Crucifix was paramount in many moments. I am very fortunate to count him as an academic confidante and a friend. An attentive reader and critic, an incredibly talented and intelligent *compagnon de route*, I'm indebted to him for many shared readings, second opinions, and calls to Earth. *Merci à toi.*

Of course, in such a bright constellation of friends and supporters, some stars burn brighter: for putting up with me for life, and making all of this possible, Yunseon, Juno and Ari are the stars I call home.

Introduction:
Going small to widen the scope

The present book has, first and foremost, a theoretical-conceptual interest in trauma theory. By engaging in this field through the subject of comics, I hope to inquire about its limitations and open up the possibility of entering into a dialogue with some objects that have received insufficient critical attention. As an inflecting focus, the book will ground itself in a specific national context, namely, the contemporary, independent Portuguese comics circle, from a production and publication point of view. It is not my goal to study reception, which would warrant different groundwork. I hope that by addressing each of these objects - trauma studies, comics studies and the specific corpus covered by this book - we can better understand them. Ultimately, by looking at a different type of comics production, one that is underanalysed in my view, I may help to increase understanding of it, and assess its political agency.

I could sum up the work that follows in the form of a few questions. First of all, what can we draw from trauma studies, as it has been used to think about literature, cinema and other arts, in order to consider comics production? Over the period of research for this book, recent trauma theory has invested significantly in the comics field (e.g., Refaie 2013, Chute 2016, Earle 2017). I hope to contribute further to that effort. Second, how can the consideration of comics and comics studies contribute to a different understanding of trauma studies? The two following questions narrow the case studies but also help to consolidate my goals. What happens when instead of considering "big traumas" we look into "small traumas"? And lastly, how does looking at one specific national context helps us in pursuing such a goal and in thinking about different, wider, contexts?

Chapter two will exclusively discuss trauma theory and expound what I will call "small traumas". For this, I will follow a number of theoreticians who have developed a critique of earlier instances of Trauma Theory (Caruth 1995 and 1996) through the lenses of feminism and post-colonial studies (Hartman 1995, Tal 1996, Radstone 2005 and 2007, Ball 2007, Craps 2013). These critiques have reconsidered the kinds of subjects and situations that are amenable to trauma, avoiding the creation of hierarchies among traumas as well as the conflation of different political and social realities. Although these critiques do not concern themselves with comics, I believe it to be a medium that presents many instances of subjects and situations closer to the dimensions that they address, which, moreover, alter the very nature (and even the notion) of the relationship between "event" and "subject", "external" and "internal agency", and so on. As Pheng Cheah puts it:

> We should therefore understand trauma as a form of radical heteronomy where the trace or mnemic residue of something that originates from outside the subject (the accident or physical injury) takes shape within the very inside of the subject as an alterity or otherness, an alien power that undermines its self-control. (2008: 193)

More often than not, and unsurprisingly, this area is filled with controversies, vexed questions, problematic expansions and inclusions and sometimes incompatible positions. My contribution here will be less about trauma theory itself, than an attempt to understand how the tools that have been developed within it can be used in relation to often overlooked realities and experiences, and how that may enrich our comprehension of the pervasiveness of traumatogenic conditions. I would like to make mine Luckhurst's words when he writes, "[r]ather than offer another invested polemic, I propose we need to begin by unraveling the complex elements that have been knotted into the notion of trauma" (Luckhurst 2008: 15). We cannot fall into the error of thinking that we are already familiar with "which events, experiences and texts are to be classed as traumatic and which are to be excluded from this category" (Radstone 2007: 24). We cannot turn "trauma" into a predetermined category with necessary and sufficient conditions, which we would try to identify, so that we would then apply or deny them in relation to a given situation. We cannot create a hierarchy of comparisons or degrees of entitlement to trauma, or worse yet, weigh up one trauma (one kind, one nature, one history) against another. As Susannah Radstone, a linchpin for the present book, puts it clearly, trauma theory needs "to act as a check against, rather than a vehicle of the Manichean tendencies currently dominant within western politics and culture" (2007: 26). Like any other "textual figuration", comics may thus provide the reader with "an experience that parallels (without being equivalent to)" (Walker 2005: 110) that of the characters. In other words, they provide us with a vicarious experience that when considered, read, sensed, no matter how "little" the traumas addressed may be, will help us in seeking ways of being empathetically open to other people's experience so that we may, in turn, according to Ann Kaplan, "generate beneficial empathy for the sufferings of peoples far removed from one's own communities" (2005: 88).

   This does not mean that readers will *identify* themselves with the other. Being an art form, comics "expands the sympathetic imagination while teaching us about the limits of sympathy" (apud Bennett 2005: 9). Such limits are assured by what Dominick Lacapra calls *empathic unsettlement*, a term he uses "to describe the aesthetic experience of simultaneously *feeling for* another and becoming aware of a distinction between one's own perceptions and the experience of the other" (Bennett 2005: 8). Moreover, by looking at apparently less than overwhelming situations, sometimes even banal ones, we may uncover a disturbing silence and invisibility that is bestowed upon them and that prevents us from considering them at all.

A number of events are often treated in the comics medium with more or less repeated formulas and structures that trigger immediate attention to the detriment of other subjects, speakers and events. *Prêt-a-porter* "themes", as it were, that lead to "numbing effects of repeated exposure to mediated traumatic material and the aesthetics of shock" (Luckhurst 2008: 89). With the notion of "small traumas", I aim to shift the attention, not with the intention of reducing the importance of certain events or experiences, and even less so of debasing them, but in order simply to pay attention to pervasive problems in (in this case) Portuguese society as they are exposed, discussed, negotiated in the comics medium. If some authors may point out that using trauma in such a way, in the absence of so-called "real" trauma, is nothing but the expression of a generation deep in a crisis of form and language, or worse, bad faith and fetishism (Giglioli 2011), we can also look at it in a more positive light. Not by creating hierarchies based on the right to speak about or address trauma, but rather by understanding the reasons for the "pervasiveness of trauma but also the reiteration of traumatic subjectivity in different kinds of register" (Luckhurst 2008: 15), especially when dealing with a medium so closely associated with popular culture. Instead of looking for the overwhelming, dramatic and spectacular "event" that would constitute the traumatic subject, we should be attentive to ongoing, daily conditions, "a continuing background noise rather than an unusual event" (Brown 1995: 102-103), which undermine the seemingly untraumatised subjects into actors who may address trauma in their work.

As Paul Antze and Michal Lambek write in their preface to *Tense Past*: "[t]oday's fragmented subjects are not unrelated to the complexities of transnational links, cultural pluralism, and the weakening of the state" (1996: xxii). Facing those complexities, and thinking of them in the light of the small trauma, we see new subjectivities emerging within these texts, which help to "narratively reconvene the self" (Luckhurst 2008: 119).

Luckhurst continues:

> the passage through trauma often works here not to undermine but rather to *guarantee* subjectivity (...) [autobiography is] less and exercise in self-revelation than an act of coerced fashioning of selves (2008: 119, 120).

As should be clear, I am not going solely to discuss comics autobiographies, and even less so the authors themselves, of course, but rather the texts. Although it is possible to address comics as an indexical medium, as is the case of Philippe Marion's graphiation theory, we will not follow that path. Comics are a mode of expression that goes through a number of necessary structuring processes, an active and conscious operation with materials, which employs methods that, by their sheer existence, are a sign of activity. Comics are part and parcel of artistic expression of modern humanity. As such, they participate in the artefactuality and social agency of other disciplines. Comics may not only reflect the principles of a certain society, they may also act upon them and propose alternative configurations. With Alfred Gell, we can consider them as "created objects", and therefore, "as agents as prompting a cognitive operation that implies agency - they are understood both as the outcome and as an instrument of social agency" (apud Feuchtwang 2003: 87).

As a historically and socially determined cultural and aesthetic production, comics are both guided by the strong personality and creativity of individuated authors and fully integrated in specific economic, technological and political conditions, which include both the conditions of production and of reception. They are, then, as able to respond to the world as any other human endeavour. They contribute, either through imaginative fiction or critical assessment, to the discussion and rethinking of a given society's mores and politics. Moreover, and especially, they very often provide storyworlds that may help us to imagine alternative spaces, identities and practices (Fawaz 2016). There is no such thing as a homogenous body of comics. Comics are multiple, varied, come in many shapes, present a multitude of genres, styles and approaches. They may be entertaining and fun, but also politically demanding and intellectually engaging. Sometimes, they are all that at the same time. In the absence of a singular concept uniting every single object that anyone has ever called comics, we should keep an open mind to the way comics may respond to certain issues, including to the very conditions that may lead to traumatogenic situations in the contemporary world.

This may help us go beyond a certain canonicity. Quite often, and also in the discussion of comics in trauma studies-related texts, there seems to be an already established *corpora* of certain kinds of comics as objects of study, such as Spiegelman's *Maus* or *In The Shadow of No Towers*, Marjane Satrapi's *Persepolis* or Alison Bechdel's *Fun Home*. The use of these examples over and over again seems to confirm a bias towards a certain class of comics to the detriment of others. An example of this is Marianne Hirsch's discussion of Spiegelman's *In The Shadow of No Towers* (2004), which she considers as "an attempt to see beyond the [Lacanian-Silverman] given-to-be-seen and to say what cannot otherwise be said" (1215). To a certain extent, it seems that only comics that follow the tenet of the unrepresentability of trauma - that is to say, the impossibility of considering representative signs (drawings, texts, schemata) as able to transmit the experience they relate to the readers-spectators - are amenable to be addressed by the discourse of trauma. As I hope to show, by considering other sorts of productions and by shifting the focus of trauma theory, we can also expand the practice of democratizing political representation. Hillary Chute, in her most recent book, *Disaster Drawn*, discusses how comics is a powerful medium "precisely in how it intervenes against the trauma-driven discourse of the unrepresentable and the ineffable" (2016: 178).

As with any other type of work of art, the comics texts with which I will engage have to be interpreted within a framework that is sensitive. One cannot read too little or too much into them. One is reminded of Umberto Eco's "limits of interpretation" (1994) that allow for a focus on what he calls "the intention of the text". "A text is a device conceived in order to produce its own Model Reader", he writes (1994: 58). The Model Reader may have multiple interpretations of the same text, but cannot base them on the purported intentions of the empirical author or on an ultimate agenda of the Reader's own. Everything must be grounded in the text itself. Therefore, I will not use author's interviews except when necessary to explain working or publication conditions. Again, as mentioned before, I am not studying the reception of the texts.

Nevertheless, in order not to read *too little*, I believe that a description of the circumstances in which the works appeared is needed. I will start, then, with a historical and social-economic contextualisation of the texts in order to ground them as much as possible. When I read any given text, I will be doing so in a specific circumstantial framework, using specific instruments, approaches, methods that might be different in another framework, or even another moment. Each chapter will deal with very different genres and formats. In an academic setting, with a transdisciplinary approach, the danger of impermanent readings is particularly strong. That is not, however, a weakness in the reading itself: it is an intrinsic part of it. As J. Hillis Miller wrote:

> The poem, like all texts, is "unreadable" if by "readable" one means open to a single, definitive, univocal interpretation. In fact, neither the "obvious" reading nor the "deconstructionist" reading is "univocal". Each contains, necessarily, its enemy within itself, is itself both host and parasite (Miller 1977: 447).

On the other hand, is it possible to read too much into a work of art? After all, there are always excesses of meaning that emerge from that which is not said, that which lies beyond what is given to be seen. It is precisely because there are so many "unsaids" that meaning becomes animated beyond what is present in the visibility of representation or plot. Here, I am following an idea by Laura U. Marks:

> We may feel this sense of excess in conversation when we become aware that what we are saying has a sense that exceeds it (as in, the sense of "Will you pass

the salt?" is "I'm leaving you"). Similarly, a work of art is rich in sense if it cannot be contained in a description (Marks 2002: xv).

Hopefully, I will pursue the parasite within, the excessive mark that piles up upon the meaning. As H. J. Miller continues, "the parasite is always already present within the host, the enemy always already within the house, the ring always an open chain" (Miller 1977: 446). This image of the ring is quite appropriate: the excesses of meaning are open always to temporary, non-univocal readings, always revealing new meanings (hidden, excessive) that would invite new interpretive efforts, and so on.

Comics have a very specific way of dealing with human experience, and engage the readers in very specific ways (Groensteen 1999; Kukkonen 2013), allowing for a multitude of treatments and cultural conversations (Miller 2007, Berninger et al. 2010). Despite the long history of attempts to promote serious discourses about comics (Huard 1998-1999, Miller-Beaty 2014, Jeet-Worcester 2009), the very recent emergence of an academically integrated and disciplinarily articulated area such as comics studies has brought about more attention and openness towards looking at comics as an available territory that is as creative as any other. Nevertheless, I do not wish to create any sort of absolute hierarchy between this form of art and any other, in an attempt to present comics as a "better" or "more suitable" form to address trauma. Hillary Chute believes that "the cross-discursive form of comics is apt for expressing [the] difficult register [of trauma]" (2010: 2) and likewise Erin La Cour, although specifically discussing comics "life narratives", explains how

> the graphic novel's modes of visual representation of personal experience are distinctly able to comment on the discourse of truth and trauma in personal narrative in that they reveal how memory is negotiated by both sight and feeling (2010: 46-47).

I agree with both Chute and La Cour in these assessments but would add that the negotiation of memory also takes place in other types of comics, including fiction, fantasy and genre comics. More than creating predetermined hierarchies following genres, styles, formats or any other descriptor in order to decide which kinds of comics warrant critical attention or, worse, are able to address certain subjects, one should celebrate the medium itself for its artistic integrity, cultural relevance, and political agency, zeroing in on each text in particular in an attempt to understand *how* and *how far* such integrity, relevance and agency is achieved. But before addressing the *types of comics* I will include in my analysis, a brief word about its national scope.

In contrast with more established centres of comics production, such as France and Belgium, the United States or Japan, Portugal is a slower, smaller and less sure market. One could even say that comics in Portugal, despite its long, rich and varied history, is "ephemeral", considering the lack of instruments that would uphold

Introduction: Going small to widen the scope

its history and memory. Famously, Groensteen described comics as "art without memory" (2006). But this description has been put to the test over the last ten years. First of all, the "central" comics hubs have been putting out numerous archival editions of historical material, sometimes even with what one could call critical apparatuses. Second, academic endeavours have grown massively (conferences, international colloquiums, graduate courses and syllabi, papers, specialised journals, etc.). And overall, the cultural traction of comics has undoubtedly been increased across many areas, from book clubs to film adaptations, art galleries and literary festivals.

But within Portugal it is precisely because comics is not a sure-fire industry that many comics artists work in more alternative venues. To be clear, there *are* more commercial, generic types of comics being produced in Portugal, but the scope of this book will focus instead on small press, fanzines, and alternative takes on comics. Moreover, those are the types of comics that also try to address in a more direct, sometimes even confrontational manner, issues such as historical memory, the pervasiveness of the ideologies of democratic capitalism and economic liberalism, thus associating themselves with the "small traumas" that emerge within societies of this type. The first chapter, therefore, creates both a historical and a social-economic context for comics production within contemporary Portugal.

The following three chapters will present close readings of the case studies I have selected, and which are very different in nature from one another. Chapters three and four use the work of individual artists, even if working in collaboration. Marco Mendes, the subject of chapter three, creates mostly autobiographical comics, but quite often integrates fantasy and absurd or surreal scenes in his work. A poet of a stark and melancholy quotidian, Mendes creates short stories - all subsumed to an ongoing project called *Diário Rasgado* ("Torn Journal"[1]) - that act as a reflecting mirror of a whole generation's feeling that the political and economic situation in Portugal is stagnant. A crisis that does not lead to fervent responses but rather to a dispassionate inability to react, and the expression of what Sianne Ngai calls "ugly feelings" (2005).

Given the proximity to autobiographical comics, Mendes's work would be the closest to the usual objects that are dealt with when discussing trauma and comics, even though the creative way *Diário Rasgado* enmeshes memory with fantasy brings it closer still to what Janet Walker calls the "traumatic paradox". Walker explains that:

> while a traumatic experience can produce either veracious memories or a trail of symptoms connecting an event with its psychic manifestation, it can also, especially when repeated over time, as in the case of incest, trigger fantasies, repression, misperceptions, and interpretations created by the real events but not realistically representative of them (2005: 7).

Whereas *Diário Rasgado* does not involve situations as overwhelming as incest or the Holocaust (Walker's subjects in relation to cinema), it nevertheless follows memory's "inherent vicissitudes" (Walker 2006: 107), making it, in Hayden White's phrase, "unrepresentable *in the realist mode*" (apud Walker 2005: 21, emphasis in the original).

Miguel Rocha, the key author of chapter four, with a solo work (*As pombinhas do Senhor Leitão*) and a collaborative project (*Salazar*), brings in another dimension. The first book is a fictional account set in 1920-30s Portugal and the second one a more or less distorted biography of Portugal's dictator António de Oliveira Salazar. In both cases, we have comics that deal with history, contributing to, according to Karin Kukkonen, "popular cultural memory", in which

> three dimensions of culture come together: the social dimension of the audience as its carriers, the material dimension of media texts and the mental dimension of codes and convention that facilitate the reading process (2008: 261-262).

These books not only act out, as it were, these historical landscapes, they also force us to rethink our attitude towards history, and many of the fantasies we may have with "what if?" scenarios. By re-creating quotidian stories with either historically negligible characters (the mute young woman of *Pombinhas*) or central actors of historical forces (Salazar himself), we pose the question, "what would I do if I was in such and such a situation?" but we are ultimately denied any agency over the events. This forces us to consider history as something that is both set and fluid, or better still, that has to be negotiated on an individual scale, instead of falling back on predetermined roles and "right" attitudes. As Fritz Breithaupt maintains in an article about the origins of the notion of trauma,

> the starting point of pedagogy and psychology alike is that the past shapes the identity of an individual. However, what psychology adds to pedagogy is that the past shaping of the individual can be reversed by certain acts of recollection. (...) The self as such is the product of the operation of the psychological, the correction of memory, the archival act (Breithaupt 2005: 93).

Comics, when working against the grain of historical discourses, by creating fictive layers on top of historical factors or realities, offers its readers a new archive with which to reconsider their role in relation to the past and new empathy tools with which to understand, but not solve, traumatic situations. As Stephan Feuchtwang writes:

> A reader brings to a book empathy, with the named subject of the book or with the creative skill and imagination of the author; both are mobilised in the play of recognition (Feuchtwang 2003: 81).

Therefore, it is paramount that we do not buy into a facile notion of character identification, such as the one proposed by Scott McCloud (1993), and followed unquestionably by so many authors. So-called character identification is in fact a dangerous way of bypassing empathy, as argued by Dominick LaCapra:

> Objectivity requires *checks and resistances to full identification*, and this is one important function of meticulous research, contextualization, and the attempt to be as attentive as possible to the voices of others whose alterity is recognised. Empathy in this sense is a form of virtual, not vicarious, experience related to what Kaja Silverman has termed *heteropathic identification*, in which emotional response comes with respect for the other and the realisation that the experience of the other is not one's own (2011: 40; my italics).

Heteropathic identification is describable as "a form of encounter predicated on an openness to a mode of existence or experience beyond what is known by the self" (Bennett 2005: 9). Therefore, there is never confusion between the reader's and the character's experience (whether fictional or autobiographical, but especially in the case of a sufferer or victim character), and this is the caveat that should prevent us from abuses of psychoanalytical readings of works of art as paths towards their authors' lives. Even accepting the "radical insight of psychoanalysis" of an "otherness within" (Radstone and Hodgkin 2003: 91), we must bear in mind that "the goal of recounting the trauma story is integration, not exorcism" (Judith Lewis Herman, apud Leys 1996: 123). In any case, this is one of the reasons why it must constantly be underlined that we are analysing works of art and not people, lest we fall into categorical mistakes and interpretive abuse (Baetens 2001: 153 and ff.).

The fact that we will be dealing with a certain class of comics has to do both with the chosen national context and time frame, but it stems also from the very quality of comics being produced in Portugal. This does not mean, however, that I am unaware of the possibilities of engaging with other sorts of comics under the same theoretical frameworks. For instance, Martyn Pedler goes as far, when discussing North American monthly comics books, especially of the super-hero variety, with their repetitive cliffhangers and endless crises, as to find in them a perfect ground for the exploration of trauma. "When this monthly doom meets the blueprint or repetition and excess", he writes, "it makes ongoing trauma into a structural necessity" (n.d.: 3). Pedler's discussion about the way that contemporary readers and fans have access to any character's full backstory (via trade paperbacks of entire runs, online wikis, and so on) is quite riveting and radically changes considerations of the seriality of Superman or James Bond-type narratives, that still follow some of the central notions of Umberto Eco's famous essay on them and their temporal mechanisms. Pedler considers that this "hyperconsciousness" or "mass-memory transforms the nature of the ongoing superhero narrative" (Idem: 6). In Mendes' case, which involves a serialised comic to a certain extent, we could see some of the possibilities of this "structural necessity" in trauma, but the nature of the narratives is very, very different, and the traumas that are dealt with are, once again, less overwhelming, less spectacular.

That is why the last chapter will deal with a very different class of comics works. On the one hand, I want to include comics that have not been published in more traditional book formats but rather have appeared in as diverse vehicles as anthologies, fanzines, one-shot booklets or even as art-objects. And on the other hand, I want to consider work that may be considered experimental. I believe that there is a strong heuristic value of studying such objects within this context, and which will help expand the kinds of material one may consider when thinking about trauma-themed comics.

One of the tenets of trauma theory is the compulsion to repetition. In her decisive introduction to *Trauma, Explorations in Memory*, Caruth explains how trauma:

> cannot be defined either by the event itself - which may or may not be catastrophic, and may not traumatize everyone equally - nor can it be defined in terms of a *distortion* of the event, achieving its haunting power as result of distorting personal significances attached to it. The pathology consists, rather, solely in the *structure of its experience* or reception: the event is not assimilated or experienced fully at the time, but only belatedly, in its repressed *possession* of the one who experiences it. To be traumatized is precisely to be possessed by an image or event. (1995: 4).

The image or event that possesses the traumatised person haunts him or her, by reappearing repeatedly in an unsolved enigma. These recurrences may take the form of gaps or intervals in an ongoing narrative.

If we go back to considering the very structures of comics, we can understand how often writers may look at the intervals between the panels (usually called "gutters") as something that can make visible their very own gaps in memory, the forgetfulness involved in remembering, and that can underline "the subjectivity of personal experience and the disjointedness of memory" (La Cour 2010: 47). In this sense, La Cour is following Scott McCloud, Hilary Chute and others in her equation of panels and time. But I feel that this is a reification of the gutters beyond their arthological role (Groensteen 1999). To equate the apparently fragmentary nature of comics with a "never fully-remembered story" seems to reinforce the idea that comics is better suited for the impossibility of reinstating a full-fledged narrative than any other medium. But I believe it is possible to look at the fragmentary nature of comics, that is to say, the visible integration of the intervals in the very visual matter of its telling, as a "force of repetition", to employ an expression of Judith Butler's, so that, instead of being a source only of "a destructive repetition compulsion" brought about by trauma it can be seen also as "the very condition of an affirmative response" to that same trauma (Butler 1993: 83-84). Instead of considering the intervals as gaps that would stand for the unrepresentability of the event and of the experience, which is the keystone of trauma theory, we can consider it as the actual space of negotiation and suture that come about with the very act of re-telling, re-creating, re-addressing that same experience. Fritz Breithaupt goes even farther when he characterises "repetition as the place where the self becomes itself" (Breithaupt 2005: 96).

But trauma may arise within comics not in the gaps but the visible panels. In *Désoeuvré* (2005), the French author Lewis Trondheim produces a complex essay about comics creation. Using the first person and drawing from conversations and the experiences of a multitude of other artists, Trondheim aims to understand "le problème du viellissement de l'auteur de bande dessinée" (the problem of ageing for the comics artist), creating a rather bleak sociological cross-section of the medium (at least, within France), but at the same time proposing new aesthetic and political paths for comics, such as this very interrogative gesture. Through the examples of Moebius, Fred, Franquin, Tibet, Gotlib and some of his L'Association colleagues, Trondheim tackles issues such as depression, lack of will, numbness and the sheer pain that overwhelms many artists due to the fact that they have to draw the same things over and over again, panel after panel, following the same page composition, the same narrative structures, the principle of the series, and so on, years on end. It is the repetition of the same, not the gaps, that brings about traumatic consequences. It is repetition of the self that destroys the self, to re-use Breithaupt's sentence.

It is the medium of comics that acts in such a way, and not solely one type of comics production. However, the final chapter will assemble as its particular corpus a number of comics that fall outside the purvey of either the "graphic novel" phenomenon or mainstream serialised forms. This arises out of the fact that comics production in Portugal follows quite different models and possibilities, but it is also an attempt to contribute to a widening of the attention of comics studies to allow for the inclusion of many sorts of comics, and to call into question a quite often unchallenged canon (of works, authors, genres, styles, but also languages, nationalities, economic prowess, and so on). In fact, I will not engage with a undisputed distinction between *graphic novels* and *comics* that could, arguably, be debated on the basis of social or business-commercial terms, for instances, or some narrow formal differentiation, or perhaps length-wise considerations about purported oppositions between "seriousness", "gravitas" and "levity" (see Baetens 2010, Baetens-Frey 2014).

Chapter five, then, will discuss a number of short stories found in anthologies, fanzine material, and even experimental gallery-based comics. For this, I will engage with the notion of "minority" as discussed by Deleuze and Guattari in *Kafka* (2003), in order to understand the different expressive and political paths followed by these works in relation to the previous authors in their books. The political dimension of this sort of production, as it relates to the very democratisation or critique of trauma theory, will gain a new inflection thanks to a dialogue with Jacques Rancière's particular notion of "politics" (2004 and 2010).

We come across many texts, either journalistic or academic, speaking about the "possibilities" that comics has of delving into a number of content matters, stylistic approaches and its use within disciplinary, cultural, aesthetic and political contexts. But the truth is that after more than a century and a half of production in dozens of fully-fledged, more or less independent traditions, those possibilities are not virtual but actual. If this book casts a constricted net where space and time are concerned – contemporary Portugal – it nonetheless aims at a wider consideration of form and expressive approaches. And by interrogating that production with the tools and conceptual frameworks afforded by trauma studies, assisted by many other disciplinary sources, it may discern fashions of identifying, negotiating, dialoguing and perhaps even responding critically and overcoming those "traumatogenic effects of oppression that are not necessarily overtly violent or threatening to bodily well-being at the given moment but that do violence to the soul and spirit" (Brown 1997: 107).

And if the structure of the argument of this book seems to advance by short bursts of theoretical contextualisation, then to go back to historical background and conditions of production, finally to close readings of specific texts, and then back again to a consideration of theoretical or contextual dimensions, that happens precisely in a way that mimics the lack of order of the opening questions. Or the circular relationship between comics and how they may help us to better understand certain conditions and responses to trauma, and how traumatogenic situations and consequences may be expressed by comics. But this should come as no surprise, since after all, as Roger Luckhurst puts it: "No narrative of trauma can be told in a linear way: it has a time signature that must fracture conventional causality" (Luckhurst, 2008: 9).

Notes

1 All translations are by the author unless otherwise indicated.

Chapter 1

The semi-peripheral role of the Portuguese comics scene

Comics come in many sizes, formats and types. From personally traded fanzines to graphic novels integrated into national education programmes, from riso-printed minicomics sold in concerts to works presented in art galleries, from obscure books that are hard to hunt down to *tankonbon* printed in seven-figure print runs with inter-medial merchandising, all comics are, at the bare minimum, particular texts that are part of more complex constellations, "parts of continually reconfigured media networks or dynamic cultural series" (Baetens-Surdiacourt: 348-349).

Despite the exponential and fantastic growth of comics studies within the last few years, there are still many national traditions that are relatively unknown outside their national borders.[1] Although there are some efforts to produce resources to create a *translational* space for comics, via monographs (e.g. José Alaniz's *Komiks: Comic Art in Russia* or Fredrik Strömberg's *Swedish Comics History*), specific articles on countries (such as the ones regularly produced by a team of scholars for *IJOCA*) or comics anthologies translated into languages with wider access such as English or French (like Hard Comic's anthology of Romanian comics, *The Book of George,* Top Shelf's two-volume *From the Shadow of Northern Lights*, etc.), the notion prevails that some countries are *central* in comics production (typically, France-Belgium, Japan, and the U.S.), in relation to which all other countries are somewhat *peripheral*. It comes as no surprise then, that the presence of peripheral traditions of comics on more central stages only happens once in a while and, when it does, either they may be presented as either odd, exotic material, or a number of texts will be presented together as if they shared some sort of kinship beyond the fact of being produced in the same country.

Let us take the example precisely of Portuguese comics. We may find small press publications or festival catalogues that focus on a particular country, so that when Portugal was the guest country at Angoulême in 1998, a catalogue was published, *Perdidos no Oceano.* That same year, Amok's *Le cheval sans tête* no. 5 included Portuguese authors in a thematic issue; a few years before, Alain Corbel had coor-

Chapter One

dinated two projects with a few Portuguese authors, *Pelume Amére* (L'encre du polvo, 1994) and *Porto Luna* (Amok, 1995), and later on, the same kind of project took place in the Swiss magazine *Strapazin* no. 70 (2003). These examples all differed widely, as the Angoulême catalogue reflected the interests of Portuguese commercial publishers, necessarily and correctly, while all the others had stricter aesthetic agendas and/or were born out of personal relationships between authors (Corbel lived in Lisbon, Filipe Abranches shared a studio with Vincent Fortemps in Brussels for a while, etc.). However, not all these efforts endured over time. They did not succeed in opening the Francophone market up to the possibility of translating and publishing Portuguese comics, and neither did they became integrated in a differentiated way into general assessments (see Gaumer 2002: 152-161, Beaty 2008: 126 ff.)[2].

However, what does that "peripheral nature" reveal? Does it mean that comics productions from these other countries are to some extent derivative of those from the self-appointed centres? Does it mean that there is a lack of sophistication or aesthetic value (however we consider such words) that prevents them from becoming integrated into a wider market? Surely, if there is room for artists such as Jason and Rutu Modan, Arne Bellstorf and Ulli Lust, Fábio Moon and Gabriel Bá, Lorenzo Mattotti and Gabriella Giandelli on the global comics stage, then this must mean that that market is actually willing to translate good comics from peripheral traditions. So if something is *not* available, then it must lack the necessary qualities, surely? Unfortunately, as has gradually been acknowledged lately, considerations of the "global" or even "European" comics field have lead to the creation of an erroneous view that any less known traditions constitute "more or less imperfect variations of that idealised [the Franco-Belgium *bande dessinée*, especially] model" (Baetens-Surdiacourt, 347).

It is almost impossible to consider Portuguese comics without referring back to certain models, or central poles of production, which, as such, will be seen as the reference to which everything else is compared. That centre thus becomes the *metropolis* for its related peripheries. That is how certain productions will surface as necessarily having an "exotic tinge", "cultural specificities", and so on. The characteristics of the Portuguese comics market, defined by deficient production of both translated and new domestic titles, but a strong culture of small press and community networks, have led to a wide distribution or knowledge, by comics readers, of the most varied traditions of comics, namely French, Belgian, North American, Japanese, but also Italian, Spanish, German, Finnish, British, and so on. In fact, most Portuguese comics authors are quite knowledgeable about the worldwide production of comics, and it is somewhat difficult to pin down any single artist to a specific influence, seldom understood as constrained to a single author, language, country, genre or style. Without referring, of course, to influences from other realms of creativity, considering that some of the comics authors we will consider are also accomplished in the visual or performance arts, animation or music.

But the problem lies in the fact that broad presentations aim at finding a common trait across *all* Portuguese comics (this also happens in relation to any other sort of cultural or medium-specific production, from cinema to music) and will present them under that aegis. Contemporary touristic or official discourses, even though historically anchored in slightly different socio-political values such as democracy, secularism and multiculturalism, will sometimes revert to guiding principles that are inherited from the old regime, which subsisted for 48 years, from 1926 to 1974. "Though the political programme of the 'Estado Novo' may have become obsolete", write Mário Gomes and Jan Peuckert, "the symbols of national identity propagated for decades still subsist". (2010: 117). In this short article on comics artist Miguel Rocha, whom we will study later, the two authors analyse with precision the use of cultural clichés (their word) such as the feeling of *saudade*, melancholy, and the trilogy "Fátima, futebol, fado"[3] in order to understand how some contemporary comics authors negotiate such symbols, such heritage, through "aesthetic challenges", an "artistic task" of repurposing such symbolism.

The article presents a fascinating close reading of Rocha's books, and I will come back to it. For now, I wish to focus on Gomes and Peuckert's broader assertions, with which I do not, however, agree. When they write that "there seems to be no such thing one could label a 'Portuguese comic tradition'" (117), the authors present a two-fold reason. First, the lack of a specific Portuguese word for this art form, against the Spanish "tebeos" and the Italian "fumetti", which would "stand as signposts for a national tradition", and second the fact that it "has neither brought up any popular comic figures nor recognised comic artists" (idem). Now, each of these reasons deserves to be considered separately, if briefly, and I will do that presently. But considering that in the subsequent paragraphs the authors condense the history of comics in Portugal into a two-period structure - during the Estado Novo "used as a political instrument" and after 25 April 1974 as a product for cultivated audiences - with no mention of detailed publications, authors or channels of distribution, it has to be concluded that such a division is not sufficiently operational, and even less so, explanatory.

Let us engage with the two factors. Any discussion basing itself on the naming of words in *themselves*, without explaining their contextual usage or historical development is bound to run into trouble. The lack of a specifically Portuguese term should not count for much. Before the adoption of the Gallicism "banda desenhada",[4] the expression "histórias em quadradinhos" (lit. "stories in little squares") was used, and although less frequent, is it still used today. The French word "bande dessinée" is in itself also an adaptation of the Anglo-American term "drawn strips", going back to the 1960s. "Tebeos", as a naturalised and grammaticalised form of an acronym, could only possibly be in usage after 1917 (the foundation of the magazine *TBO*), and currently most Spanish people will use the word "cómic", without signifying with that change a move away from the old "tradition". Moreover, the Argen-

Chapter One

tines call their comics "historietas", and there is enough exchange and cross-fertilisation of comics between Spain and Argentine to make us wonder if traditions are always clearly separated in national terms (the same could be said about a few Brazilian works in Portugal, not to mention the Franco-Belgian francophone two-way traffic). And even in the English language, as it is common in academic and even popular *milieux*, terms are constantly being debated, refined and disputed.[5]

As for the lack of "popular comic figures" and "recognised comic artists", this sounds somewhat like an *argumentum ad nauseam*: it has been repeated so often in Portugal that it has become acknowledged as a truth. However, if we add the qualifying phrase: "for whom?", things may change a little. If the answer to that hypothetical question is "foreign/ global audiences", then perhaps that would mean that there is no comics tradition in Russia, Serbia, Romania, South Korea, India, Indonesia, Peru, or Thailand. But just because a certain national tradition is not internationally known, that does not erase it from history. In fact, it is rather revealing of unbalanced globalisation processes. If the answer, on the other hand, is "domestic contemporary audiences", even though I would agree that there is a certain weakness of memory, or the lack of permanent access to the historical patrimony, of comics,[6] with every successive generation, that problem is also true in a few other creative areas (in Portugal but also elsewhere), especially in the case of non-specialised audiences. It is true that most people in their twenties and thirties, even if interested in comics as (non-meta) readers, are probably unaware of Carlos Botelho's outstanding output, or have never read Cottinelli Telmo's "A grande fita americana", or even know about Bordalo's *Rasilb* (more on these authors below). Then again, the same thing could be said about other areas, including erudite and popular music, early cinema, poetry and architecture.

Having said this, it is probably true that Portuguese comics lacks the economic vigour and perseverance to "faire école" (as in "école de Marcinelle", "the Caniff school", "The Marvel house style(s)" and so on), but on the other hand the emergence of artists with distinctive, singular and vibrant styles is ongoing. Such diversity empowers the artistic felicity of Portuguese comics. Instead of schools, and despite the many collaborations, joint efforts and even "creative families" throughout its history, Portuguese comics is mainly characterised by fully individualised values, or what Jorge de Sena, in a different context, called "dazzlements".[7]

So, all in all, perhaps the problem is precisely that of defining the peripheral production of Portugal according to metropolitan, central models, in some sort of cultural imperialism, imposing models from the outside. Although it cannot be denied that comparisons are useful for the sake of clarity in order to make a new, unknown tradition more approachable, they should not be used to "drown" its specificities. If we invoke the traditions of French or American, or even Italian comics, as a model, then we will not, as a matter of fact, find the same kinds of structures or examples in Portugal. However, to deem the Portuguese tradition inexistent is to lack sensitivity to cultural, historical and economical specificities. In that sense, even though some international audiences may recognise the names of Amália Rodrigues or Siza Vieira, Manoel de Oliveira or Pedro Costa, these artists do not reach "mass audiences", and in no sense can that be used as an argument that Portugal has no musical, cinematic or architectural traditions.

Europe does not have a "low cost of mobility". That is to say, apart from costs of travelling spatially and physically, quite often the costs of cultural, linguistic and social boundary crossing, taken together, are an almost insurmountable obstacle. Ugo Pagano has referred to this reality as a "low horizontal cultural homogenisation" (2004: 315). Cultural homogenisation only operates within certain circles, those that can still be called, unironically, *popular* (not to be confused with the sociological notion of "the masses"). It is by no means obvious what would or would not be a part of those circuits, given that they can be stratified, crossed over, combined or complicated due to cultural traffic and the wide range of individual experiences. But I think we can make educated guesses in slightly generalised fields. On the one hand, there is the widespread mainstream media-divulged, bourgeoisie-sustained, international, if not Americanised, culture, that is translated by the global consumption of largely American-based, -produced or -distributed pop culture products – say, Beyoncé, the *Fast and Furious* franchise, or all kinds of reality shows (even if these are adapted *from* and *to* local specificities). But we also have popular phenomena that are identical at all stages (local production, swift breakthrough into international broadcasting, and subsequent commodification of related products, etc.), but which come from countries different from the usual ones – good examples are Stieg Larsson's *Millenium* series, the novels of Sveva Modignani, the music of BTS, and so on.

On more localised stages, each country will have its own middle- to lowbrow products that are subject to the same kind of media exposure and economic strategies, but are only consumed domestically. Portugal is no exception, with its own roster of famous journalists turned into bestselling writers, pop bands and genre-hopping performers who reach a sufficiently high domestic stardom that creates the illusion of "being the same" as their international counterparts. They are not integrated at all into that global market, even if it may seem that way.

So to which Europe does Portugal belong? How does Portugal respond to this homogenised Europe, or to any other image of Europe? Boaventura de Sousa Santos, in his book *Portugal. Ensaio contra a auto flagelação* (Portugal. An Essay against self-flagellation, 2011), comments as follows:

> There is no doubt that [Portugal's] integration into the European Union has changed Portuguese society dramatically and, in most cases, it was a positive change, a change for the better. However, I think that up until now those changes have been

> conceived less as a part of a well-thought-out project that has been adopted than as the auspicious results of new routines that have been imposed from without. It seems that Portugal is in the European project, but it is not the European project yet. (...) [Portugal takes the role] of the guest, not that of the host (2011: 52-53).

The sociological approach to literature of Jean-Marie Klinkenberg and Benoît Denis introduces "gravitational theory", and I believe that many of the concepts discussed by them are quite appropriate in the realm of comics too. They mention comics briefly (2005: 37), but do not analyse them particularly. Within their perspective, comics may be understood as "weak institutions", in the sense of not being strongly coded and having fewer implicit rules (29-30), than literature *per se*. When Klinkenberg and Denis mention that "'small literatures' do not have the means to exist without reference to the grander literature ensembles that are closest to them and to whose influence they have always been subjected" (24), it is not difficult to understand how a marginal production such as the one discussed in the present project relates to better-known poles of production, such as the North-American or the French markets, whether from the so-called mainstream or alternative circles from both zones (and elsewhere).

The notion of "world literature" becomes quite operational here. Franco Moretti bases his approach on Immanuel Wallerstein's world-systems theory, creating a framework that cannot be seen as a simple context but as the very condition of possibility of literary production. "The one-and-unequal literary system", he writes, "is not just an external network here, it doesn't remain *outside* the text: it's embedded well into its form" (2000: 66; original emphasis). Moretti is aware of the problems of creating an analytical category based on a given literature (usually "central"), which then acts as the focus of investigation in a different production context. When he refers to the method of reading texts in order to search within them for a "unit of analysis", which he actually explains as "reading through the text", a sort of dictum comes up: "The task is constrained from the start; it's a *reading without freedom*" (61, my emphasis). Looking for a Portuguese "Pekar" or "Satrapi", a "comics reportage" or a "*Maus*", then, would be incredibly constrained, or even more so: such a search would be fated *not* to find anything. In such a negotiation, where the point of departure is always already to establish the models from the centres and then "apply" them to other literatures, it comes as no surprise that this will be, more often than not, a failed negotiation. Theo D'haen points to the problem for certain literatures that never had any chance of becoming popular or accessible within this system, especially when, in contemporary discussions, literature from former "peripheral" points of the world, like African and South American countries, India or China, vie for a place in the sun, making it doubly difficult for literatures from countries now perceived as historically privileged, but which actually never had a chance:

what has to give is what was never any getting to begin with, that is to say Europe's "minor" literatures (...) If anything, this has led to an even growing marginalisation, or perhaps we should say "peripheralisation" of Europe's minor literatures (D'haen 2012: 6; also, D'haen 2011 and 2013).

Of course, displacing these considerations onto the realm of comics demands the utmost care. First of all, D'haen refers to Belgian literature - already in itself a difficult construct, as it crosses linguistic divides - and he does not count Portuguese in the same category of "minor", especially on account of the lusophone programme, which seeks to associate itself with the Portuguese-language literatures not only of Portugal, but also Brazil, Angola, Mozambique and elsewhere. However, it cannot be underlined enough that comics is a wholly different affair. Comparisons can be made, then, for the sake of clarity, but we have to ensure that the inclusion of any given society in a transnational category must secure the specificity of that society's historical process (cf. Santos 1985: 873). This is precisely what I will try to achieve with this chapter.

In the final chapter, I will use the term "minor" in a more Deleuzian-Guattarian sense, but for now it follows its most common meaning, of something that has a smaller print run and circulation, and does not meet with an extensive critical reception. The gravitational character of the system refers to the both centrifugal and centripetal dynamics that are established in literature (and beyond), between the centre and the peripheries, which in turn leads us to "think of the literary groupings in terms of tendency towards dependency [i.e., the "small literatures"] and independence [i.e., "great ensembles"]" (Klinkenberg-Denis 2005: 35). Centripetal forces attract peripheral literature towards the centre, entailing their *assimilation*. Centrifugal forces, however, can lead those same groupings towards *differentiation* and *independence*, usually to what may be called "emergent literature" (36). This literature reaches some degree of *autonomy*, which "manifests itself through its capacity to self-organise independently of other social powers" (27). Comics production in Portugal, especially in independent labels and artists' collectives, shows precisely this independence, at once editorial, political and financial, as we will see.

It is true that these agents, within the country, are less articulated with mainstream media outlets or with bigger comics-related institutions and companies (whether publishers or festivals, etc.), but they do relate to other congeneric bodies across Europe, in networks of cooperation that come up with counter-hegemonic forms of transnational cooperation. Publishers such as the Portuguese Chili Com Carne, as well as the Finnish Kuti Kuti, the Italian Canicola, and the Slovenian Stripburger, among a few others, provide English translations alongside the original text, more often than not in the shape of a footnote track. That is one way of providing a solution for the language hurdles between countries, and along with the festivals and meetings themselves, those

Chapter One

strategies seem to create what Gustavo Lins Ribeiro calls "social transfrontiers", which contribute to "translocal systems and translocal cultures" (2006: 247). Ribeiro is referring to actual places (specifically border cases like Ciudad Juárez and Foz do Iguaçu), so this usage is somewhat metaphorical, in the sense that this cross-border flow of authors and publications creates an alternative venue to the more conventional globalisation of comics (usually, through publishing contracts between well-established publishers of several countries). Ribeiro explains that these locales:

> are often seen as spaces out of state control and, as a result, are negatively valued by authorities and the media as zones prone to illegal activities. Such spaces, thus, can easily be manipulated by different political and economic interests since they are liminal zones, hybrids that mix people, things and information from many different national origins, and reveal nation-states' fragilities (240).[8]

In a way, the sort of collaborations and exchanges that emerge from this (within a limited number of Western European countries, admittedly) are less merely *translational* than *transnational*, considering how these editorial processes and decisions seem to be, up to a certain point, co-coordinated or at least mutually informed. These publishers also look for the divulgation of politically charged authors, or artistic endeavours that are outside the norms of a more orthodox perception of comics. In this sense, they contribute to what Charles Hatfield deems a "new movement", whose main traits are:

> the rejection of mainstream formulas; the exploration of (to comics) new genres, as well as the revival, at times ironic recasting, of genres long neglected; a diversification of graphic style; a budding internationalism, as cartoonists learned from other cultures and other traditions; and, especially, the exploration of searchingly personal and at times political themes. (Hatfield 2005: x).

Chili Com Carne is usually present at several international meetings such as the Luzern and Malmö Festivals, or Crack! and Angoulême-Off, and, as a small publisher (although we can count a handful of people working for it, many of the tasks fall upon the editor, Marcos Farrajota), it shares many of the characteristics and affinities with some of the aforementioned publishers. CCC, as it is also known, was born in 1995 as a loose-knit group of artists who created fanzines, but within a few years it became a non-profit youth organisation and a legally established publisher.[9] On average, CCC puts out six books per year, mostly domestic but also international comics, as anthologies or monographs, especially from alternative or underground circles, including "maudits" like Mike Diana. However, its catalogue also lists novels, chronicles, essays, and illustration books. One of their titles in particular, *Boring Europa*, depicts a European tour by van of a small group of Portuguese artists, stopping at a handful of European cities, from Valencia to Ljubljana, and putting up a small publication fair, presenting a DJ set and other actions, taking advantage precisely of this informal network. To a certain extent, this confirms how "peripheral agents" sometimes "de-nationalise" themselves, and are attracted to the mainstream centre, albeit in an alternative network (Klinkenberg-Denis 2005: 31-32). It could be argued, however, that these are strategies that share, if on a smaller scale, the same goals as larger, more institutionalised bodies:

> The contemporary comic book field, especially in its alternative wing, embodies a curious mix of values, a blend of countercultural iconoclasm, rapacious consumerism, and learnt connoisseurship. It is a highly specialised if thinly populated consumer culture, one that holds tightly to a romanticised position of marginally and yet courts wider recognition (Hatfield 2005: xii).

One way to overcome the centre-periphery dichotomy is to engage with the concept of *semiperiphery*. Even though he did not coin this term, Portuguese sociologist Boaventura de Sousa Santos is responsible for the theoretical development of the notion, in particular with regard to Portugal in an influential 1985 article, entitled "Estado e sociedade na semiperiferia do sistema mundial: o caso português" [State and society in the semiperiphery of the global system: the Portuguese case-study]. I will draw heavily from it in the following paragraphs, as I will also draw a social, political and economic portrait of the country, believing this to be important in order to understand the context of the comics I will engage with.

Portugal seems not to be integrated into more usual descriptors such as First/ Third World, developed/developing countries, and other such nomenclatures. Following social indicators such as the relationship between capital and labour force, or that between the state and civil society, social classes, stratification and statistics, social patterns of social reproduction, and so on, and applying them to Portugal will provide elements that would allow it to be considered as both part of the First World or the Third World, depending on the perspective or the actual indicators used. Santos proposes to engage with the term "semiperipheral". He traces the origin of this term to Immanuel Wallerstein (in *The Politics of the World-Economy*, 1984), but he not only engages with it sociologically (and not merely as a metaphorical translation into the world of literature), he also immediately criticises its limited use, considering it *descriptive* (with insufficient theoretical traction), *vague* (for both the criteria and the poles to which it is contrasted, i.e. "periphery" and "centre", are insufficiently defined) and also, or more importantly, *negative*:

> in the sense that the traits found in semiperipheral states and societies are not based on a materiality of their own, nor do they possess a specific logic of evolu-

Chapter One

tion, and end up being rather a mishmash of traits applicable to both central and peripheral States and societies (Santos 1985: 870).

In this text, Boaventura Sousa Santos engages in a long, detailed and almost exhaustive analysis of hard data and historical developments in order to transform the term into a sounder theoretical notion, against which Portugal comes up as a good example. It is impossible for us to go into any detail here, so let us point out the two fundamental characteristics of contemporary Portugal:[10] first of all, the "lack of coincidence between social relations of capitalist production and the social relations of reproduction" and secondly, "the internal lack of articulation of each of these relationships" (idem: 871 ff.).

The first characteristic is related to the fact that the development level of the social relations of capitalist production is lower or more backward than that of social reproduction, or the reproduction of labour power in the Marxist sense. The examples underlined by the Portuguese sociologist are as follows: an industry particularly centred in traditional sectors that are undervalued today and whose global market competition level is low; low productivity levels, on average; low wages; a public sector that is modernised but hampered (by legalities, taxes, etc.); a heterogeneous bourgeoisie in which a very small number of modern sectors co-exist with a wider backward-looking sector, with stagnant productivity and whose competitiveness is based on low wages; an equally heterogeneous labour force that more often than not suffers from lack of collective memory where pressure and negotiation of labour conditions and salaries are concerned, and fragmented along other non-capitalist production forms (particular attention is paid to the still existing small subsistence farming, or parallel economic transactions);[11] among others (Santos 1985: 876). Due to the maintenance of strong bonds with small, subsistence agriculture in many social sectors of Portuguese society, Santos writes:

> (T)he capital/labour relationship is therefore crisscrossed by a network of relationships that stem from social practices and ideologies imbued by non-capitalist logics of action, which bolster an internal fragmentation or atomisation of the proletariat, as well as, to a certain extent, the bourgeoisie (idem: 882).

Bhattacharya also adds that "the major functions of reproducing the working class take place outside the workplace" (2013: n.p.), and it not uncommon for working adults to have help from retired parents, for instance, whether financial or with time and domestic tasks. To Sousa Santos, this has blatant consequences on the relatively stable, non-conflictual relationship between social sectors, which as a result plays a role in the generally conservative nature of Portuguese society.

The second characteristic, that of "internal disarticulation", consists in the discrepancy between the juridical and institutional framework of social relationships (whether capitalist production or reproduction) and the social practices into which they are translated. In a semi-industrial country, with grave problems of modernisation and productivity, a certain laxity of the state only adds more problems, especially where the application of justice is concerned, and which successive economic recessions, including transnational crises that have hit Portugal hard have only worsened (887).

In this picture, despite the many efforts towards the legitimation of comics,[12] both domestically and, more successfully, abroad, we must consider Portuguese contemporary comics not as "marginal", but, in the term that as we propose to use here, "semiperipheral" in the same charged political sense used by Santos… They are semiperipheral; in fact an almost residual production of a semiperipheral literature of a semiperipheral European country. Therefore, it may seem odd to consider Portuguese comics as having any meaningful role. Even though comics are always already a part of the "public sphere", it seems that most comics production in Portugal, historically, aimed at a sort of calm social and political consensus. The words Terry Eagleton wrote about British eighteenth century literature seem to be applicable here: "The literary is the vanishing point of the political, its dissolution and reconstitution into polite letters". (2005: 25). "Polite letters" (and images) could well be a description of most comics production throughout the 20th century, even globally speaking.

Comics have roots, in part, in political caricature. So, of course, there were always comics or comics-related production with more or less overtly political tones, explicit discussions or depictions of political issues, crises, or even theories and philosophies. Think of *Les Pieds Nickelés* and Frans Masereel's books, Harold Gray's *Little Orphan Annie* and Ditko's *Mr. A*, or consider magazines such as the American *The Masses* or work by the Neue Sachlichkeit artists. Throughout the first half of the 20th century, however, there was overexploration of comics as an escapist form of entertainment. It was thanks to its "literary turn" in the mid-1990s that a larger diversity became more consolidated. For instance, with the emergence, acceptance and critical reception of comics in reportage, documentary or essay modes, or comics that addressed the "Other" not as an object seen from without, but engaged with the "Other-as-subject", with his or her own voice (Moura 2012a).

In a 1996 catalogue from the then newly founded French publisher Amok, we find words that sound like a manifesto:

> The profound nostalgia for childhood that largely permeates comics production dooms their effectiveness in the world, and relegates them to the periphery of contemporary issues. AMOK's gambit, on the other hand, is to place itself at the heart of a creative response to the real.

Chapter One

The authors I will study are quite conscious, precisely, of their "creative confrontation with the real". How does this confrontation take place? Comics are mainly constituted by a corpus of *published* work, meaning texts that penetrate and circulate in the public sphere. All of them arrive at that precious and precise "public use of reason" that Kant discusses in *Beantwortung der Frage: Was its Aufklärung?* (1784). Instead of something close to what is usually called "public opinion" (a normative discourse of which not all individuals in one given society are the subjects, and that both contributes to social control and therefore entails the emergence of a new "tutelage"), it is a use that, according to Maurizio Borghi (who discusses Kant's text) assumes a truthful pedagogical (*paideia*) role that will contribute towards the emancipation of human beings (Borghi 2005-2006). Witnessing, reportage, voice (re)claiming, or resistance to hegemonic discourses are all an integrant and fundamental part of this public sphere, even if we are within a media ecology and a genre economy that does not always allow comics to share the same cultural and critical reception space of other expressive and artistic languages and disciplines (cf. Groensteen 2006, Maigret 2012). This has changed significantly in the past decade, both in the United States and in some European countries, whether due to the presence of comics in the review pages of newspapers, or due to the organisation of exhibitions in major visual arts institutions, the attribution of literary awards to graphic novels, not to mention the proliferation of academic assessment of comics, via monographs, essay collections, calls for conference papers, and so on.

As should be expected, within that public sphere we will always find works that are dissimilar; some will uphold hegemonic discourses while others will counter them. However, we must also consider that hegemony generates less *marginality* than *centrality*, and that those margins must be seen as "approximate categories, not absolutes" (Cabral 2000: 883-890). Mark McKinney, addressing a selected area of comics production (French-speaking *bande dessinées* by contemporary French-Arab authors), speaks of an "alternative public sphere, in which history is debated and political positions are staked out" (2008: 162). The works I wish to discuss will fall within a somewhat similar category.

As I have already mentioned, I will not be arguing that comics are better equipped than any other art form to convey a certain theme or feeling, or address a certain issue. Creating interartistic hierarchies is somewhat absurd, despite social perceptions. As Noël Carroll concludes one of his texts, "the relevant issue when commending a given artwork is not whether it is an instance of the medium that is best for the effect the artwork exemplifies, but whether the artwork in question achieves its own ends" (1984: 15).

To a certain extent, then, I wish to engage here with a "radical contextuality" in Lawrence Grossberg's sense (from *Bringing it All Back Home*), that is to say, "the way that cultural studies investigations work across historical and political contexts rather than taking up a fixed theoretical position. In these terms, 'context is not merely the background but the very conditions of possibility of something'" (the inner quote is Grossberg's, apud Harding and Pribram 2009: 3). The notion acknowledges that contexts operate in specific ways but also change constantly. In that sense, an understanding of the "Portuguese comics scene", embedded in the country's particular history, is necessary. I will start with an extremely brief overview of its history, but will get into more detail as we approach the context in which the authors I will address in the book have emerged, both as readers and as agents.

I am aware of the fact that creating any story based on "nationality" - in this case, a belonging, imagined or official, to a specific legal construct called *Portugal* and a unity projected by a common language and cultural distribution networks - leads necessarily to subjective, partial perspectives. That is an inherent trait of human memory, whether individual or collective.

> "Like personal memory, social memory is also highly selective, it highlights and foregrounds, imposes beginnings, middles and ends on the random and contingent. Equally, it foreshortens, silences, disavows, forgets and elides many episodes which - from another perspective - could be the start of a different narrative" (Hall 1999: 5, see also Confino 1997).

The creation of an idea of heritage - "Portuguese comics" - leads to a more or less conventional, consensual group of authors, titles and attitudes, as well as a notion of much stronger bonds between the texts than can be warranted, eliding discrepancies, paying little attention to highly individualised traits, as if in fact it was one big, happy family, relating to "one of those things which everyone possesses, and which everyone will defend, seemingly without thought" (Turnbridge and Ashworth, apud Harvey 2001: 322, nt. 12). Hall also throws light on the fact that the notion of nationality, or nation-belonging "was always fissured along class, gender and regional lines" (Hall 1999: 6). As we shall see, by not engaging with the usual normative narrative conventions of commercial comics, even though they may *use* them critically, the central authors I discuss create an alternative space for the vocalisation of the dispossessed, but also create an alternative view of Portuguese comics, if not of comics themselves.

Although ideology is always pervasive and constitutive of subjects, if there is a difference between historical, classic productions and these contemporary authors I want to study, it is the latter's conscience of their interventionist role. Instead of the hegemonic "business as usual" adventures of heroes upholding the current ideologies of the day, these authors, or most of them, focus on the livelihood of ordinary citizens, if not unremarkable ones. However, by focusing on such characters, and by showing how they are marginalised by hegemonic discourses, they are going against the grain not only where comics are concerned - their supposed entertaining or uplifting societal role - but also in relation to discourses of citizenship "role models". Thus, these texts also shape history, if even on the margins of the *grands récits*, and this becomes particularly acute in relation to books that thematise History (such as that of Miguel Rocha). To be sure, I have no wish to play this particular group of artists off against a monolithic presentation of past authors. Rather than setting up an artificial opposition, we must be aware of the ongoing negotiations between tradition and experimentalism, the prolongation of languages and styles and formal and political originality. Nothing is ever clear cut, unambiguously on one side or the other. When quoting extensively from John Bodnar's *Remaking America: public memory, Commemoration, and Patriotism in the Twentieth Century*, and closely analysing his words and cases, Alon Confino points to that sort of simplifying dichotomy in order to criticise it. He argues that "Official culture relies on 'dogmatic formalism' and the restatement of reality in ideal rather than complex or ambiguous terms" and that "Defenders of [vernacular] cultures are numerous and intent on protecting values and restating views of reality derived from first-hand experience in small-scale communities rather than the 'imagined' communities of a large nation..." (Confino 1997: 1401). He concludes: "Not only is vernacular memory not as saintly and official memory not as brutal, but they constantly commingle" (idem: 1402).

In fact, we must avoid falling into the trap of either "excessive polemical dispute" or "commemorative activity" (Frey 2002: 301) of the past, but instead we should actively and intellectually engage with the works themselves, in their own context, and try to understand the role they play. But in this way, by engaging with *alternative* (more on this word later) artists and texts, I hope to avoid "defining heritage almost completely along the lines of economic commodification (...) one-dimensionally, as just another aspect of a burgeoning leisure industry" (Harvey: 324; see also Baetens 2010).

A short history of Portuguese comics from its origins to the early 20th century

Knowledge of Portuguese comics is accessible in more widely spoken languages such as English or French only in an episodic, lacunar, and sometimes erroneous way. However, there is much Portuguese scholarship that takes the form of either global assessments or particular histories dedicated to particular time periods, titles or authors, written for exhibitions on themes, authors or commemorative dates. In this section, we will draw much information from researchers such as António Dias de Deus, Leonardo De Sá, João Paiva Boléo, Carlos Bandeiras Pinheiro and Carlos Pessoa, among a few others. In a three-part article, Pierre Huard establishes a typology of comics research (Huard 1998-99, see also Chavanne 1998), in which he proposes a classification of *discourses*, which have to do with the nature of the work itself, and its relationship to the object of study, and *approaches*, or the methodological tools employed. The discourses are divided into three main areas, the first encompassing the "technical", the "socio-economic" and the "encyclopedic", the other two being the "archivist" and the "critical". These discourses are then cross-classified with a number of "approaches", which Huard identifies as biographical, literary, encyclopaedic, anthological, historical, sociological, socio-historical/ideological, socio-economic, technical, pedagogical, philosophical, semiotic, psychoanalytical, epistemological and art-critical. Most of the aforementioned bibliography of Portuguese comics fits nicely with the so-called "archivist" approach, where "the comics author is in fact the real object of the study, sometimes to the detriment of the comic itself. It is in fact all about making the author sacred" (Huard 1998-99). It is, undoubtedly, important to acknowledge the contribution of these precursors, whose work, with its exhaustive take on titles, source identification, precise dates and data, has opened up the field for further incursions, but it is very important to understand that rarely does it amount to an actual critical discourse, which should be based on a wider historical context and follow disciplinary boundaries. Even the aggregation of these historical studies still leaves some parts of Portuguese comics production unattended to (cf. Matos 2011).

If we rummage through history from a merely aesthetic point of view, looking for any sort of sequence of images or visual art techniques that we can compare with modern comics, finding any instance that we would then call "comics" *avant la lettre,* or "proto-comics", or that at least we could integrate into an unhistorical account of this territory, perhaps we could go back to the 18th century *azulejos* (tiles) of Sr. Roubado, in Odivelas, just outside Lisbon, a series of panels that depicts a crime-and-punishment story from the time of the Inquisition. Or, perhaps, flexing nationalistic linguistic muscles, we could include the several 13th century codices of the *Cantigas de Santa Maria* illuminated manuscripts of Alfonso El Sabio, written in Galician-Portuguese, and sharing with modern comics many of its formal techniques and procedures (Alexandre-Bidon 1996). We could even go further back, to the Upper Paleolithic, in order to include the ca. 20 000 BCE engravings of Foz Côa, in Northern East Portugal.

However, such vain exercises would not lead us to a good comprehension of the actual social, cultural and economic conditions of the contemporary comics scene in which our authors work. Comics, after all, are neither "unchanging" (to remind us of Alan Gowans' classic *The Unchanging Arts*) nor "post-historical" (see Carrier 2000, especially chapter 7). Considering comics as a social-cultural artefact, imbued in history, and in a transnational creative process, we will consider Portuguese comics to have originated and evolved within the 19th century matrix of urban, middle-class, mass-marketed press.[13] There are many examples of short cartoons and strips in several newspapers and magazines throughout the decades of the 1850s to the 1880s, with names such as Nogueira da Silva, Flora (a possible

Chapter One

pseudonym of Silva), Figueiras and Manuel José Ferreira, and others. However, as in most countries, there is always one particular name that becomes highly prised and heralded as the "patron" or "father" of its national tradition (such as Töpffer, Doré, Christophe, Wilhelm Busch, Pehr Nordquist, Frederik Von Dardel, A.B. Frost or R. F. Outcault).[14]

In Portugal, that role belongs to Rafael Bordalo Pinheiro (1846-1905)[15] and even if he was not technically the first author of modern comics in Portugal, there is no doubt that he is its tutelary figure, not only for the sheer quantity of graphic and editorial work (not to mention his similarly overwhelming output as painter, ceramicist, decorative artist and, to a certain extent, polemicist), but its quality, its verve and the survival of many of his creations. We need only mention the creation of his "Zé Povinho", a character that, despite originally representing a specific class of uneducated, underprivileged *paisanos*, quickly became a type to represent all Portuguese people, somewhat like "John Bull" or "Uncle Sam", but always in a self-deprecating manner. Indeed, Bordalo's role in the shaping of an iconic cultural, collective Portuguese imaginary puts him in the same creative category as, for instance, Rowlandson and Gillray in England, Honoré Daumier in France, or Thomas Nast in the U.S.[16] And, many of his images, like theirs, would become models for decades to come. Apart from caricature and one-panel cartoons, he also did some one to two-page narratives in the many publications in which he participated, some of which he directed. He worked in a myriad of publications (more often than not, weekly eight-page periodicals), in both Portugal and Brazil, including some as director, but always being the most famous name and the heart that would colour the title. In 1870 alone, for instance, he launched three different titles, *O Calcanhar de Aquiles*, *A Berlinda* and *O Binóculo*. Others followed, the most important ones being perhaps *A Lanterna Mágica* (1875), *O Besouro* (1878), *O António Maria* (1879) and *A Paródia* (1900). Some of them were exclusively filled with caricatures.

Notwithstanding a rather small strictly comics output (by comics we will understand, rather conservatively, any sequence of images that creates a narrative, with some sort of causality and/or recurrent characters), the ones he did produce are enough to consider him to be a pioneer of comics in Europe,[17] including some pieces that could be called autobiographical. One of his sequences, entitled "Diario d'um gommoso/conto movimentado" ["Diary of a toff/a thrilling short story"], published in 1893, seems to be quite informed by Cham's style, or that of other French authors of the period, for its quick, minimal line work. But the physical and moral expressivity of the characters and its sheer visual lavishness are somewhat related to theatre art. However, the most important thing he did in this field is, undoubtedly, the very first comics album in Portugal: *Apontamentos de Raphael Bordallo Pinheiro Sobre a Picaresca Viagem do Imperador de Rasilb pela Europa* (translatable as "Notes By Raphael Bordallo Pinheiro on the Picaresque European Tour of the Emperor of Razilb", the last being a simple anagram of *Brazil*), which had three successive editions in its debut year, 1872. Despite containing no more than 16 pages, this was a true precursor of the European-style *álbum*, which had an intense life throughout the 20th century. Its main purpose being to satirise the Emperor of Brazil, D. Pedro II, it is a book filled with wonderful, innovative graphic solutions, some of which are akin to those of European artists such as Töpffer, Cham and Busch (one other Bordalo 1878 piece features the note "Loose imitation of Busch") and, above all, Gustave Doré (there are actually a couple of "processes" than seem to be a homage to, if not a rip-off from, devices from Doré's 1854 *L'Histoire de la Sainte Russie*; see Moura 2010). Like Doré, Bordalo used blacked-out panels and children's drawings (see Groensteen 2003; this could initiate a discussion about "l'hybridation graphique", that is to say, the diversity of styles within a single work, cf. Smolderen 2014 and Groensteen 2014b). Furthermore, Bordalo employed a comics parenthesis, opening up an excursus to the main storyline, a device that I believe he originated.

Many other artists followed in Bordalo's footsteps, including his own son, Manuel Gustavo, who contributed to the children's comics magazine *O Gafanhoto* (1903-1910), but never reached the level of recognition (or creativity) of his father. This last publication included some translations of foreign comics, among them those of Winsor McCay. With the end of the Portuguese monarchy and its transformation into a Republic,[18] there was also a change in the "usage" of comics socially, which from a social and political caricature-related art became increasingly a narrative, entertainment medium for children, perhaps associated with the pedagogical policies devised and upheld by Republicanism. This does not mean that there was a complete absence of adult-oriented, political satire-tinted comics. Quite the contrary, and Leal da Câmara's or Silva Monteiro's names would suffice to satisfy that line of development.

The emergence of the Estado Novo

Starting around the 1910s and continuing into the early 1930s, but with some authors extending their work well into the early 1940s, or even 1950s, a profound transformation of Portuguese comics occurred. One the one hand, there was an almost concerted, deliberate creation of child-oriented comics. On the other hand, the artists contemporary to the implementation of the Republic began to shift their interest from political satirical comics (under Bordalo's aegis) towards a focus on social, everyday life (Matos 2011).[19] But the new, brief generation that would be later called "Modernist" was comprised of people interested in working on many creative fronts as well as in diversifying their visual approaches to illustration and comics, considerably more stylised and streamlined than those of the previous generation, which were still following linework typical of the 19th century. The introduction of

Chapter One

colour was a major factor, even if sometimes it was only the covers of the publications, or the interior contained only one other colour. Almost none of the artists in this generation worked exclusively in comics production. Just as Bordalo had worked on ceramics and painting, we find people here who were accomplished in other areas, from painting to architecture and film, as well as theatrical set design, tile-painting, ceramics, caricature and illustration. There are a large number of important artists in this large family, and we can name Hypólito Collomb, Bernardo Marques, Margarida, Rocha Vieira, José Viana, Thomas "Tom" de Mello, José de Lemos, Guy Manuel and Sérgio Luiz (the last two siblings and often collaborators), as well as Almeida Negreiros and Júlio Resende, who became absolutely central names in the history of painting in Portugal. Arguably, however, the artists who became the paramount, quintessential references of this generation, especially although not exclusively for comics, are Bernardo Marques, Cottinelli Telmo, Emmérico Nunes, Carlos Botelho, Abel Manta and Stuart de Carvalhais (cf. Deus-De Sá 1997, Boléo-Pinheiro 1997 and Boléo-Pinheiro 2000).

With the advent of the military regime in 1926, followed by the institution and consolidation of the Estado Novo, things necessarily changed at all levels of society. On May 8th 1926, an antiparliamentary, military coup d'état ended the First Republic. The economy was in disarray, and in 1928 a professor of Economy from Coimbra was invited to become the Minister of Finance. António de Oliveira Salazar managed to create what was dubbed a "financial miracle" by balancing the public budgets - which were never approved by the Parliament, as one would expect in democratic conditions - and by stabilising the Portuguese currency, the escudo, without international aid. Of course, today this "miracle" is seen as a self-propagating myth that was part of the propaganda of the budding regime, as it was achieved through a brutal raising of every sort of tax, budget cuts in health, and other public expenses. In any case, as the historian Fernando Rosas writes, "budget policies were not limited to being merely financial techniques, but were rather tools for a wider project of state building" (Rosas 2012: 51). In point of fact, this situation allowed Salazar to gain ever more power over the state, until in July 1932 he became the President of the Council of Ministers (equivalent to a contemporary Prime Minister, still the Head of Government in Portugal). This was the birth of what was later dubbed the Estado Novo [New State], a regime set up under the auspices of a corporatist system. Moreover, as a "solution" to the many financial problems brought upon the first Republic, and its associated liberal capitalism, but also avoiding the core Marxist notion of class struggle, corporatism was the ideology underlying economic and social organisation: defending state intervention in economic matters, accepting capitalism, defending the social functions of property, labour and capital, but imposing social harmony between all sectors. According to another important historian of the regime, Jorge Pais de Sousa, we should avoid either including the Estado Novo under the traditional heading of *authoritarian* regimes, as influenced by American political sciences, or considering it as a simple Portuguese variant of *Fascism*, as it was spreading across Europe in the 1920s and 1930s (2011). Pais de Sousa attempts to rise above this dichotomy of taxonomies that have typified historical discussions in the last decades by reusing a term coined by Miguel de Unamuno, who christened the Salazar regime a "fascism ex cathedra".[20]

This regime was characterised by its conservative, authoritarian, nationalistic, rural, and even anti-urban and anti-industrial nature. Historian João Medina, for instance, talks of a "regime of immobility, stemming from a Christian matrix, nostalgic for a medieval *pax ruris*, mistrustful of anything that might remind one of the modernity of the 1900s" (Medina 1993: 13). Despite the economic, societal and industrial changes that took place in the 1960s and 1970s,[21] it can be considered that the 48 years that Portugal lived under a non-democratic regime were defined by a number of political processes. There were no parties, no political pluralism, and, importantly for us, the press was not free.

Despite a certain flexibility assured by Gomes da Costa, the President after the 1926 coup, in that same year a "preliminary censorship" was instituted, which became increasingly more controlling, of both domestic production and the importation of foreign material. In 1934, a Secretariat for National Propaganda (SPN, later SNI) was launched.

This had an immediate repercussion on children's literature and, naturally, on comics as well, as the medium was considered, as elsewhere, an off-shoot (if not a bastardisation) of literature for younger audiences. While only a certain number of researchers (Rocha 1984, Araújo 2008) consider that the first few decades of the 20th century were the "golden period" of children's literature in Portugal, due to the literary efforts of intellectuals like Aquilino Ribeiro or António Sérgio, both involved with several left-wing movements, but also the monarchic and anti-Salazar Afonso Lopes Vieira, among others, all of them agree that the institution of the Estado Novo in the early 1930s represented a weakening of liberty. Many of the newspapers exclusively dedicated to children, or their special supplements, disappeared, and with them the opportunities for Portuguese authors. To a certain extent, the Mocidade Portuguesa-related[22] titles filled that void, but under the tight propaganda agenda of the regime. In 1950, the Direcção de Serviços da Censura [Direction for Censorship Services] published the *Instruções sobre literatura infantil* [Instructions on children's literature], which "impose(d) general ethical, psychological and aesthetic guiding principles". These are somewhat analogous to the French *Loi n°49-956 du 16 juillet 1949 sur les publications destinées à la jeunesse* (see Crépin and Groensteen 1999) but they went further, especially into formal aspects, and it is worth going into this small - a booklet of a few dozen pages - but important document in a little detail.

The surprising aspect of this law concerns not only choices in relation to social representation, morality and the encouragement of national pride, but also

Chapter One

details of formal production. Where the first aspects were concerned, this led to the redrawing - or the "butchering", depending on the perspective - of some panels from foreign material (sometimes domestic as well), eliminating guns from cowboys' or bandits' hands, lengthening female characters' skirts, erasing anything shocking, or adapting the names of foreign heroes into Portuguese versions. So J. C. Murphy's *Big Ben Bolt* was known as *Luís Euripo*, M. Butterworth's and G. Campion's *Battler Briton* became *Major Alvega*, and A. Raymond's *Rip Kirby* became *Rúben Quirino*. This also led to the adaptations of places, institutions, etc., so it comes as no surprise that many of the young readers actually thought the comics originated in Portugal. But the document also aimed to secure the "reader's visual hygiene"... Verbal text could only be written in black on white or cream backgrounds, text type and size was allowed only according to strict rules, the sizes and thickness of border lines, the type of paper, and so on... there is even detailed, dogmatic advice on the use of lighting and colours: "Green is less tiring, red is more tiring". Garish colours were out of the question. As I have mentioned, these "instructions" applied to all children's publications, but they affected comics as well, and there are a few specific mentions of the medium, cf. article 4, where there are precise instructions on the rectangular limits of the panels, the composition of captions, and so on. Simões Müller, the director of *Cavaleiro Andante*, was a member of the Commission that brought to light the *Instruções*, which complicates the common notion of considering certain editors, authors and other agents as being merely "people of their times". As in the case of Müller, they actively contributed to the characteristics of those times.

To go back to the broader society, it also has to be borne in mind that any kind of associative movements, strikes, or worker's unions were forbidden. Not only were rights and freedoms trampled, but the very possibility of claiming rights was cut short: public meetings had to be authorised in advance (if at all) and any demonstration or protest was violently repressed. A political police, the PVDE/PIDE played an important part in the pervasiveness of an ongoing repression, reinforced by a very large network of informers, which installed a long-lived, permanent fear of voicing political views.

It has to be understood, then, that the production of comics throughout the Estado Novo, even though it may have not upheld all the political, oppressive policies of the Government, still had to work within the expected values, morals and principles of the regime. Most of them, in the midst of censorship, conformed to a certain model of representation of the nation, with its normative notions, and a narrow view of what "healthier" and more socially accepted forms of comics for the younger generations should be. Some of the previous, modernist authors continued to work, albeit conforming to the rules and standards of the time. A blatant example is Stuart de Carvalhais's "Quim e Manecas". This famous title is perfectly in the line of the "pair of mischievous urchins" tradition of *Max und Moritz, The Katzenjammer Kids, Zig et Puce, Quick & Flupke,* which has continued throughout the history of comics and its many nations. The first scripts for "Quim e Manecas" had been written by Acácio de Paiva, the director of *O Século Cómico*, where the strip debuted, and despite its subject matter, the exploits of two little children, the way it dealt with everyday life had strong political undertones, which made it appeal to adults as well. Under the Estado Novo, Stuart continued the adventures of his characters in *Pajem*, a small-sized magazine, an insert of the larger comics journal *Cavaleiro Andante*, but in a somewhat tamer version, partially due to its mission: *Pajem* was aimed at an audience younger than that of the main publication (the titles play upon this, as we can guess, the insert playing "Page" to the "Knight"; cf. Deus-De Sá 1999). Some of Stuart's stories in this magazine were written in collaboration with its director, Adolfo Simões Müller, an extremely influential writer, editor and publisher of children's literature, who created many works that toed the line of national exaltation and pride. And, as we have seen, a member of the Commission of the *Instruções*. Müller was also responsible for *O Papagaio*, another influential children's comics magazine, which published many groundbreaking Portuguese artists,[23] and *Diabrete*, a cheaper magazine, but within the same general editorial outlook.

The history of comics in Portugal, as in other European countries and the United States, has a close relationship with the newspaper industry, and only after the 1960s can we speak of a blossoming of a comic *book* industry, whether with the classic Franco-Belgian format of the series of *albums* (from the 1970s on) or the "graphic novel" one-shots (since the 1990s). Bordalo's magazines were in newsprint, and up until the 1960s magazines were printed in cheap paper, and there is a wide variety of colouring and cover-styles: black-and-white, a second colour or even four-colour printing for the inside, and colourful covers, whether in matte or glossy paper stock, but usually printed in four colours (earlier in two or three), etc. Formats could go from in-octavos to broadsheets. Many were supplements to newspapers or magazines (such as the case of *ABCzinho* for the *ABC* magazine, or *Pim Pam Pum!* and *Notícias Miudinho* for, respectively, the dailies *O Século* and *Diário de Notícias*). But others were sold as self-standing titles (*O Mosquito, Senhor Doutor, Papagaio*, etc.).

In this respect, then, these publication formats, and the formal strategies of comics-making and narrative, thematic and intermedial implications of these artists, in other words, these formulas were consonant with the practices of the field throughout Europe. Carlos Botelho broke completely from these more or less homogeneous practices with his one-page chronicles, "Ecos da Semana" ("Weekly Echoes") for the weekly *Sempre Fixe* (Fig. 1.1). Despite his groundbreaking formal choices, Botelho did not have any real followers. Again, no "school" stemmed from this individual artist. His use of open-ended page compositions, where the represented urban elements themselves become the units for actions and episodes, organised not according to episodic structures but thematically or relationally, not

Chapter One

Figure 1.1.: Carlos Botelho (1937), "Ecos da Semana", *Sempre Fixe*, issued 3rd November 1937. Reproduced with the gracious permission of the inheritors.

to mention his attention to seemingly banal, everyday life enable him to be seen, however as a sort of precursor to practices, both formal and thematic, that gained traction in the 1990s.

Throughout the 1940s, then, but also the 1950s and 1960s, magazines such as *Cavaleiro Andante, O Mosquito,* and *Jornal do Cuto* (along with a few others), substantiated the general, coherent images of comics as a vehicle able to consolidate the "Estado Novo" re-imagining of Portugal: a strong, Christian, colonial empire, proud of its history but also proud of its contemporary simplicity, that had nothing to do with the vices of more industrialised countries. "Alone but proud", as one famous *dictum* of Salazar went (upholding also the myth of being a neutral country during World War II). This does not mean that there were no differences and tensions between titles, although we cannot go into detail about that in this text. For instance, to a certain extent, the purpose of Müller's *Cavaleiro Andante* was to create a counterpoint to *Mundo de Aventuras*, another comics magazine but one that published mostly translations of Anglophone material, starting with adventure titles such as *Flash Gordon* and *Steve Canyon* (which was published under the name "Luís Ciclon", because the photolytes were brought from Spain), but also humour strips such as Al Capp's *Alley Oop. Mosquito*, which had a long life, from 1936 to 1953 (its first series), published the most important naturalistic Portuguese comics artists of the time alongside Spanish giants such as Emilio Freixas and Jesús Blasco. *Cavaleiro Andante*, on the other hand, although it also had foreign material - such as Bob Lubber's *Tarzan*, stories by Hergé, Caprioli, and adaptations from children's literature - aimed at producing "healthier" stories, usually confined to adventure genres: detective (not "crime") stories, sports stories, sea-faring stories, adventures set in the jungle, the U.S. Wild West and other exotic places, or during the times of the musketeers or Christian crusaders (the very title evokes a sort of medieval flavour). Its weekly 20 pages had some variety, but they were confined to the "boys' adventure" field. In any case, many other magazines also conformed to this description.

The bigger names that constituted this (long) generation are those of, first and foremost, Eduardo Teixeira Coelho (Fig. 1.2), but also José Antunes, Carlos Alberto Santos, Fernando Bento, Augusto Barbosa, Manuel Alfredo, José Ruy, José Garcês, Raul Correia and Vítor Péon, many of whom were influenced by the naturalistic style of a Harold Foster (particularly true in relation to Coelho, Garcês and Péon). Apart from what was indicated above, many stories adapted classic, central texts from Portuguese literature - more often than not, texts that could be read within a pro-colonialist perspective, such as Camões's *Os Lusíadas* or Fernão Mendes Pintos' *Peregrinação*[24] - or that would contribute towards an exaltation of the "Portuguese soul", as with Alexandre Herculano's and Eça de Queirós's books. Adaptations of foreign literature were common, based on stories by authors such as Walter Scott, Jules Verne, George Dumas, Lewis Carroll or Erich Kästner. As we have seen, more

Chapter One

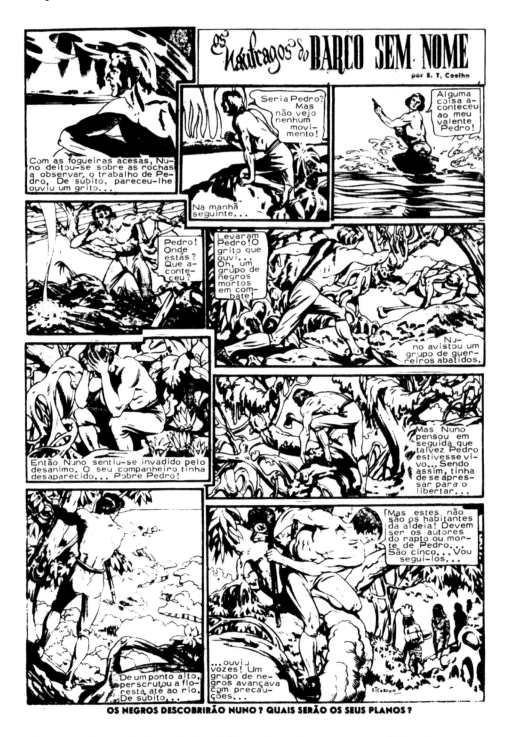

Figure 1.2: Eduardo Teixeira Coelho (1946), "Os náufragos do barco sem nome", *Mosquito*, n.p.

typical genres were pursued, from westerns (Péon's *Tomhawk Tom*), to jungle and sea adventures (Barbosa's and Santo's *João dos Mares*, José Ruy's later *Bomvento* stories) or episodes from Portuguese history (Antunes' *Geraldo sem pavor* or Carlos Alberto Santos's story about D. Fuas Roupinho, "A espada nazarena").

Needless to say, most of these works amounted to a political eulogy of the civilising mission of Caucasian Christians (if not specifically the Catholic Portuguese), and simple Manichaeism was the narrative norm. It is perhaps going too far to consider them as nurturing "political complicity" with the Estado Novo's politics, but they were as much constituted by the normative discourses of the time as they were contributing to it, especially if we take into account the child-oriented publications in which they were published, and the overall *docere, delectare et movere* framework of those titles. In any case, there *were* actually comics magazines, or magazines that included comics, that were official propaganda organs, such as those owned by the Mocidade Portuguesa (MP): *Jornal da MP, Camarada, Pisca-Pisca, Lusitas* and *Fagulha* (these last two associated with the female wing of the MP). Many of the artists we have mentioned participated in all of these titles, but we must beware of certain automatic, contemporary reactions to these historical texts, lest we fall into "anachronisms of memory" (Frey 2002).[25]

Stylistically speaking, we could also subsume most of these works under a general rubric of a naturalistic approach to drawing the human figure, a clear use of ink lines to depict objects and a simplistic application of colour, somewhat limited by the technology of the period. *Mundo de Aventuras*, as well as *Titã, Falcão*, or *O Pirilau* published other Spanish and British material, which included science fiction and war comics, but all in all they conformed to the overall category of "boys' own" type of publications.

April the 25th and contemporaneity

After a few failed attempts at coups, and as a form of protest against the bloody, crushing, ongoing wars in the African colonies (Angola, Mozambique and Guinea) from 1961, a group of low rank military officials managed to bring down the regime on April 25 1974, reinstituting democracy. This was more or less a bloodless, pacific change, but it was followed by high tensions between the military, the Communist party (illegal for years, but surviving as a clandestine organisation and quite well-organised), other larger political forces, a myriad of smaller parties, conservative sectors of society, etc., which led both to a complicated period of economic and political stress (known as PREC, or "Ongoing Revolutionary Process") and the coup/counter-coup of November 25 1975, which some commentators point to as the consolidation of the democratic regime in Portugal. Economically speaking, however, not much was solved. In fact, some left-wing analysts see in November 25 the point at which the possibility of a concrete Socialist alternative was blocked for good (under the pressure of NATO, the USA, etc.), so that the dynamics of reconstituting a capitalist state were assured.

Nonetheless, the "25 de Abril" or "Carnation Revolution", as it is known, is still celebrated today as the foundation of modern, democratic Portugal. The consumption levels of the working classes were raised, and apart from the political and economic changes at high level, popular movements, quite politicised throughout the 1970s, were able to act upon other fronts as well. These included health, leading to the creation of the SNS, or National Health Service; education, dramatically raising literacy levels and giving wider access to various levels of schooling to the working classes; housing, whether through radical occupations or new social housing projects; social security, which updated its values and widened its eligibility criteria; justice, granting easier and more universal access. Not to mention access to culture, thanks to the disappearance of censorship, the multiplication of agents and a plurality of views, etc.,[26] and increased gender equality (a woman had previously needed her father's or husband's authorisation to get a job, for instance, or even apply for a passport, and there were also changes for the better regarding employment and family rights).[27] As Santos concludes in his 1985 article, these claims and conquests "not only forced more or less profound changes on a legal level, but also compelled the state to become more involved in the regulation of social reproduction" (1985: 901).

Necessarily, these dramatic changes had consequences for comics-making as well. The maintenance of child-oriented, mass-marketed magazines and journals after the regime change should not, however, allow us to conclude that *all* comics belonged to that category. Especially after the 1974 Revolution, with the disappearance of censorship, and the multiplication of political movements, each with their own newspapers and presses, satirical political cartoons appeared everywhere, sometimes leading to the publication of books, or even series of books. To give but one example, Pedro Massano created a strip for the weekly paper *A Luta*, entitled "O Abutre" [The Vulture], in 1978 (it has been suggested that these cartoons had been created before, in 1973, for another newspaper, and perhaps they were considered too risky at the time), which presented a dark, political humour, and which led to seven landscape, soft cover books. Maoist activists also translated Chinese propaganda comics, an adaptation of Marx's *Capital* was created by Carlos Barradas (1978), and politicians became fodder for satirical stories. Moreover, pornography was another line of development, usually mixed with some humour, with outrageous and fantastical stories. These were not sold under the counter, and actually had commercial distribution, with mostly foreign material, even though their quality left much to be desired.

And sometimes both those tendencies were combined together. The most important figure in political satire mixed with risqué representations is, undoubtedly, José Vilhena, who worked as a cartoonist throughout the 1950s, but went on to engage in a very productive phase in the next decade, creating many magazines that tackled, through not all that subtle, eroticised humour, political issues such as censorship, the vacuous discourse of politics, the economic crisis, and so on (which led to his arrest by the political police a couple of times). After April 25, his activity became unbridled, and the endemic political and economic crises gave him plenty of topics for his work (Zink 2001).

Up until the 1990s, the Portuguese editorial market was mostly characterised by short weekly magazines with Portuguese and foreign content, as well as an increasing number of translations of albums, especially from the Franco-Belgian axis. As we have seen, most domestic production was subsumed to historical themes or genre adventures, a trait inherited and especially pushed by magazines such as *O Mosquito* (published between 1936 and 1986), *Cavaleiro Andante* (from 1952 to 1962), and, later, the Portuguese *Tintin* (from 1968 to 1982),[28] some of which "pre-published" two to four pages per issue of the material that was later collected into an album. The first two mixed foreign material from the most diverse sources (France and Belgium, of course, but also Spain, England and the U.S.) and helped create the first "professional comics artists"[29] in Portugal, such as Jayme Cortez, Teixeira Coelho, Péon, Ruy and Garcês. Some of these emigrated in order to work full time as comics artists, like Teixeira Coelho, Carlos Roque and Vítor Péon, whereas others were able to stay in Portugal while collaborating with foreign publishers, like José Pires. But slowly the room for Portuguese artists started to be restricted. With magazines such as *Diabrete* (1941-1951), *Faísca* (1943-1944, where American super-heroes debuted in Portugal), *O Mundo de Aventuras* (1949-73) and *Condor Popular* (more of a collection, this *petit format* collected mostly rearranged English-language newspaper strips, with each issue publishing a particular character or storyline, and appeared from April 1951 to April 1972), covering especially British and North-American work, including super-heroes, a new "demand" was being nurtured in Portuguese readers that could not be satisfied with the same formulae as before. *Tintin* opened the floodgates for the "Franco-Belgian" invasion, as it was dubbed, tongue in cheek, by António Dias de Deus (1997).

The importance and impact of this last magazine on several generations of readers, including that of the present author and of some of the artists featured in this book, cannot be underplayed. When *Tintin* appeared in 1968 it brought two innovative aspects: it introduced many of the contemporary artists working in the French-speaking world of comics (for instance Goscinny and Uderzo and Hugo Pratt), its paper was of high quality, and it published its stories in four colours, using a thicker, brighter paper stock for its coloured cover. Focusing mainly on French and Belgian comics, it brought about what I believe to be a ground-breaking mix, for its editor-in-chief, Diniz Machado, was able to secure the rights for material from

Chapter One

quite distinct Francophone magazines, such as Lombard's *Tintin*, Dupuis's *Spirou* and Dargaud's *Pilote*. This led to a very specific, tightly knit conceptual formation in Portuguese minds of a " Franco-Belgian scene", if not style, and it allowed for the creation of a wide fan base. The magazine published other material as well, on rare occasions, such as stories by Will Eisner's *The Spirit*, but it was basically associated with Franco-Belgian authors. In part, it was also the influence of this magazine that introduced the Gallicism "banda desenhada", already mentioned. Despite its focus, *Tintin* opened up a few exceptions for Portuguese artists. The first few months had included the contribution of Péon, but he left shortly afterwards. José Ruy was a more or less regular presence in the magazine, with both long stories and short, sometimes even publicity one-pagers, in colour. But perhaps the most important, if irregular, contribution consisted of the two pages, almost always in the first or last black-and-white pages, produced by a younger generation of Portuguese artists. Starting in the late 1970s and early 1980s, we saw the work of people like Pedro Morais, António Serer, Mário Jorge, and more importantly, due to his unrelenting production rate and quality, Fernando Relvas.

Therefore, there was not much space for Portuguese artists to start with, but even less so to engage in work that did not conform to a certain norm or that did not cater to public expectations, whether in terms of genre, style or even readership. There were exceptions, however, the best known and most brilliant being the magazine *Visão*. With luxurious paper stock and brilliant colours, it carried almost exclusively Portuguese material, a remarkable move in itself, but more remarkable still through the fact that these works were aimed at adult audiences, dealing with taboo themes – for Portuguese comics – from drugs to politics, to urban dread and surrealism.[30] Launched precisely one year after the "Carnation Revolution", the magazine was deeply marked by the left-wing tinted discourses of the time, a struggle for ever-widening but also revolutionising democratisation, which included facing contemporary issues such as the Colonial Wars, Workers' Rights, and a fight against international capitalism and the pressure of Western powers (the presence of the C.I.A. in Portugal was not that secretive) against the possibility of the Communist 1975 coup. *Visão* included, for instance, a comics biography of Amílcar Cabral (an unsigned Cuban work, translated into Portuguese), considered up until then one of the major "public enemies" of the Empire. There was also an unfinished story written by Machado da Graça and drawn by Vitor Mesquita, "Matei-o a 24" ("I killed him the 24th"), about the hardships of a white Portuguese soldier trying to reintegrate into civil society, and his memories of a relationship with "the enemy", a black libertarian. Highly influenced by a myriad of sources (North American underground *comix*, the Losfeld books, *Métal Hurlant*, and so on), every artist had a particular style, ranging from naturalistic approaches to highly stylised or classically cartoony styles. All in all, names such as Vítor Mesquita, Zé Paulo, Pedro Massano, Carlos Barradas, Carlos Zíngaro, José Pedro "Zepe" Cavalheiro,

The semi-peripheral role of the Portuguese comics scene

Isabel Lobinho, Nuno Amorim made their debut in *Visão*, even if not all continued to create comics regularly. Despite its material quality and its diversity, several tensions within the team, a poor distribution scheme and probably mis-management and a general lack of interest by the public led to its incredibly rapid demise. *Visão* lasted for only 12 monthly issues, from April 1975 to May 1976. However, it had a profound impact beyond its short life, and it is still remembered (and sought out) today by new generations. A selection of its work was published in 2016 in a single volume called *ReVisão*.

To a certain extent, each decade could be characterised by one single magazine title. However, after the demise of *Tintin* in 1982 and *O Mundo de Aventuras* in 1987, and despite a few other projects typically involving pre-published episodes of Franco-Belgian album types, with no Portuguese authors (such as *Spirou*, 2 series from 1971 to 1979; *Flecha 2000,* 1978; *Jornal BD*, from 1982 to 1987; and *Selecções BD*, 2 series from 1988 to 2001), comics almost disappeared from the newsstands, ending thus the long, declining curve of its "Golden Age".[31] Imported Brazilian small magazines ("gibis"[32] in Brazilian parlance) were still around, though, translating American superhero comics and international Disney material (through publishers like Ebal, Abril and Morumbi), and American superheroes were sold in Portuguese translations (through the Agência Portuguesa de Revistas, which also had other adventure titles). Book shops carried the albums (Bertrand and, later on Meribérica/Liber), but without the magazines supporting the fanbase, the presence of comics started exiting the mass market to enter its "niche market" phase.

This does not mean that commercial projects, or those we can consider as such, including by Portuguese authors, disappeared completely. There was actually even room to create "national heroes". As an illustration, we could quote two examples of these hero-characters. First, *Tónius*, by the simply named authors Tito and André, was created as a home-grown pastiche of *Astérix*, focusing on a Lusitan leader resisting irritable Arab invaders (even though historically incorrect, we can read it as a humorous attempt to avoid featuring the historically correct Roman invaders, which would have brought it even closer to its model). Sadly, it had a very short life in the Portuguese *Spirou* magazine and in a single book published in 1981. Second, *Jim del Mónaco*, created by writer Tozé Simões and drawn by Luís Louro, began publication in 1985 in newspapers and comics magazines. It was actually quite long-lived by contemporary standards, adding up to seven albums published (and re-published in new colour editions) between 1986 and 1993, and an eighth in 2016. A blatant parody of classic adventure comics of a bygone area, and with a style analogous to the neo-*ligne claire* approach (especially after Daniel Torres), the series dives directly into narrative clichés and serves as homage to known series (above all, Alex Raymond's and Don Moore's *Jungle Jim*, but with elements from *Tintin*, *Blake & Mortimer*, and *Tarzan* as well, not to mention incredible intertextuality with popular films, comics and literature). However, at times it feels that the pastiches

Chapter One

of all the problematic heteronormative and Eurocentric representations of women as necessarily sexualised and helpless, the African sidekick as under-civilised and speaking a pidgin dialect are uncritical, deprived of their original political implications. Despite its overall "caricature" status, and the fact that these are books that circulate in a wholly different cultural context, which would suggest that they are not reflecting a normative perception but act as an ironic *clin d'oeil* to past representations, it seems nonetheless that the representations themselves are upheld and not deconstructed (Cunha 1995 and 2006).

In the Spring of 1990, a new, luxurious magazine with almost exclusively contemporary Portuguese material showed up: *Lx Comics*. Albeit also short lived (four issues, ending in the Summer of 1991, with no significant distribution of the last issue), it was reminiscent of *Visão* for its domestic roster and the remarkable diversity of visual styles and narrative approaches. Its director was Renato Abreu, and the editor was João Paulo Cotrim, who became a key agent in the development of comics throughout the decade, thanks to his work at the Bedeteca de Lisboa, as well as a writer of important books, one of which I will address in the chapter on Miguel Rocha. *Lx Comics* presented artists who had been around on the fanzine circuit like Filipe Abranches, Diniz Conefrey, Maria João Worm, Jorge Varanda, Alice Geirinhas, André Lemos, Jorge Mateus, Pedro Burgos, Nuno Saraiva, but also "recuperated" Zepe and Zé Paulo, from *Visão*, and Fernando Relvas, from *Tintin* (all of whom, however, collaborated with other magazines, newspapers or published books, especially Relvas). Although it also included work by international artists (introducing Miguelanxo Prado or the work of Alain Corbel, who lived and worked in Portugal for many years), *Lx Comics* can be seen as presenting a new generation of authors, many of whom are still fairly active today, influenced by new international tendencies, and quite informed not only about comics but also other creative disciplines. With some important contextual differences (both cultural and economic), *Lx Comics* could be seen as introducing in Portugal the "alternative" or "independent" scene, mixing, once again, new French traditions (what Bruno Lecigne deemed "le nouveau réalisme"), American alternatives and even, closer to home, Spanish experiences (the outstanding anthology *Madriz*, edited by Felipe Hernández Cava, published between 1983 and 1987, was a probable model, not only editorially but also financially, as both had municipal-level support; "LX" stands for "Lisbon"). To a certain extent, *LX Comics* was the signpost of the entrance of Portuguese comics onto the contemporary stage of "alternative comics".

The contemporary scene

According to Sara Figueiredo Costa, throughout the 1990s the perception of comics as something beyond mere juvenile stuff or nostalgic throwbacks changed in Portugal, but more in its social dimension than in a full blossoming and diversification of the market forces. There were more channels of distribution, true, and following international trends comic books became more present in general bookstores and were also better handled, allowing for them to reach a slightly wider readership, especially in demographics if not in absolute numbers (Costa 2011: 60 ff.). In addition, more consolidated formulas for exhibitions and festivals were key in this wider reach, underlining the importance of exhibiting "original art" and contact between authors and audiences through talks and signings, to the detriment of commercial aspects (there were no American-styled "conventions" in Portugal until recent years and the ones that tried this formula were short-lived), and sometimes disposing of significant budgets.

What follows is a concise, though unavoidably zigzag-like, portrayal of important references in the construction of the comics "scene" today.

The International Comics Festival of Amadora (FIBDA) was launched in 1989, organised officially by the City Council of Amadora (although it has developed its own team over the years, including a small department called CNBDI, following its Angoulême namesake in mission, albeit not in budget, scope or even efficiency; it continued uninterrupted until its closure in 2014, giving way to Amadora's own Bedeteca). Although its main focuses are on more commercially leaning, mass-market comics published in Portugal, it always aimed to include exhibitions on lesser-known national traditions, or authors working outside the U.S. or French mainstreams. Porto had its own Salão Internacional, which actually began before FIBDA, in 1985, but this only lasted until 2001 (annually until 1989, and then biannually). Growing exponentially and also more informed than FIBDA about contemporary tendencies, it presented a larger number of both contemporary Portuguese and foreign artists, especially from "alternative" circles (such as Joe Matt, Seth, Adrian Tomine, Julie Doucet, Étienne Davodeau, etc.). In 1996, the Bedeteca de Lisboa was opened. This was a city-level specialised comics library and institution dedicated to the exhibition and publishing of comics, and whose executive director was J. P. Cotrim. Again, somewhat akin to the CNBDI, it had its own Festival, the Salão Internacional de Banda Desenhada e Ilustração, which started in 1998 but had a short-lived and convoluted history until 2005 (what started as an annual event on comics and illustration soon split those areas, which were subsequently presented in alternate years).[33] In 2011, for both economic and political reasons, the Bedeteca was "absorbed" by the adjoining (literally so, as they are in the same building) local municipal library of Olivais, and lost its budgetary autonomy. Although it still exists as a separate library, and it continually buys books, it no longer organises exhibitions, workshops or meetings, nor does it publish.

The cities of Viseu and Moura, like a few other smaller cities, also have their own long-standing international festivals, although both seem to focus more on a nostalgia-tinted approach, with retrospective looks at classic domestic and foreign

Chapter One

masters, and a rather narrow consideration of new artists (only those published through larger or commercial platforms, or working in conventional genres and styles, and so on). For instance, Viseu, every year, presents an exhibition of an artist working on the famous western Italian series *Tex Willer*. More recently, another international festival joined these references. The Beja Festival opened its first edition in 2005, and despite having a smaller budget than FIBDA or the Porto and Lisbon "Salons", and dramatically so in recent years, it has consistently presented a varied choice of international names, from highly recognizable names from mainstream North-American superhero comics to experimental artists from Greece, from famous names of the French-speaking industry to upcoming Portuguese talents, and with a very special relationship with some Spanish contemporary artists.

All these different events and venues, although working *with* and *on* comics, aim at quite different audiences, although there is, as is to be expected, some overlap. The Lisbon, Porto and Beja meetings are rather more varied in their programmes, and somewhat more attentive to contemporary tendencies, but also their initiatives and style of exhibition and communication is quite appealing to audiences who would not define themselves as "comics fans", but people more generally interested in cultural production, from literature to the visual arts, to cinema *d'auteur* and performance arts. As S. F. Costa writes:

> Comics reception was no longer an exclusive province of fans of juvenile adventures and people with nostalgia for a supposed Golden Age. Comics [with the Lisbon and Porto salons] took their first steps in their inscription within the ample, transdisciplinary field of the arts. Without forgetting the patrimony that motivated publications and exhibitions before [the 1990s], and without neglecting the heritage of mass communication that structured the perception of comics to the detriment of any other approach, comics stepped out of the ghetto of 'bedephilia' (a term that is more expressive of the fans' enthusiasm than the field itself, given that comics make up a language with as plural a vocation as any other) and became available to a wider, necessarily heterogeneous audience. (2011: 61).

I would like to add a few short words on exhibitions, arguably one of the strategies to put comics onto the cultural map. Exhibitions can be monographic or collective and can be organised within the frameworks of festivals and salons,[34] or within small, "alternative" shows.[35] More often than not, exhibitions are associated with a book launch, a historical chapter that is being rediscovered, a contest, a thematic or national grouping, or any other commemorative reason. There are also cases in which some artists who make comics are known as visual artists and are used to being part of that other art world, but the exhibitions of those particular *other* works have little or no traction in relation to the comics world or are not done with any dialogue between those worlds in mind.[36] The most important gestures, I think, are those which attempt to present a choice guided by more consolidated criteria that will lead to an appreciation of comics' own intrinsic, aesthetic elements, presenting them to wider, non-specialised audiences. There are only a handful of examples, but they have contributed to that dialogue I referred to.

In 2000, the Calouste Gulbenkian Foundation presented *Banda Desenhada Portuguesa*, a show that covered the history of national comics, organised by João Paiva Boléo and Carlos Bandeiras Pinheiro. A lavish two-volume catalogue was produced, but, as one can surmise, the criteria were solely those of historical relevance. That same year, in a completely different environment, in the contemporary art and cultural centre Zé dos Bois gallery, the *Zalão de Danda Bedenhada* (a play on words with the acronym of the gallery, ZDB and BD), was presented, co-organised by Marcos Farrajota, comics author and editor at Chili Com Carne, focusing on more independent, avant-garde informed artists (in fact, Farrajota's new editorial project, Mmmnnnrrrg, was born out of this junction). By the early 2010s, several smaller, independent spaces opened their gallery spaces to several projects, including visual arts, performance and music, but also considered comics as a valid art form. Some of them were short lived, while others are still active today and some of them are actually more or less specialised in comics and illustration. We can quote Plumba, Dama Aflita and Mundo Fantasma in Porto, or Work&Shop and Trem Azul in Lisbon. In 2011, the Colecção Berardo Museum of contemporary art opened an exhibition called *Tinta dos Nervos*, curated by myself. This show presented almost 40 artists, most of them working on comics, although a few visual artists were also included who had created work based on visual, structural or conceptual approaches that are akin to comics (such as painter Eduardo Batarda, for his groundbreaking art book *O Pinguim Blindado*, or Isabel Baraona for her small, pseudo-narrative, drawing booklets). Only two of the artists were "historical" references (Bordalo Pinheiro and Carlos Botelho), as all the others were alive and mostly still working on comics. Artists represented included those who had been working since the 1960s as well as newcomers who were yet to publish their first book (assuming that publishing a "book" is some sort of step for the consolidation of a "career"). This was the first time, in Portugal, that an institution dedicated to the arts exhibited comics as an *art form*, and not as a mass medium or as a source of historical documentation, so it comes as no surprise that the comics include ranged over many forms, genres, styles and degrees of public projection. Before this, I also had the opportunity to script a television documentary, directed by Paulo Seabra, for the national channel RTP2, broadcast in the Summer of 2007 in five 25-minutes episodes, entitled *Verbd*. A first part (almost the whole of the first two episodes) was focused exclusively on history, while the rest of the programme zeroed in on a group of eleven contem-

Chapter One

porary authors. However, it also assessed many other realms, from the editorial world, the economic conjunctures, the diversity of genres and styles, methods of work, academic and study venues, etc. Despite a planned DVD edition, this has not been issued yet, if it will ever be (it is available on Youtube, however). With all due modesty, I believe that both were significant events in the public broadcasting of comics culture and creation beyond the usual confines of its circle, even though I must also admit that they have had little if any influence on the most important aspect of comics-production: its publishing and circulation.

Part of the growth pointed out by Costa was felt specifically in the multiplication of publishing platforms that were not only attentive to different interpretations of what could be done with and expressed through comics, opening up the possibility for the translation and publishing of artists usually unconsidered by more commercial publishers, but also, more importantly, were interested in creating room for new Portuguese authors with an incredible diversity of interests and research paths. These included both independent small presses like Chili Com Carne, Polvo and Pedranocharco, as well as publishers supported by city-level institutions, such as the "comic book" collection Lx Comics (recuperating the experience of the magazine in which Cotrim participated) from Lisbon's Bedeteca and the mini-comic collection Quadradinho from Porto's Salão. Moreover, Bedeteca also "inherited" *Quadrado* from the Porto Salão. What started as an oversized magazine with international and national comics, and some critical articles, more or less associated with the exhibitions in Porto and an incredibly international view of comics production, transformed into a smaller, book-like publication with more room for essays and theoretical work, both from known international names and domestic more or less established and budding critics (Beaty 2008: 129). Anthologies seem to be a guaranteed way of creating a new, more cosmopolitan readership of contemporary comics, whether from institutionally supported projects or artist-run projects. As Beaty intuited brilliantly, efforts such as *Lx Comics, Noites de Vidro, Para além dos Olivais, Stad, Satélite Internacional*, among many others, "point[ed] to the possibility of producing highly focused works for local constituencies that are nonetheless rooted in a particularly regional vision of an increasingly transnational creative movement" (idem).

With the closing down of the Lisbon and Porto "Salões", the dwindling of Lisbon Bedeteca's budget for publication and the demise of some publishers (Witloof, Pedranocharco), etc. recent years have been marked by a significant publishing inertia. A major publisher, Asa, still puts out the same kind of Franco-Belgian albums that Meribérica-Liber did (in fact, until very recently, the editor was the same person), and sometimes even "swamps" the market with cheap-priced collections of so-called classics distributed with national daily papers: a few examples are the collections dedicated to *Astérix, Spirou, Corto Maltese* or *Blueberry*. The super-hero collections from Marvel and DC or several "Classic Heroes" collections (which, by including examples such as Jiro Taniguchi's *Aruku Hito/The Walking Man* or Joann Sfar's *Le chat du rabbin*, somewhat "diluted" their potential impact on a wider audience uninterested in collections such as these, losing an opportunity of reaching new, differentiated audiences). Although there is no hard data on this, it seems likely that this "dumping" practice diminishes the attention that could be guided towards the production of Portuguese artists. In fact, Sara Figueiredo Costa, a literary critic who is also interested in research on publishing policies, complains about the lack of data provided by publishers or book-related institutions that are necessary to any serious, historically-sociologically anchored study of publishing in Portugal. This is a critique also presented by other specialists in the field, but it extends to all book-related areas not only in this country but elsewhere.

I cannot, therefore, pretend to give here a (pseudo-)sociological account of the present Portuguese comics market, but I hope that a general account of a recent year can show the comics environment in Portugal. I would like to make two preliminary points. The first is that between my first draft of this section, many things have changed, and they may change again within the next couple of years, which is to be expected in a market whose main agents are middle- to small-sized independent publishers, instead of larger commercial houses. The second is that I have relied on the precious information provided by the site http://bandasdesenhadas.com/, spearheaded by Nuno Pereira de Sousa. *Bandas Desenhadas* is a platform that is dedicated to all things related to comics, whether in the form of reviews, news, or comments on film adaptations, authors' profiles, etc. One of the things it provides is monthly checklists and yearly balances of what has been published. I have drawn on information directly provided by Pereira de Sousa in the form of personal communications for the following paragraphs, which cannot but be seen as a very broad account.

First of all, there is a (not completely distinct) difference between the comics that are sold in bookstores - usually in the form of books, *albums* or "graphic novels" - and the ones sold in *bancas* - U.S.-style comic books, magazines (more or less A4-sized, four-colour printed) or Brazilian-style *gibis* (small size magazines). Although there are other words that can be used, *bancas* stands for the many newsagents' shops, whether stores or self-standing kiosks that sell newspapers, magazines, tobacco, lottery tickets, public transportation monthly passes and many other things. It is here that one finds monthly or weekly comics, in Portuguese (of the European Portuguese variant but in the imported cases also in Brazilian Portuguese), as well as those books distributed with newspapers. A typical month will offer around five to six titles from the Italian publisher Bonelli (locally published by Mythos, with the famous westerns *Tex* and *Zagor*), around twelve North-American super-hero (DC and Marvel) comic books (all from Panini, with some titles from the Spanish-based company and other imported from Brazil), four titles of Disney comics (mainly Italian material, translated and published in Portugal), and more than fifteen titles associated with Brazilian author and children's comics power-house Mauricio de Sousa (of *Turma da Mônica* fame). There are also a few other occasional titles of child-oriented comics or magazines with a few pages of comics, in many formats, more often than not related to cartoon shows and toy lines (*Winx, Cars, Cartoon Network, Legos, Playmobil*). Sometimes there are publishers like Planeta de Agostini - a specialised producer of collectible products, like car miniatures, coins and toys, but also with a large selection of publications - who act upon this market: throughout 2013-2014 they produced a collection of seventy hardback volumes, distributed weekly, of *Star Wars*-related comics. Salvat is putting out a *Graphic Novels Marvel* collection, with up to sixty hardback volumes. Furthermore, daily newspapers such as *Diário de Notícias, Jornal de Notícias, Correio da Manhã* but more recently *Público* may offer weekly collections of comic books. Many formats have been distributed with these newspapers, but the Franco-Belgium album format, both hard- and softcover, is particularly prevalent, the most recent example being a collection of cheaply priced albums featuring Raoul Cauvin's and Lambil's *Les tuniques bleues*. There have also been, since 2015, several collections of "graphic novels" previously unpublished in Portugal, put out every Summer by Levoir and distributed by *Público*, with an average of fifteen titles each, mixing genres and styles, countries of origin and original dates of publication.

Apart from the several specialised comics bookstores, which carry foreign material (mostly North-American comics in English, but there are a few important examples that carry much Francophone material and, although rather less often, sometimes other languages too), a number of key *bancas* in the main cities also carry American or French comics magazines or magazines about comics such as *L'Im-manquable* or *dBD*.

As for books, in any given month a handful of books are published. The major output is foreign material produced in the U.S. (mainly super-hero material, and sometimes re-editions) and in Japan, with a number of current *shonen manga* series. Then there follows original Portuguese material, less open to re-editions. Humour strips (either international or domestic) are rare, but they do occur and, to a much lesser degree, children's comics. All in all, however, not more than ten books on average are published. Until very recently, the years that this book covers, only a fraction of those were by Portuguese authors. Today there are a few changes, as in 2015 39% of comic books published in Portugal were by domestic authors, putting it in the first place. But in 2016 it dropped to third place, with only 15%. Whatever the future holds, the bottom line seems to be that there is no assuredness for the long-term survival or financial success of Portuguese-made comics even within the country.

As we have already discussed and will develop below, some of the Portuguese authors' output is made through small press endeavours, or even self-publishing efforts, whether in the form of "classic" fanzines of print-on-demand editions. All in all, following contemporary Portuguese comics production requires an effort to look for alternative bases of distribution and divulgation, outside the *bancas* and bookstores circuit. These include the specialised stores, which more often than not will *not* carry fanzines, and whose relationship with the smaller publishers is sporadic at best.

Despite the multiplication of agents, however, the truth is that print runs are quite small and the economic investment in each title is residual. Many books are black and white, some pretty slim, and more often than not, Portuguese authors are not paid or, if they are, it is a "symbolic" amount, and not a percentage of the whole book. Publishers, on the other hand, rarely expect anything more than to cover printing expenses, and sometimes they do not even reach that sum. There are cases, however, of successful, intelligent practices, so even a small publisher can prove to be able to profit and consequently invest in new editions. Cases in point are Chili Com Carne and Kingpin Books, despite their almost opposite choice of styles and understanding of comics production. At the same time, these two publishers may be used as examples of the confirmation but also complication of the application of external notions such as "alternative" and "commercial" to Portuguese reality. More recently, other medium-sized publishers have been created, some of which devote significant attention to Portuguese authors, such as Escorpião Azul and A Seita, for instance, with very different strategies and successes, but this is not the place to delve into them.

Costs are, in fact and as always, difficult to manage, from production to distribution, not to mention negotiating with the bookstores themselves to "conquer" shelf space, and then everything else a publisher may use to promote the new book, from marketing strategies as simple as e-flyers, to book launch, to exhibiting at festivals or other venues that can act as a selling point, etc. Major publishers have specialised staff, or specific budgets for each item. In some cases, such as Asa, which is now part of a larger publishing conglomerate called Leya, they have their own distribution company, and even bookstores. But in most cases the publisher consists of one or two people doing every single step of the process, from paginating a book to driving down to a bookstore and delivering the books.

A major problem associated with the social perception of comics is a lack of diversified space for promotion. Literary criticism in general suffers from diminishing space, but comics suffer doubly; also, very rarely can newspapers feature articles about books whose prints runs are residual, although some newspaper critics do make an effort to include them. But there are other pernicious habits - such as the one that leads to shelving *any* comic book in the children's section, in a specific comics section, or next to them - that quite often makes sure that a certain book will never reach its intended audience.[37] However, there are a few exceptions to this rule. We can quote again from Costa, who gives the example of the Portuguese edition, in two volumes, of Joe Sacco's *Palestine* (a joint enterprise by MaisBD, Mundo

Chapter One

Fantasma and Devir in 2004). This book found shelf space not in the specific comics sections, but the more general sections, sometimes even the "new books" section or the "international relations" section. Moreover, its journalistic reception was quite widespread, and went beyond the usual (very restricted) space reserved for comics editions in newspapers and magazines, often taking the form of lengthy articles, including by influential international relations journalists. As Costa concludes, "the interest in it from the audiences ended up making [*Palestine*] a milestone" (2011: 65). When Costa wrote her text, Marjane Satrapi's *Persepolis* had not yet been published in Portuguese, and Emmanuel Guibert et al.'s *Le Photographe* trilogy has never been published. She nonetheless quotes these two titles, on account of the attention that they had generated in newspapers and literary magazines, with articles written by leading critics of international politics and culture, despite the very fact they had *not* been published. For Costa, this shows clearly that "some authors, if they were handled by publishers and marketers with the same methods that are used for literary fiction authors, would have all the conditions to access a good reception from a market point of view". Unfortunately, Portuguese comics authors can very rarely count on this sort of "handling".

Here are a few brief examples. Being a "household name" means little. Authors such as Filipe Abranches, Diniz Conefrey and Miguel Rocha, although they have outstanding books to their name, sometimes find overwhelming obstacles in the way of new projects. In fact, Conefrey moved into self-publishing recently, faced with the lack of interest of major publishers (of comics or otherwise) in putting out his sophisticated creations (a saga of a Mexica *tlacuilo*, the adaptations of short prose and poems by Herberto Helder, and an remarkable abstract comics output). Undoubtedly, these authors would find an interested audience, if the "market" was not moulded towards comics-as-entertainment. Filipe Abranches also set up a self-publishing house, through which he released his own new solo book (*Selva!* or "Jungle!") as well as a weird/science fiction magazine called *Umbra*, trying to tap into different genres and demands.

Again quoting Costa, it is as if comics publishers and mediators were "unable to separate market and audience segments, as it is done by the rest of the editorial industries" (64 ff.). So the upscaling of comics, in Portugal, seems to have failed. Another important Portuguese comics critic, Domingos Isabelinho, adds that "from the people's street, comics went into the bourgeois bookstore. Even there, though, its survival cannot be taken for granted" 2011: 89).

Of course, such constraints and lack of venues for publishing find a complete reversal when we reach the ever more democratic information technologies, which allow artists to reach for alternatives to traditional processes of publishing (web-based platforms, print on demand, online sale and distribution, etc.). Additionally, although historically not a new thing, conquering international markets is also a solution. For instance, never before did we have so many Portuguese authors working for foreign publishers (in a work-for-hire fashion), especially thanks to the many younger artists working for widely known American publishers such as Marvel, but also Dark Horse, Boom! Studios, Moonstone Books, Shadowline/Image, Dynamite Entertainment, etc. - people such as Jorge Coelho, Filipe Andrade, André Lima Araújo, Eliseu Gouveia, Daniel Maia, Nuno Plati, João Lemos, Ana Freitas, Ricardo Venâncio, Miguel Montenegro, Miguel Mendonça and Daniel Henriques. But it is not only in commercial, mainstream markets that this traffic is found. International partnerships, travelling and independent fairs and venues also put alternative artists in contact. As a result, publishers may buy translation rights. For example, Amok published *Mr. Burroughs*, by David Soares and Pedro Nora, as well as the first volume of *Histoire de Lisbonne*, by Oliveira Marques and Filipe Abranches, which was published in its entirety also in Italian by Comma 22, under the title *Storia di Lisbona*. 6 Pieds Sous Terre put out *Le collectionneur de briques*, by Pedro Burgos, subsequently issued in Portuguese. They may also invite Portuguese artists to participate in collective projects, such as *...de ellas*, an all-women anthology organised by F. H. Cava for De Ponent, which included Isabel Carvalho, or *Lanza en Astillero*, consisting of short adaptations of episodes from the *Quijote*, with one piece by Abranches, published by Castilla-la-Mancha, both from 2006. They may even publish original work in monographs. The Latvian house kuš! is also quite attentive towards a number of Portuguese authors, who have published both short works in the anthological **š**! and the monographical mini-kuš! Once again, we can find this possibility both within the realm of more commercially-driven projects, such as Rui Lacas' *Merci, Patron* (published by Paquet in 2006, before the Portuguese *translation*), or alternative, art-related works such as André Lemos' two silk-screened collections, *Mediaeval Spectres Soaked In Syrup* (from Russia's Pipe and Horse) and *Some Dishonourable Creatures Attacked Us* (from the French Boom Books). Furthermore, alternative European publishers have found ways of collaborating, either by sharing the expenses on printing, or distributing the books as widely as possible across the continent. Two good examples are *Greetings From Cartoonia*, which, although published by Stripburger, is supported by other publishers, including Chili Com Carne, and Tommi Musturi's *Walking with Samuel*, which is a co-edition among the Finnish Huuda Huuda, the Portuguese Mmmnnnrrrg,[38] Belgium's La 5ème Couche and Swedish Optimal Press.

Self-publishing, as we have seen, is an obvious choice. Not only where classic fanzines are concerned (photocopied, black-and-white, folded and stapled sheets of paper) but, thanks to new developments in printing techniques and a less expensive array of solutions, from offset to silkscreen to digital printing, all kinds of books (leading to endless discussions, especially where festival and awards categories are concerned, on what constitutes in precise terms "independent" publi-

Chapter One

cation, and the multiplication of terms such as prozines, artzines, and so on). This also frees artists and publishers (or artist-publishers) from conventional formats or "saleable" categories. Individually, in small groups or larger collectives, artists such as André Lemos, Marco Mendes, Miguel Carneiro, Joana Figueiredo, Pedro Nora, Isabel Carvalho and Rodolfo, for instance, exploit the affordances of comics, and some of them engage in anthological projects (with both national and international participations). This does not mean that new agents on the Portuguese scene do not use the same possibilities for creating work that is rather more conventional and genre-related, in conjunction with very interesting and intelligent policies of management, as is the case of Mário Freitas' label, Kingpin Books, quoted before. It is worth taking some time to understand this project.

Kingpin actually started as a comics bookstore, with a logo of a pig (the "Kingpin") which was, at one time, both the commercial logo but also a caricatural avatar of its owner, Mário Freitas. In 2006, he began the eponymous publishing platform, with comic book style publications, by several authors, including the adventures of that avatar, written by Freitas himself and drawn by a number of different artists. Most of the titles Kingpin produces are by Portuguese artists, although there was at least one successful anthology with the very first book edition of the first chapters of Cameron Stewart's *Sin Titulo* and a series of books by Mexican artist Tony Sandoval. This is a one-man affair, considering that Freitas is also the letterer and designer of his publications, as well as the organiser of Anicomics, a mid-sized event dedicated mostly, but not exclusively, to North American comics and Japanese manga, in addition to an annual "industry" award. The way that Freitas coordinates all these events, for instances, inviting the winners of the Anicomics comics contest to publish through Kingpin, the way that he publicises his artists' work via social media - on which he is extremely prolific - or even through policies that put everyone's names on the book covers (not only the writer and penciller and/or inker, but also the colourist, the letterer, etc.) makes it quite a tight project that reaches its audience fast and creates a "buzz" on the scene, for better or for worse. The publisher is able to pay its authors, even if not at a rate comparable to (average) U.S. or French rates per page, and to make some profit, which is channelled into the production cycle. However, considering that the titles have not had a print run above 500 copies (although two titles have announced a second edition, and not merely a reprint), it is too soon to assess the scope of its "success". Nevertheless, this is a case in which commercial strategies - working within well-established genres, following the typically "Taylorist" method of North American comics, using mass media and a media-savvy discourse - have been used positively to reach out to new audiences, even if within the ambit of "popular culture".

Although physically some of the projects of these last few names do not look like the typical fanzines of the 1980s (on which many of the artists I will deal with took their first steps, especially during the 1980s and early 1990s, and even in the 2000s), the most important aspect of these self-publishing projects arises out of their political dimension, especially if we take account of Stephen Duncombe's postulation of a "central ethic" common to all zines, the "emphasis on the personal" being its most important aspect (1997: 235). As "a novel form of communication and creation that burst with an angry idealism and a fierce devotion to democratic expression" (idem: 228), "[z]ines offer a space for people to try out new personalities, ideas, and politics" (idem: 247). In fact, freed from the concern to integrate themselves into expectations about genre, style, narrative formulae, commercial and critical success (especially from the perspective of a mass market, or even niche market) and even readership, these publications aim towards a different expression of their authors' creative will. Duncombe points that, at least in the examples he is addressing in his article, authors "do share this emphasis on the act over the result" (idem: 242), but that does not preclude the achievement of outstanding results in an aesthetic sense (complex and sophisticated storytelling techniques, drawing and colouring, the very materiality of the publications, and so on). This will have some effect on the way the authors deal with trauma, as we will see.

So, to a certain extent, there are small fields characterised by different interests, some of which we may deem to be "commercial" and others to be "alternative". I have no wish, though, to leave the impression of clear-cut, separate worlds. There is some overlap. Not only do many of these authors participate in the same festivals and exhibitions, but some will have a continuous involvement in both self-publishing projects, usually more personal, and more commercially-inclined projects, that aim to conform to a certain genre. A case in point is André Pereira, who creates personal works of weird poetical sci-fi, alone or in collaboration with João Machado, through his own labels Clube do Inferno and Massacre, or more established houses such as Polvo, while participating in collective projects with other "alternative" artists, as in the case of *QCDA* (probably short for "Quatro Chavalos do APOPcalipse", or "The Four Punks of the *Apop*calypse", a label bestowed by Farrajota, the editor of Chili Com Carne), or putting out "work-for-hire", as in the case of *Super Pig: O impaciente inglês*, written by Mário Freitas (and published by Kingpin).

There are always problems when we resort to dichotomies of this kind, which run into the danger of creating artificial fields. Metropolis *versus* periphery or commercial *versus* alternative leads to seemingly unambiguous narratives that do not tell the whole story and very often present too smooth a pair of opposing camps that actually share much of the same scope for action, and sometimes the same stages, readers, venues, and even authors. Fan discourses and even some (the little there is) journalism on comics like to make use of "independent", "alternative", "underground", "artistic", "intellectual" comics, or similar terms (that in Portugal always go through a radical de-contextualisation of their original deployment and

Chapter One

must find uneasy adaptations) against the perceived "commercial", "successful", "widely distributed" comics.

An article by Marie Manuelle Silva and Rui Malheiro contends that Portuguese comics also seem to follow these two major *lignes de fuite*. On the one hand, "an experimental branch, searching for a different way to express their worldview, and [on the other hand] a popular branch, that tries to develop the potential of comics as a form of entertainment" (2006: 171). The article is rather incomplete and reductive in its description of the Portuguese market (and history), and limited in its theoretical scope, but it does set the tone for an artificial opposition between practices, which, despite its artificiality, is rather pervasive in all the discourses on comics in the country (in festivals, blogs, specialised or general press, and, as we can see, academia as well). The major problem with the article, however, and one that we perceived before, is also repeated by other voices: it is the failure to look at Portuguese comics globally without recourse to a direct comparison with outer, "more developed" models. This leads of course to a distorted vision, and a consideration of Portuguese comics as "lacking" something, and not as its own particular thing.

Having said this, it is still possible to consider that some artists do aim to work within the entertainment industry, such as it is in Portugal, or are willing to work within institutional *commandes*, such as the many books that exist on "The history of the city of X", for instance. But some, if not all, of the artists I will address in this book fall into this porous territory we can call "alternative". Or at least in a space of tension between more traditional comics and open-ended artistic realms, leading to what Domingos Isabelinho has called, on different occasions, and non-paradoxically, both "the expanded field" (see 2008; drawing from Krauss 1979) and the "strict field" of comics. Considering an alternative look at the history of comics, we can arrive at an understanding that a real openness of expressivity and visual experimentation could only take place after the experiences of the 1960s in most of the world. As a handful of international examples, Fred's *Le Petit Cirque*, Oesterheld's and Breccia's *Ernie Pike*, Buzzelli's *Zil Zelub*, the general output within the Japanese *Garo* magazine and Yoshiharu Tsuge oeuvre in particular, the U.S. underground comix of Crumb and Pekar, and others, could be seen as flagships of a broadening of the visual, composition, narrative, genre and even political strategies afforded by the comics medium. Of course, the following decades would witness and even more radical growth of freer, more independent-minded diverse creators of comics.

In fact, trauma, while a free-ranging topic that can be addressed by the most varied forms and strategies within the medium of comics, will find in these "counter-aesthetic" works (Beaty: 49) a more critical reassessment of history, of subject formation and even of comics themselves as an art form available for such an ambition, considering how some of these artists' formal choices "challenge[s] our understanding of comics as a cultural form" (Beaty: 64).

Finally, allow me to return to Costa, whose work helps to sum up many of my thoughts in this chapter. She underlines that "a large part of contemporary artistic production is developed along a sort of margin, with a few points of contact with the centre, but more often than not without having that marginality forced by its agents". (2011: 52).

Notes

1 Cultural studies has, of course, created obstacles to any consideration of the "nation" as a transparent, uncomplicated notion, by bringing to the front not only its "imaginative identification" as well as the multitude of "systems of representation" that act both within and upon it.

2 Patrick Gaumer, *La BD. Guide Totem*. n.l.: Larousse 2002. As of course, we are not comparing in any way these assessments: while Gaumer's typical encyclopaedic treatment, inherited from Moliterni and co. leads to an undifferentiated grouping, Beaty's work is much more focused and his choices are based on explicit criteria (not to mention his short yet incisive analyses, of which there are none in Gaumer).

3 The "three Fs", religion, sports and folk song. The sanctuary of Fátima stands for the Catholic tradition; football is the main sport and distraction of the country; and Fado, the typical melancholic song from Lisbon and Coimbra, and which would become the "national" song throughout the Estado Novo.

4 Quite certainly under the immense influence of the Portuguese magazine *Tintin*, after 1968.

5 There are many discussions about this subject, entangled as they are with another *vexata quaestio*, that of the "definition". See Labio 2011.

6 Only recently did comics, as a field, start to have organised, concrete publishing policies in relation to the "recuperation of memory" of comics. If one can consider Denis Gifford's *Victorian Comics* (1975), Bill Blackbeard's The Hyperion Library of Classic American Comic Strips collection (several volumes, 1977), and the two Smithsonian anthologies (1977 and 1982) as important precursors, as well as the first steps of publishers like Fantagraphics, TwoMorrows and Pierre Horay, as an attempt at commercialising this memory, it was only in the 1990s that this recuperation became more sound and effective, entangled as it was with the emergence of graphic novels and the novel distribution of comics in non-specialised bookstores. But very diverse, as well. On the one hand, there was the integration of "classics" by certain artist-run publishers in order to create a tradition of which the artists themselves would become a part (say, L'Association with Francis Masse, Gébé and Edmond Baudoin, among others, Ego comme x with Jean Teulé, Frémok with the *Che* of Oesterheld and the Breccias, and Alex Barbier). On the other hand, commercial publishers soon found interest from now moneyed adults in buying *intégrales* of their childhood comics (e.g. *Tif et*

Chapter One

Tondu, Gil Jourdan, etc.), or even beyond. In the U.S., integral collections became the rage as well: projects such as *Peanuts, Gasoline Alley, Dick Tracy, Moomin, Pop-eye* and *Krazy Kat* are but a few examples of very successful projects, commercially, editorially, critically and even where design is concerned. A study of the "dialogue between authors through design" in these ventures would be quite interesting (Seth in relation to Schulz, Chris Ware to Frank King and Herriman, Adrien Tomine to Tatsumi, etc). In Portugal, a wonderful collection published throughout the 1980s on Portuguese historical comics (mostly precisely from the Estado Novo decades), organised by Jorge Magalhães (for the now extinct Futura), despite its quality, met with little commercial success. Today, only a handful of collections are significant in this aspect, such as Paiva Boléo's edited collection of Carvalhais' *Quim e Manecas* (Tinta da China). See Robert Fiore, "The Experience of Comics", *The Comics Journal* # 300, November 2009; especially pp. 252 ff. This revitalisation of the past can be interpreted from a mediological perspective, as pointed out by A. Rajagopal: "Friedrich Kittler has argued that the sense of loss that haunts writing is erased by new media, that render the past into accessible presence. If new media make information 'want' to be free, they seem also to create pasts that 'want' to be restored". (2006: 283).

7   This is from Sena's introduction to *A Literatura Inglesa: Ensaios de Interpretação e de História* (English Literature: Essays of Interpretation and History), Cotovia: 1989), where he is characterising Portuguese literature in contrast to the several historical English "schools".

8   Ribeiro is drawing from Victor Turner's concept of *liminality*, that points towards an unstable state.

9   In 2000 a sister-project, Mmmnnnrrrg, would be founded but we will consider them together (see below).

10   The essay is dated 1985, but despite the radical changes operated in the last decades (European Union integration, followed by the euro, the cultural openness granted by events such as Lisbon 94 European Capital of Culture, the World Expo 98, and so on), with the recent global financial crisis, and the specific tensions within Europe, many of the illusory developments of the late 80s and 90s have vanished. Santos, as well as numerous other critics, has reiterated these traits.

11   In Portuguese, one other term for this is "subterranean economy", which can mean something as simple as *not* asking for a receipt in any given transaction, allowing for the provider not to declare it, and in some sectors this also means that the client does not pay VAT. Both are illegal, of course. This may play a part in some of the texts we will discuss, considering that they are sold and distributed outside any capitalist structure, when not traded.

12   See Groensteen 2006 and Éric Maigret, "La reconnaissance en demi-teinte de la bande dessinée" in *Réseaux* Vol. 12, n° 67: 1994; pp. 113-140.

13 In this, we are following the pioneering work of David Kunzle (1973 and 1990), as well as further developments by Thierry Smolderen, Pascal Lefèvre and Charles Dierick, Thierry Groensteen and Benoît Peeters, Jared Gardner, and wonderful blogs such as *Andy's Early Comics Archive*, *Yesterday's Papers*, *Coconino's Classics* and others. In Portugal, the main people who have worked on this subject are António Dias de Deus and Leonardo De Sá (1997) and João Paiva Boléo and Carlos Bandeiras Pinheiro (1997 and 2000).

14 However, more and more work has been produced that not only points to a quite complex history of "inventions" and "influences", but also supports the thesis that Töpffer may, in fact, have been a decisive factor in the development of "modern" comics, a common root. See Groensteen-Peeters 1994, Kunzle 2007 and Groensteen 2014 (especially chapter 4, pp. 64 and ff.)

15 Also found as "Raphael Bordallo", to follow its 19th century spelling.

16 In the case of Zé Povinho and Bordalo, however, there are no doubts about the paternity of the character. There are many books on both his work and oeuvre. A still wonderful introduction is the culture historian José-Augusto França's *Rafael Bordalo Pinheiro* (1981), while a more visual, modern approach is found on João Paulo Cotrim's *Fotobiografia* (2005).

17 In fact, his name is included in the BNF's *Maîtres de la bande dessinée européenne* exhibition, and respective catalogue (Groensteen 2000). He is the sole Portuguese artist in this exhibition.

18 In fact, a succession of unstable, short-lived governments. Up until 1926, when the May 28th military coup d'état implemented the beginning of a long-lived autocratic regime (until 1974), there were, to simplify, forty-five Constitutional Governments, plus the 1910 Provisional one, with more than fifty changes in heads of government (including collective juntas).

19 This does not mean that a strand of "political, critical and interventionist comics for adults" (Matos 2011: n.p.) was abandoned, as is precisely the point of Álvaro de Matos's study of the publication *Os Ridículos* (1910-1926).

20 Miguel de Unamuno used this expression among others, such as "university fascism" or "bellicose-scholastic dictatorship", in "Nueva vuelta a Portugal", July, the 3rd 1935 piece from the newspaper *Ahora*. Sousa 2011. Salazar, we should remember, was not only a university professor but had been a seminarian.

21 Salazar left the government in 1968, after a accident with serious consequences for his mental abilities, but he did not die until 1970, still believing himself to be the President of the Council.

22 A regime-oriented youth movement, the Mocidade was created in 1936 and was only dissolved in 1974. It was practically compulsory for children between 7 and 14 years of age, especially the male branch, although there was an active female branch as well.

Chapter One

23 Another important detail is that Müller, with Father Abel Varzim, also published in *O Papagaio*, in its very first translation, *Tintin en Amérique*, as "Aventuras de Tin-Tim na América do Norte" (starting in April 1936, at issue 53). It has some significant differences from its original *mise-en-page*, but it also added (limited) colour, which positively surprised Hergé. The character and story settings went through significant "localised" alterations, according to the *Instruções'* principles, perhaps the most significant one being the transformation of Tintin into a Portuguese reporter, or the relocation of *Tintin in the Congo* to Angola (with all the necessary national colonialist changes). This had no weight whatsoever in Hergé's or Casterman's creative output or translation concerns, according to Jan Aarnout Boer (cf. http://www.publico.pt/cultura/noticia/centenario-de-herge-portugal-foi-o-primeiro-pais-do-mundo-a-publicar-o-tintim-a-cores-1294692 [last access: march 7th, 2014], but the fact is that Müller managed to guarantee the ongoing translations into Portuguese of all adventures throughout all his editorial endeavours, from *O papagaio* to *Diabrete*, and then to *Foguetão*, *Cavaleiro Andante* and *Zorro*.

24 But also against. This is not the place to discuss it, of course, but *Os Lusíadas*, being a strongly polysemic poem, has been re-framed constantly according to several perspectives and can warrant both pro-imperialist readings as well as alternative, even resistant readings opposed to the Empire (such as Eduardo Lourenço's famous *O Labirinto da Saudade*, studies by Luciana Stegagno Picchio, or José Madeira's *Camões Contra a Expansão e o Império. Os Lusíadas como Antiepopeia.*). *Peregrinação* has been always read as an anti-epic text, but this does not preclude readings that underline its "adventure" side, especially when it is partially adapted into comics format.

25 The figure of Hergé, to quote arguably the most famous example of this problematic, has served as a model for this discussion (both its excesses and its fruitful developments).

26 A famous "revolutionary" song of the time, by Sérgio Godinho, entitled *Liberdade* [Freedom] (1974), spoke of (my free translation) "There will only be freedom when we have/bread, peace, housing, health, education./There will only be freedom when we have/Freedom to change and decide".

27 Suffice it to say, not immediately. An effective law on abortion, for instance, only came about in 2007, and indicators still point out to a significant discrepancy in wages between men and women.

28 *Mosquito* went through several phases, its peak being the biweekly format with a 30 000 print run.

29 Although we may apply epithets like "professional" and "exclusive" to some contemporary comics artists such as Jorge Coelho, Filipe Andrade and Miguel Mendonça, especially if they are working for international markets (mostly the U.S.), it is a bit of a stretch to speak of professionalisation these days in relation to most authors. Many of the artists we feature in this study have day jobs and

The semi-peripheral role of the Portuguese comics scene

several means of subsistence other than their comics production.

30 In point of fact, the artist Isabel Lobinho adapted some short stories by Mário Henrique-Leiria, one of the central names of the 1950s Surrealist movement in Portugal.

31 In the television documentary series *Verbd* (RTP2, 2007), António Dias de Deus sums this issue up by considering that from a strictly materialist, Marxist point of view the Golden Age of comics in Portugal can be situated around the 1940s, when comics were sold in the streets with newspapers (printed in them or as special inserts or supplementary magazines) and were "read by the largest number of people and came at a cheap price".

32 A word borrowed from the title of a children's magazine launched in 1939, which survived into the early 1960s.

33 See Beaty for a brief presentation and long-term, international contextualisation (2008: 120 ff.).

34 More often than not with a local impact only, but sometimes able to integrate projects of international projection, such as Lisbon Bedeteca's presentation, in 2009, of the Finnish *Glomp X*.

35 As for instance the ones organised by Feira Laica throughout the 2000s and early 2010s, in Lisbon, or associated with the A Mula collective (Marco Mendes, Miguel Carneiro et al.) in Porto, which were sometimes also re-presented in other cities or even outside Portugal.

36 Here we could talk about people like Eduardo Batarda, Alice Geirinhas, Bruno Borges, Pedro Zamith, Isabel Carvalho, Mauro Cerqueira, Carlos Pinheiro and Nuno Sousa, who work mostly on painting, but also drawing, sculpture, installation and performance.

37 By this we do not mean any empirical, real audiences, which may well be very varied and surprising. There is, however, or so I believe, a set of expectations that readers have about, say, a mainstream *shonen* manga title about a young magical ninja and an alternative autobiography in comics format of an Iranian woman living in Europe. Surely there are people who read and enjoy both - I do - but the set of expectations leads to differentiated strategies of production (format, paper stock, design, even pricing, perhaps) as well as divulgation (different channels of communication, criticism, shelving practices, etc.).

38 As mentioned before, in fact, both Chili Com Carne and Mmmnnnrrrg have the same editor-in-chief, Marcos Farrajota (who also works at the Bedeteca de Lisboa and was one of Beaty's sources, although the author misspells the name as "Pellojota" in the ackowledgements pages), but they are two different publishing venues. It is quite typical to mix them both, considering the pre-eminence of the editor, the sharing of the publisher's site, a certain "nature" of the works published, etc.

Chapter 2
A short history of trauma

"...trauma has become such an abiding concern also in the humanities as to necessitate the development of a new paradigm".

So writes Thomas Elsaesser (2001: 195). The purpose of this chapter is to discuss the ever-changing features of such a paradigm.

Throughout this book, I will be addressing and using critical tools on works of art - comics texts - and not the actual people, the authors and artists who have created them, by employing clinical, medical tools. It is important to be attentive to the kinds of methodology and tools that are used, but also to the scope of those very same tools and, crucially, to their limits.

I will use trauma studies as a lens through which to read a number of comics texts with the aim of reaching and underlining their political, social and ethical implications. It is less important for me to reveal the authors' purportedly inner mental world (the province of a certain style of psychoanalytical and biographist work that I have no interest in), than to understand their diagnosis of the world as performed through the comics medium. "We do not write with our neuroses (...) [literature is] an enterprise of health" (Deleuze 1997: 3).

I would like to make this chapter as clear as possible. I have no intention of proposing a new definition of trauma, but I want to understand how is it that the cultural and political disciplinary discourses that have been associated with trauma studies can help in the analysis of works by certain authors that seem to respond to situations of social and financial inequality, a certain feeling of insecurity and violence, and historical forgetfulness. In the case, the works are comics. More often than not, when people think of trauma and comics (or any other medium for that matter) they will think of traumatic events such as the Holocaust through the para-digmatic *Maus*; but also Miriam Katin's *We are on our own*; 9/11 with Spiegelman's *In the Shadow of No Towers* or Alissa Torres's and Sungyoon Choi's *American Widow*; incest or sexual abuse with Debbie Dreschler's *Daddy's Girl*, or Phoebe Gloeckner's and Lynda Barry's oeuvre, etc.; disease through Harvey Pekar and Joyce Brabner's *Our Cancer Year*, David B.'s *L'ascension du haut mal/Epileptic*, and Frederick Peeter's *Les pilules bleues,*; or of any engagement with larger historical frameworks, from Satrapi's *Persepolis* to Peter Pontiac's *Kraut* and Antonio Altarriba's and Kim's diptych *El arte de volar/El ala rota*. This perspective perpetuates an invisible division between a comics canonicity demarcating what merits scholarly attention from everything else beyond such a threshold.

By no means am I arguing that it is wrong to focus on these themes, or that the works I have mentioned are unimportant in any way. I myself have had the opportunity to write about many of them. But it begs the question as to why they warrant so much attention to the detriment of other texts, other chronicles, other cultures and nationalities, etc.? And, more importantly, if by doing so that focus perpetuates prejudices and imbalance?

Enmeshed with that query is another question. Besides these overwhelming traumas, do comics respond to *pervasive* or *insidious* trauma, "micro-aggressions" or other instances of trauma? How do they work with "small traumas", everyday affects that hinder people's daily lives, their prospects for the future, even the very possibility of thinking about a future or a self?

A few years ago, I participated in an academic symposium, and one of the panels was dedicated to history, memory and trauma. After the presentations, one of which focused on the autobiographical work of Carol Tyler, Miriam Katin and Alissa Torres, one of the participants bemoaned to the presenter the fact that, in her view, "trauma" was becoming an "umbrella term". In this person's view, "trauma" should be a protected term, to be used exclusively as regarding a certain class of events and psychological and emotional impacts on people, and not to be used willy-nilly in relation to whatever difficulties individuals would experience as traumatic. Now, as of course, without further information about and contextualisation of this intervention, this becomes a rather straw man argument. I understand that. But the fact is that whenever the words "trauma" and "comics" come together, more often than not the events brought to the fore belong to a certain expected typology, within a conservative view of the word.

The problem is that trauma has been an umbrella term since its inception in the late 19th century and throughout its history, as it made its way from a medical-psychological framework to a literary studies-inflected discourse.

Trauma began as a term applied to *woundedness*. In fact, its etymological Greek root means "wound", the result of a physical blow to the body. But with the work of Jean Martin Charcot, Pierre Janet, Josef Breuer and Sigmund Freud, a more comprehensive approach began to include the psychological consequences of the traumatic event. Charcot's work on hysterical women was but the first step into the investigation of the intersection of trauma-as-event, psychological disturbances and personality development. Roger Luckhurst presents an outline of the "psychodynamic theory [of the mind]" (2008: 38 and ff.), which played a crucial role in the development and expansion of the usage of the term *trauma*. It was never "a 'matter of fact,' as [Bruno] Latour puts it, but a 'matter of concern,' an enigmatic thing that prompts perplexity, debate and contested opinion" (33). Even within Freud's work, trauma went through a number of changes. His treatment of the condition of hysteria, for instance, moved from the body to a trauma- and anxiety-based causality, and its psychologisation. Freud "was modifying a category already in semantic flux" (Bettina Bergo, 2007: 6-7), a category that went back and forth in between internal and external excitations of trauma, founding its aetiology on his early "sexual seduction" theory, later disavowed in order to focus on internal causes. With World War I, a "mechanised factory of death" and source of "mass trauma" (Luckhurst: 51), Freud's observations of "shell shocked" soldiers made him return once again to external explanations (see also Janet Walker, 2006: 119).[1] In addition, Abram Kardiner made important contributions to the study of trauma within the war environment with 1914-1918 U.S. veterans, and, of course, Sandor Ferenczi's insights (and the discussions with Freud) were crucial in this development. Moreover, a more mature Freud brought together his interests in trauma, history, culture, art and literature. Significantly, Freud does not attribute an all-powerful role to his own discipline when approaching literature, and he confesses in his 1928 "Dostoievsky and Parricide" essay: "[b]efore the problem of the creative artist analysis must, alas, lay down its arms" (apud Jean-Michel Ray 1982: 304).

Even these first expansions were not devoid of obstacles, and neither were they devoid of ideological strife, engaging with gender, race and social class. Quoting Herbert W. Page, from his 1883 essay, *Injuries of the Spine and Spinal Cord without Apparent Mechanical Lesion, and Nervous Shock in their Surgical and Medico-Legal Aspects*, Roger Luckhurst explains how:

> [t]he vastness of the destructive forces, the magnitude of the results, the imminent danger to the lives of numbers of human beings, and the hopelessness of escape from the danger, give rise to emotions which in themselves are quite sufficient to produce shock (apud 23).

Working as a surgeon for the London and North Western Railway Company, in whose interest it was to dismiss these consequences, Page immediately downplayed the force of these traumas, insisting "that the psychical traumas of railway accidents were forms of hysteria (...) a shameful, effeminate disorder, often dismissed as a form of disease imitation (what was called 'neuromimesis') or malingering" (idem).

Even though I run the risk of presenting a rather too tidy history of trauma theory, it is worth remembering that my aim is to re-purpose trauma theory towards our texts of choice. For that reason, I would argue that in this brief and general outline, another significant development was brought about by awareness of the grave psychological disturbances of Vietnam War veterans, which led, in

Chapter Two

great part, to the emergence of the psychological disorder known as Post-Traumatic Stress Disorder, which not only "entered official diagnostics in 1980" but also "gave a coherent disease-entity to diverse political programmes and ensured the wide diffusion of the trauma paradigm" (Luckhurst: 59; see also Caruth, *Trauma*: 3). It entered the "official diagnostics" through its inclusion on the third edition of the *Diagnostic and Statistical Manual of Mental Disorders*, also known as *DSM-III*. Importantly the *DSM-III* does not distinguish explicitly *mental* memory and *bodily* memory (see "Preface" and "Introduction", Antze and Lambek 1996). Moreover, "PTSD has *not* been a fixed but a very mobile term, progressively extending the types of symptoms and categories of sufferers *outwards* from the initial restrictions on what constituted the traumatic event" (my emphases, Luckhurst, 2008: 29)[2].

The intersection of combat trauma, the Holocaust (which also gained a greater hold on public consciousness throughout the late 1960s and 1970s) and the second wave of feminism led to a profound change in the response to trauma, moving from the secretive and private to more public spheres, from individual healing processes to collective, institutional and political processes. There seems to have been a recurrent cycle of expansion and resistance in relation to the concept of trauma and its social implications. Judith L. Herman, in *Trauma and Recovery*, writes: "[t]hree times over the past century, a particular form of psychological trauma has surfaced into public consciousness. Each time the investigation of that trauma has flourished in affiliation with a political movement" (apud Hacking 1996: 69). At this point it should briefly be noted that we are referring mostly to North American sources and developments. In Portugal, women rights were simply nonexistent until 1974, and until this day little has been done to develop an adequate and complete (not to mention timely!) response to the problems of colonial war veterans with combat trauma. Only in 1999 was there appropriate legislation recognising "war stress" as a psychological disease, which would make veterans suffering from it eligible for an invalidity pension. Contextualisation, even if it is necessarily *constructed*, is paramount in addressing this topic, as we shall see.

More recently, and especially where women's mental health is concerned, there has been work to expand the definition of PTSD, which presents a "whole constellation of symptoms," as Kali Tal says (1996). Judith Herman and Christine Courtois seem to be the leading names in this endeavour, taking into consideration prolonged exposure, multiple sources of trauma as well as misdiagnosis and misunderstanding by mental health professionals who do not align the patient's present personality structure with early traumatic experiences. "Complex PTSD" is a broader framework that acts upon individual psychological health but also on social conditions.[3]

The engagement of (clinical)[4] trauma theory with "the humanities", namely literary and cultural studies (or nonclinical trauma theory), yet another crossing of disciplinary divides, came about in the late 1980s and early 1990s, especially with the work of Shoshana Felman and Dori Laub, Dominick LaCapra, Geoffrey Hartman and, arguably the most authoritative voice, Cathy Caruth. All of them were extremely influential, "far beyond the world of academia", as Susannah Radstone attests (2007: 104) even when she criticises what she sees as the shortcomings of those very same theories (about which more later).

For Caruth, trauma is triggered by an external event that is not perceived at the time through the normal structures of memory by the traumatised person, thereby recalling Freud's words from *Beyond the Pleasure Principle*: "We describe as 'traumatic' any excitations from outside which are powerful enough to break through the protective shield". Indebted to neurobiology (especially the work of Bessel van der Kolk, whom she quotes often and with whom she seems to establish a "symbiotic" relationship, one of the bones of contention for Ruth Leys), Caruth posits that this experience is "unclaimed", it cannot be promptly accessed by conscious recall, like regular memories. It is "engraved" on the mind, with such literal power that while unrecognised (i.e., not going through *cognition*) it is only through impromptu, indirect means – Caruth mentions flashbacks and dreams, among others – it is experienced, but as if unmediated: it is as if the person were re-living the traumatic event all over again. In other words, only later, when the wounding is enacted once again, does it take place. The traumatic experience is not "remembered" as a past event, integrated into a "normal" structure of a self-centred, embodied narrative time, but rather irrupts as a "present" experience, and that accounts for its overwhelming disruptive power and opens up profound aporias concerning the referentiality of trauma. As she writes in *Unclaimed Experience*,

> [i]f return is displaced by trauma, then, this is significant in so far as its leaving – the space of unconsciousness – is paradoxically what precisely preserves the event in its literality. For history to be a history of trauma means that it is referential precisely to the extent that it is not fully perceived as it occurs; or to put it somewhat differently, that a history can be grasped only in the very inaccessibility of its occurrence" (187).

There is a split of the personality, as it were, creating two divided selves, one of which is the traumatised self that will "survive" within the "containing" self and which will return, unchanged by history, every time the "containing" self, which inhabits history, comes across his or her own trauma.

This division of the self was to be found right at the beginning, when Breuer and Freud wrote in *Studies in Hysteria* about "the presence of a dissociation, a splitting of the content of consciousness", in the case of hysterical attacks characterised by "the recurrence of a physical state which the patient has experienced earlier" (apud van der Kolk et al., 1996: 30). Ruth Leys and Susannah Radstone, however, criticise this apparently literality of the preserved event, as it seems to bypass the unconscious. In any case, the two "fields" or "schools" that later developed (the so-called "mimetic" and the "anti-mimetic" fields[5]) seem to agree on perceiving trauma as an experience that brings the experiencer into contact with some sort of limit, perhaps that which Maurice Blanchot called the *disaster* (I'll get back to this). This in turn shapes the subject's own processes of subjectivity, both emotional and cognitive.

I want to stress once again the fact that this is a study of artistic texts, not people. About the place of those texts in a public arena, a political arena, considering, along Jill Bennett, that "visual art presents trauma as a *political* rather than a subjective phenomenon. It does not offer us a privileged view of the inner subject; rather, by giving trauma extension in space or lived *place*, it invites an awareness of different modes of inhabitation" (2005: 12). And where artistic creation is concerned, the structure of that disastrous experience will have its correspondence with the way the chosen medium is structured. In the present case, comics.

Caruth and some of her fellow theorists came under criticism quite early. Felman and Laub's book *Testimony: Crises of Witnessing in Literature, Psychoanalysis and History* was published in 1992, Caruth's edited anthology *Trauma: Explorations in Memory* dates from 1995 and her own monograph *Unclaimed Experience: Trauma, Narrative and History* came out a year later. Quite surprisingly, Kali Tal's *World of Hurt: Reading the Literatures of Trauma*, was published immediately in 1996. Having had several editions, including one updated 3rd revision online[6], Tal's revised PhD dissertation not only expanded the theory but also criticised its limited scope. Above all, Kal demanded "the reintroduction of a political and ethical dimension to the interpretation of texts dealing with trauma and memory" (online version, n.p.). Tal and, more recently, other scholars - such as Stef Craps and Maurice Stevens, for instance - have pointed out how the edifice constructed by trauma theory has focused mainly on Western models, just as it has worked with Western-made tools and categories.

With both this history and these criticisms in mind, we can understand how *"trauma" was always already an umbrella term.* According to Sam Durrant, Homi Bhabha would call it a "travelling theory", considering that it was "borrowed by Freud from conventional medicine and put to work as analogy or metaphor, and that the metaphoricity of trauma as a description is necessarily heightened by attempts to extrapolate from the clinical understanding of trauma in individuals to notions of collective or cultural trauma" (2005: n.p.).

Consequently, from its very beginning trauma is a concept that invites a multidisciplinary approach. As Dominick LaCapra writes, "trauma invites distortion, disrupts genres or bounded areas, and threatens to collapse distinctions. (...) no genre or discipline 'owns' trauma as a problem or can define definitive boundaries for it" (2001: 96), to which Luckhurst adds: "Trauma is also always a breaching of disciplines". Later on, discussing Bruno Latour's re-bonding of science and culture, Luckhurst claims that this only strengthens the very notion at stake: "A scientific concept therefore succeeds through its heterogeneity rather than its purity" (14). Sara Murphy also argues this, when she quotes M. Seltzer (*Serial Killers*) in considering trauma as a "borderland concept", and on a more challenging and provocative note, she says that "only those who would want to make of psychoanalysis a normativizing and coherent apologia for bourgeois individualism would see such conceptual impurity as flaw" (in Ball 2007: 94). This is what allows Murphy to search for the gendering and affective turn of trauma theory.

At any rate, for the purposes of this analysis, I will consider trauma as "an abrupt and transitory stoppage in the individual's efficient personality operations" (apud Rappaport 1968; cf. Kardiner 1941), i.e., an overwhelming event experienced by the individual that is not fully understood at that precise point in time, leading to a momentary perceptual blindness, and whose repercussions at psychological, emotional and even perhaps physical levels are felt through symptoms, or displaced effects. More often than not, the results of trauma are fragmentary, mysterious, uncanny, and are spread in several directions. It is through the analysis of discontinuous elements in the individual's expression (particularly salient in Marco Mendes), verbal, physical or otherwise, that enables us eventually to perceive and map back the presence of a traumatic phantasm, which is to say, perhaps we will not be able fully and directly to reconstitute the traumatic event *per se*, but the invisible, unapproachable core where it should lie.

Moreover, in addressing whatever kind of trauma, we should avoid detaching it from social and historical contextualisation, leading to a sort of reification, lest we fall into what John Mowitt calls "trauma envy", where "trauma acquires transcendental status. Everything is potentially traumatic. Under these circumstances, trauma has come to be invested with such authority and legitimacy that it elicits a concomitant desire to have suffered it, or if not the unspeakable event itself, then the testimonial agency it is understood to produce" (2007: 130).

Becoming small

But what kinds of traumas do I want to address? It is thanks to the intensification of trauma theory via cultural studies, especially with post-colonial studies, that it has expanded even further - an "outfolding", as Sam Durrant calls it (2005: n.p.) - and has attended to a wider number of the disenfranchised. Portuguese philosopher José Gil made a deep, broad analysis of the Portuguese situation in his 2005 book *Portugal, Hoje. O medo de existir* [Portugal, Today. The Fear of Being]. The book is somewhat in need of a revision, given that that the economic crisis has got worse since 2010/2011, when Portugal embarked on its three-year austerity package for

Chapter Two

economic recovery (the slight improvement during the Socialist-run government of 2015 is now jeopardised by unknown post-Covid consequences). However, many of the notions presented by Gil not only still hold water but are quite apposite to the times reflected by the comics texts I will be reading. In his assessment, which he associates with both Deleuze's and Foucault's notions on societies of control, José Gil talks about what I am calling "small traumas", even if he uses different terms:

> little terrors at the office, at the company, at the newspaper, at the university, the terror of not being good enough, of being pointed at, of being punished, of losing your job, of getting fat, of not getting fat, of not knowing (how to raise the kids, how to be a woman, how to be joyful and dynamic, attractive and sexy, and so on and so forth) (2004: 122).

A little further ahead on, he devises the sort of motto that I have used as an epigraph: "There is no quotidian life in contemporary societies of control that does not presuppose a form of microterror" (idem). Other commentators and researchers have also been sensitive to this inescapable situation, such as Gabrielle Schwab, who, in a study on transgenerational trauma, and how especially violent histories create an intergenerational dialogue and intersection of experiences and narratives, says that "[t]here is no life without trauma" (2010: 42).

One path to lead trauma theory closer to these other experiences is proposed by Susannah Radstone in her many papers. She reconsiders how memory is articulated with the public sphere, that is to say, how it is always already mediated, especially through the materiality of the body and the "broader social formation in which [the terms mediation and articulation as related to memory] are forged" (2005: 134-135). She claims that a study of:

> the specific tropes, codes and conventions of personal memory's diverse articulations produce new understandings of the knowledge that memory can provide. This is a knowledge not of the past itself, but of how memory, or 'memorial consciousness' is constructed and of its relation to the social and to the past (136).

Radstone criticises the way that trauma theory, following what she and Leys call an "anti-mimetic" model, "takes the traumatic *event* as its theoretical foundation" (original emphasis, 2007: 12), and holds that that event is recorded in memory in a totally different manner from anything else witnessed or experienced. In fact, it is said to be recorded pristinely, and not through the unconscious, which means for Radstone always already mediated processes of memory. Gabrielle Schwab, for instances, speaks of trauma "encapsulat[ing] the unbearable affects generated by a catastrophic event in a space that will remain sealed off from the everyday and, in most cases, from the free flow of memory" (2010: 113). But for Radstone's and Ley's critical view, such a stance becomes "compatible with, and often gives way to, the idea that trauma is a purely external event that befalls a fully constituted Subject" (Ruth Leys, apud Radstone 2007: 15). This focus on the event itself, and not on how the subject's mind classifies and even reifies the event or a certain class of events, not only selects or even appoints which individuals can be traumatised by it but also, at the same time, those who are excluded from such process. Radstone gives the contrasting examples of 9/11 and the Rwanda genocide.

This critique challenges the elegant, organised idea, and the clean-cut narrative thereby generated, that the Subject of trauma is a sound, fully constituted and integrated individual who is suddenly overwhelmed by the traumatic event, making him or her identifiable and eligible as vulnerable, and able to elicit our empathy/sympathy. But at the same time, the blind spot of this notion is the implication that there are a number of individuals who are not amenable to traumatogenic situations, because, perhaps, they are already in overwhelming situations that "make them used to it", from people living in war-torn places to people living in difficult, if not miserable, economic situations. This is one of the reasons why the very basis of trauma studies must be critically addressed, along with its choice of texts, objects of study and even subjects, to prevent it leading towards "a silencing of discussion which leaves hanging any number of questions about the continuingly problematic nature of academic discussion of trauma and the apparent acceptability of debate only of certain types of material and not others" (Radstone 2007: 22).

However, I wonder if these criticisms are totally warranted in relation to the foundation of trauma studies, considering how direct Cathy Caruth is in the introduction to *Trauma. Explorations in Memory*, when she explains that trauma is not typified:

> by the event itself - which may or may not be catastrophic, and may not traumatize everyone equally - nor can it be defined in terms of a distortion of the event, achieving its haunting power as result of *distorting* personal significances attached to it. The pathology consists, rather, solely in *the structure of its experience* or reception: the event is not assimilated or experienced fully at the time, but only belatedly, in its repressed *possession* of the one who experiences it. To be traumatized is precisely to be possessed by an image or event. (1995: 4)

As Stef Craps and Gert Buelens argue, it is one thing to affirm this, but another actually to engage with subjects and critical instruments that do not belong to a "Western canon" of trauma (2008: 2; see also Craps 2013: 2). Some of those points of criticism, however, underline the lack of recognition of collective experiences such as slavery, genocide, racial violence, or of the apparently lesser forms of socio-economic aggression (even within the so-called First World), and emphasise the lack

Chapter Two

of engagement with "local knowledges", which take place through the integration of non-Western peoples and cultures into prefabricated categories, "trauma" itself being the crowning category (cf. Stevens 2009).

But for Radstone there is an even more profound problem, which has to do with the loss of the valuable lessons of psychoanalysis, namely, "the radical lesson of Freud", "the radical ungovernability of the unconscious" (2007: 16, 18). As the above quote from Caruth indicates, there is an ineluctable bond between any person's individuality and his or her trauma. That is to say, instead of generalising about either a type of traumatic event or a class of people, there is a paradoxical move that we need to make. On the one hand, we have to pay attention to the particularities and idiosyncrasies of the subject. And on the other, we have to inquire about the social and political context that occasioned the trauma, or in other words, how it became possible.

Refocusing beyond the individual does not mean forgetting its impact and the terrible consequences it has upon those who suffered the trauma, but instead engaging politically with the roots of the possibility of trauma.

According to Radstone, in his work on South Africa's Truth and Reconciliation Commission, Christopher Colvin

> argues that the dominance of the language of trauma and victimhood in post-apartheid South Africa carries with it the assumption that a therapeutic language linked to the witnessing of survivor memories can be appropriately applied to a group or a nation, as well as to an individual (...) This leads to the problematic assumption that "[t]rauma... is the central mode and consequence of power" (Colvin, apud Radstone: 143).

Consequently, "a stress on personal memories of suffering and on individual testimony to abuse displaces attention from continuing structural inequalities" (144). As I have mentioned, the intersection of post-colonial studies and trauma theory has led some of the discussions back to collective issues, as Stef Craps and Gert Beulens have done in their co-edited *Studies in the Novel* issue (see "Introduction", 2008: pp. 3-4). Of course, neither Colvin nor Radstone are arguing for an end to such discussions of acts of witnessing. Nor are other authors, myself included, that aim for a certain decentralisation, asking for the ongoing and ever deeper understanding of those "big issues" to come to an end. Rather, Radstone and the others are engaging with Tal's steps towards the politicisation of the cultural representation of traumatic experiences, and want to emphasise the result that this position corrects the tendency "to screen from attention broader issues of economic and political power that exceed those of relations between individuals" (144). Craps and Beulens consider that there are "ultimately depoliticizing tendencies" in the Western models of trauma treatment" (2008: 4), and these steps allow us to return to a political re-inscription, to a renewed attention towards the contextual specificities of these texts, rather than to argue *against* a dominant trauma discourse. Of course, I cannot avoid being Eurocentric, and I will not be dealing with overarching transnational issues but with the way in which contemporary authors deal with recent history or in which autobiographical artists examine the economic precariousness of their own situations, within Portugal, which I have described as semi-peripheral.

Nonetheless, it must be borne in mind that some attention to "Other" traumatic experiences was right there at the beginning of literature studies-informed trauma theory, and also at the core of its clinical employment. In Caruth's collection *Trauma. Explorations in Memory*, we find Laura S. Brown's essay "Not Outside the Range: One Feminist Perspective on Psychic Trauma". In fact, this was the very point of departure for my own project, conceptually speaking. Brown, a feminist clinical psychologist, starts her essay by discussing the criteria used in the *DSM* to define trauma or, in its parlance, "post-traumatic stress disorder". Written in 1991, the essay is referring to the *DSM III-R*, which is the revised 1987 version of the *DSM III*, originally from 1980. Brown is particularly taxed by "criterion A", which requires an event that is "infrequent, unusual, or outside of a mythical human norm of experience" (Brown 1995: 111). What passes as unusual creates from the outset a very narrow understanding of "normalcy" in experience:

> The range of human experience becomes the range of what is normal and usual in the lives of men of the dominant class; white, young, able-bodied, educated, middleclass, Christian men. Trauma is thus that which disrupts these particular human lives, but no other (Idem: 101).

And Brown wants to go beyond such a narrow range and encompass experiences from people who do not belong to those societal criteria.

By the end of the article, she knows that the criteria and symptomatology is "undergoing change" for the then-upcoming *DSM IV*, and in fact she went on to address this change in future work, but that was the point of contention at the time. According to criterion A, trauma was seen as "an event outside the range of usual human experience that would be frightening or threatening to almost anyone". If this seemed to unproblematically encapsulate the experience of Holocaust survivors, war veterans, and individuals who underwent natural catastrophes or were exposed to violent events (such as rape, attempted murder, assault), it left out other complicated situations, such as incest, which despite its mind-boggling statistical presence in the U.S., was called a "secret trauma" by feminist writer Diana E. H. Russell, whom Brown quotes.

Given that I am neither dealing with clinical cases nor with these specific issues, more important for the present work is Brown's assessment that to consider

Chapter Two

trauma to be "outside the range of *usual* human experience" reinforces the neat narrative mentioned before, as well as a specific allocation of those who are "traumatizable" (cf. the quote above). But Brown wants to shift our attention towards the lives of many under an apparently invisible yet "constant presence and threat of trauma", which under the purveyance of dominant culture becomes "a continuing background noise rather than an unusual event" (102-103).

Brown, along with Kali Tal, Stef Craps and others, contributes towards an alternative notion of trauma, one that is not event-based, or *punctual*, but rather involves culturally embedded ongoing processes that enable traumatogenic settings in relation to certain people. It is constructed by social forces and it is within the social texture. Not everyone within that social model will feel or react the same way, of course, as Cathy Caruth herself has pointed out.

This does not mean that there is not always resistance against this conceptual expansion, as we have seen. In fact, much of the resistance against the conceptual expansion of trauma has been fought out in courtrooms, and it is precisely that legal dimension that makes Roger Luckhurst say that "it emphasized the extent to which trauma was not a 'matter of fact,' as Latour puts it, but a 'matter of concern,' an enigmatic thing that prompts perplexity, debate and contested opinion" (2008: 33). Just as at the end of the 19th century the insurance companies fought against the "elasticity" of trauma to avoid engagement with the consequences of accidents, so did some agents of the U.S. legal system actively resist its extension into an "umbrella term". Brown gives the particular example of a female patient of hers. In that account, she tells us how the psychiatrist that the insurance company of the woman's employer referred her to "excoriates those who would stretch the definition of trauma to include such daily occurrences", including harassment at work (1995: 104); an occurrence that José Gil would call a "microaggression" (2004: 122 and ff.), which becomes increasingly worse as it is repeated. There is not much difference here, I think, from the way that Herbert W. Page, the railway company surgeon who dismissed psychological shock as a mere *effeminate* disorder[7], and it is also felt today when people dismiss the "complaints" of people addressing an unjust economical situation/context as traumatic, displacing the "fault" onto the complainant. As I mentioned at the beginning, in Portugal war-associated traumas are still not a judicial reality, so from a legal point of view, *there is no* problem.

Brown is well aware of the possibility of extending trauma into other realms, but, like Radstone, she argues above all for it to be brought to bear on social, economic, political and gender issues as well. Conscious of the work by people such as Marianne Hirsch, Brown writes:

> Mainstream trauma theory has begun to recognize that post-traumatic symptoms can be intergenerational, as in the case of children of survivors of the

A short history of trauma

Nazi Holocaust. We have yet to admit that it can spread *laterally* throughout an oppressed social group as well, when membership in that group means a constant lifetime risk of exposure to certain trauma. [These are people] for whom insidious trauma is a way of life (my emphasis, 1995: 107-108).

With the term "insidious trauma", Brown is quoting from yet another therapist colleague, Maria Root. This is a notion referring to "the traumatogenic effects of oppression that are not necessarily overtly violent or threatening to bodily well-being at the given moment but that do violence to the soul and spirit" (idem: 107). The kernel of the issue is to acknowledge the existence also of estrangement and suffering in these smaller traumas.

We have to beware of oversimplification here. The word "small" in this case is used with the intention of respecting all types of trauma, and the necessary discourses about them across disciplines. It does not seek to create hierarchies, nor to downplay the suffering of those who have "small traumas". I acknowledge the overwhelming importance given to the discussion of a transhistorical event such as the Holocaust, and there is no comparison attempted here between that and the musings of an unemployed, white, male, cultured artist in the peaceful, contemporary city of Porto. But focusing our attention on one problem does not come at the expense of addressing any other problem.

In this sense I am, hopefully, attending to a very specific "political-historical and social" and "cultural context [that] should not be excluded from trauma research, for it determines how symptoms are experienced and expressed and provides a framework for understanding traumatic events, opportunities for healing and therapeutic possibilities" (Sibylle Rothkegel, apud Kaplan 2005: 68). Memories "are never simply records of the past, but are interpretive reconstructions that bear the imprint of local narrative conventions, cultural assumptions, discursive formations and practices, and social contexts of recall and commemoration" (Antze and Lambek 1996: vii).

It is worth quoting Maurice Stevens at length:

Rather than thinking of trauma as an identifiable and discrete event that must have occurred at some specific point in time and place, it can be more usefully understood as a cultural object whose meanings far exceed the boundaries of any particular shock or disruption; rather than being restricted by the common sense ideas we possess that allow us to think of trauma as authentic evidence of something "having happened there," a snapshot whose silver plate and photon are analogues to the psyche and impressions fixed in embodied symptoms, the real force of trauma flowers in disparate and unexpected places. And, like most cultural objects, trauma, too, circulates among various social contexts that give it

Chapter Two

differing meanings and co-produce its multiple social effects. Like most cultural objects, trauma's component memes, those pivotal conceptualizations that tailor its function, have origins that can be traced to coordinates that vary in time, space and semiosis; coordinates whose ideological concerns come to refract or anchor trauma's meanings simply by occupying the same temporo-spatio-semiotic location" (Stevens 2009: 3).

In my view, the insistence on the same kinds of texts over and over again runs the danger of crystallising what can be thought of as trauma, which situations can be deemed traumatic, who is entitled to discuss trauma, and so on, making ever more invisible the plights of those left out. As Stevens writes, these are the stories that remain "un-included in the realm of historiography... [h]unched over and squinting, [history] worries at the frayed ends of incomplete narratives and hidden transcripts", they are "history's lacunae". It is our collective task not to lose sight of those left behind by the overarching account of normative trauma theory. In other words, it is incumbent on us to take a Benjaminian, redemptive stance towards historiography.[8]

I will also not forget that there are no non-embodied, non-marked statements, no isolated, absolute, timeless truths (least of all my own). However, this should not allow us to fall into a desperate relativism that would suspend any possibility of ethical responsibility and even principles. So the questions that follow are: how do the texts I am discussing address their own role within their social structures? If they are not addressing war, physical violence, political oppression, violent gender oppression, what kind of problems are they talking about that can be seen through the lens of trauma studies? How do the autobiographical protagonists see themselves? What kind of role do they assume? Do they see themselves as part of the problems they may address or as victims of society, or is the question more complicated? To put it in other terms: what kind of self-formation is at stake in these texts and how to they relate to trauma? In an ongoing negotiation, these questions are crucial.

Trauma and Comics

As socially embedded texts, comics are of course open to cultural criticism and political assessment, so it is reasonable to analyse both the art form and precise artefacts within the framework of trauma. As is well known, in recent decades, comics have been through a marked expansion where genre and readership diversity, storytelling complexity, ethical, cultural and transnational frameworks are concerned. Autobiography, self-fiction, non-fiction, reportage, diaries and journals, and even essay, are but a few of the genres that have been increasingly exploited by the medium of comics.

A short history of trauma

Arguably, the first discussions bringing trauma theory to the realm of comics - or is it the other way around? - were the studies that focused on Art Spiegelman's *Maus*. Famously, Marianne Hirsch coined her concept of *postmemory* thanks to her reading of this book (1992-93; see also the opening page of postmemory.net). Robert S. Leventhal, for instance, addressed it in a 1995 ground-breaking article, which underlined the mechanisms through which the author reinvented a self, or constructed a self within the text, that was able to cope with the overwhelming nature of his parent's experiences in Nazi Germany and the Holocaust. One of Dominick LaCapra's chapters in *History and Memory After Auschwitz* (1998) is dedicated to Spiegelman's book (the back cover, somewhat coyly or defensively, writes *comic book* between inverted commas). Pierre-Alban Delannoy published an entire monograph in 2003 focusing on the integration of the book within that historical framework, using some of the methodologies warranted by trauma studies: Maus *d'Art Spiegelman. Bande dessinée et Shoah*. But there was one immediate problem with this outstanding and crucial work around Spiegelman's most famous work to date: the crystallisation of *Maus* as the proverbial exception that confirms the rule of comics' overall poverty of ambition and lack of diversity in relation to themes, representation and subjectivity. Admittedly, when the first volume was issued in 1986, there was a dearth of comics within the United States that addressed such powerful, personal, genre-defying, adult-oriented issues, and the works that had broken the mould of the usual genres and styles - say, Pekar's *American Splendor* and Justin Green's *Binky Brown Meets the Holy Virgin Mary* - were not particularly famous beyond the comics milieu.[9] But the world of comics is not limited to the North American output and, since then, of course, things have changed dramatically in terms of supply. But even taking that into account, it is still rather surprising to read that Leventhal considers comics to be a "medium usually reserved for hero-construction and morality play". That being said, comics scholarship has come a long way, growing exponentially and even energetically in recent years, and today the ever-expanding bibliography has multiple choices where methodologies, perspectives, social positionings and *corpora* are concerned.

But despite this diversity and despite the increasingly larger market of translated works (especially between France and the U.S., but also other countries such as Spain, Germany, Belgium, Korea, Japan, which not only have a lively local production but also a thriving market for translated comics), and an increasing international dialogue among comics scholars, the selection of comics taken to exemplify trauma gravitates more often than not around a limited number of titles, authors and themes, as I have mentioned in the Introduction. *Maus* is still the favourite subject, by far, but after 9/11 there is an unsurprisingly strong incidence of studies on Spiegelman's more recent *In the Shadows of No Towers*, along with Alissa Torres and Sungyoon Choi's *American Widow*. Marjane Satrapi's *Persepolis* and Keiji Nakazawa's *Barefoot Gen* are also recurrent examples for autobiographical accounts that

Chapter Two

place the protagonists within a larger, historical, traumatic event (respectively, the Iranian 1970 Revolution and the Hiroshima bombing). Auto- or semiautobiographical works, even if not intersecting with nationally resonant historical events, but focusing more immediately on the life of the individual within his or her personal surroundings, especially those which raise issues of sexuality, disease and tense parent-child relationships are also fodder for trauma studies specialists: Alison Bechdel's *Fun Home*, Chris Ware's *Jimmy Corrigan*, David B.'s *L'Ascension du haut mal/ Epileptic*, David Small's *Stitches*, are just a few of the favourites.

It should come as no surprise that autobiographical comics and related genres have achieved such prominence. The current critical prestige of comics life writing, in both academia and popular reception, has opened it up as a special space for these discussions, which raise a number of other pertinent current issues, including those that can be thought of under the term "small trauma". Jane Tolmie (2013), addressing a specific and judicious number of autobiographical (or semi-auto-biographical, including Lynda Barry's *autobifictionalography*) work by women cartoonists, is quite attentive towards the issues launched by L.S. Brown, concerning the extent to which very diverse comics texts can be addressed through the prism of trauma theory, from the starkly explicit (Debbie Dreschler's *Daddy's Girl*) to the elliptical (Lynda Barry's *One! Hundred! Demons!*), from the grave and sharp (Phoebe Gloeckner's *Diary of a Teenage Girl*) to the fantastical and funny (Julie Doucet's books).

> [These texts, especially the ones by Debbie Dreschler and Lynda Barry] empha-size repeated and quotidian traumas, trauma of gender inequity, traumas set in the home and enacted and re-enacted every day. In a sense, these texts are about what is perfectly ordinary and one thing that is perfectly ordinary is that it is impossible to separate mind and body, word and image, emotion and politics. (2013: xvi).[10]

Additionally, autobiography opens up to what Catherine Mao calls "two parallel paths": on the one hand, that of *exemplarity*, in which the narrator erases him- or herself to guide the focus toward the represented reality at the core of the narra-tive (the examples of Joe Sacco and Étienne Davodeau, who work on slightly de-cen-tred genres that move towards journalism, are paramount); on the other hand, that of the *exception* of autobiography, in which everything is aimed to construct the author's individual life (Mao 2013: paragraph 8).

Most of these works address more or less autobiographical or "real" settings that allow us to think of these texts as addressing whatever notion we can have of reality: a tangible, consensual, contingent historical experience (*Jimmy Corrigan* is fiction, after all). Here we are not, as yet, addressing a Lacanian Real, or the subject's 'sense of reality' supported by fantasy as discussed by Žižek (1997: 84), to which we'll

A short history of trauma

return later. But even within the marvellous (in a Todorovian sense) premise underlying the universe of super-heroes, the personal traumas of Bruce Wayne/Batman, Peter Parker/Spider-man, and other characters can be addressed using the methodological tools developed with both clinical and critical trauma studies, leading to very interesting results. Martyn Pedler's study, which I have quoted in the introduction, combines the analysis of the events within the fictions (the murders of Bruce Wayne's/Batman's parents and of Peter Parker's/Spiderman's uncle) with their economical and structurally determined serialisation (monthly comic books), so that, within his perspective, the repetition and insistence in revisiting these characters' personal traumas become an intrinsic part of the comics' textuality (2012: 3).

A notable finding enabled by the data search engine at the excellent Bonner Online-Bibliographie zur Comicforschung of Bonn University (as of 2020, https://www.bobc.uni-bonn.de/), is that the convergence of attention between Holocaust studies and studies of text/image works has led to a plethora of papers on Charlotte Salomon's *Leben? Oder Theatre?* However, one would be advised to read these papers carefully in order to understand how far these efforts are informed by comics studies or comics-related interests.

More importantly, I am not saying that the titles and authors mentioned above are the only ones addressed by the meeting of trauma and comics studies. In fact, using the *Comicforschung* database I've come across studies on Jacques Tardi and Farid Boudjellal[11], or Neil Gaiman and Dave McKean's *Signal to Noise*.

But there is a more or less recurrent cluster of names, titles and genres that still needs to be integrated into a wider landscape of comics production and methodological approaches.

An intersection

Marco Mendes' *Diário Rasgado* project, Miguel Rocha's solo and collaborative books addressing recent Portuguese history, and the alternative, experimental work of artists like Joana Figueiredo, Miguel Carneiro and others may not have much in common at first glance. But despite using very different strategies and resulting in very different outcomes, more often than not they all address issues that deal with human memory, contradictory relationships with the Other (whether in terms of family or in broader social units - gender, nation, religion, sexuality), or self-exploration. Sometimes, these themes overlap and inform each other, creating complex, intricate texts. There is a more or less coherent corpus of contemporary comics that create a vision of and towards the past, *telescoping it through the present*, to paraphrase Walter Benjamin. But looking back never reaches the original events and objects in their pristine condition: there are always distortions, displacements, silences and tricks of the language (of the whole medium).

Chapter Two

This will become paramount in a discussion of trauma. This looking back is tinted by nostalgia in its Greek etymological sense, "the wounds of returning". "Wound" can also be rendered in Greek as "trauma", and it is this concept that will help us map the strength, nature and even aesthetic value of some contemporary comics made in Portugal.

These texts deal with aspects of the collective, whether through the dialogue that Miguel Rocha's books establish directly with historical moments and characters, Marco Mendes' "x-ray" of the contemporaneous life of socio-economic precarity in Porto, or the collective, experimental practices of Joana Figueiredo and Miguel Carneiro. They not only reflect or create different facets of the possibility of the collective, they have already been founded upon it, they are interdependent along several lines of its development (from zines to artists' collectives to collaborations). This will unavoidably inform the way in which they treat their narratives and the way they convey experiences, memories, and history. "It is not so much that our memories go in or come from many directions, but rather that they are always already composites of dynamically interrelated and conflicted histories", in the words of Gabriele Schwab (2010: 29-30).

The authors I will be dealing with do not examine the roots of the situations, the social, political and economic mechanisms that have engendered contemporary precariousness, nor with the establishment of the Estado Novo and its pervasive *Weltanschauung* that was imposed on urban and rural life alike (a dichotomy that will make sense when addressing Miguel Rocha's books). They are not creating essays or reportage or historiography with the medium of comics. To a certain extent, they are following one of the tenets of trauma theory, in that it is impossible to understand the source of trauma, or is even considered obscene to (try to) do so (cf. Claude Lanzmann, in Caruth 1995). Their focus is on the consequences, on the way contemporary daily life is contaminated through and through by such trauma. When they "look back at the past", they aim less to retrieve it "as it was", than to signal that very desire of looking back.

Rather than addressing an external, juridically verifiable truth, the texts I will address, especially Marco Mendes' work, go beyond dichotomies between autobiography and autofiction, etc., to create a "self-reflexive reconceptualizing of the genre" (La Cour 2010: 45). But the case of Mendes, and autobiographical comics in general, are a privileged site of discussion around trauma and comics, as we have seen. As Mihaela Precup writes in her doctoral dissertation, precisely addressing this "genre" and trauma, "[t]he autobiographical story both gives access to either marginalized or forgotten experiences, or permits us to examine the interplay between individual experience and collective cultural and social practices" (2010: n.p.). This looking back allows them to "represent the truth while recognizing the intangibility of such an endeavor" (La Cour 2010: 46).

Kali Tal, following the major tenets of trauma theory as posited by Caruth et al., writes that the history of trauma is made of past, inaccessible events, that are not "fully perceived as they occur - [and are] given meaning later in a process of narrative construction". However, some of the authors I will be dealing with do not create stories in their most classical sense. They negotiate several forms of narrative, some of which may be called non-narrative, or poetic or experimental forms. Drawing from Janet Walker's phrase, we will find in these texts "fluid boundaries" (114) between fantasy and memory and history. Fantasy plays a decisive role here, as it is not played *against* reality, but, according to Žižek and other writers, it is constitutive of the subject's reality itself. So the consideration of both classical forms of narrative and experimental forms of comics can perhaps be a good way to think how a certain culture, an "imagined community" (Benedict Anderson) or "structure of feeling" (Raymond Williams), both responds to society and also "creates, by new perceptions and responses, elements which the society, as such, is not able to realize" (2001: 86).

Almost naturally, art plays a role here, because it is an alternative way of knowing, born out of a not-knowing. As Jean-Michel Rey writes, "Where I know, I do not write; where I write, I can know only belatedly [*après-coup*], as if in a different context" (1982: 305). That is the very condition of possibility of the creative act itself, something also pointed out by Georges Perec, "The unsayable is not buried inside writing, it is what prompted it in the first place" (from *W, of the Memory of Childhood*, apud Schwab 2010: 59), but that Maurice Blanchot sees as the re-institution, a repetition,[12] of the trauma itself: "Write in order not simply to destroy, in order not simply to conserve, in order not to transmit; write in the thrall of the impossible real, that share of disaster wherein every reality, safe and sound, sinks" (1986: 38). I think this is neither incompatible with the idea that trauma is "unrepresentable" (especially if we consider this is relation to the psychosomatic behaviours studied by van der Kolk, because they do not go through symbolic elaboration, as dreams do), or with the way artistic and creative efforts aim to respond to their respective circumstances.

Geoffrey H. Hartmann argues that "[t]raumatic knowledge, then, would seem to be *a contradiction in terms*" (my emphasis, 1995: 537). Hartman discusses literary texts as ways, not of retrieving (pristine) memories but rather a re-expression of them, opening up "the possibility of poetry as a more absolute speech" (542), in which "[t] raumatic and artistic kinds of knowledge conspire to produce their own mode of recognition" and "a view of art as at once testimony and representation" (545).

J.-M. Rey, in his study of Freud's relationship with writing, and with an awareness of the role of language, especially creative language, in the splitting of the self, points to its transformative potential through its formal specificities (and, by extension, to other art forms as well, I believe): "In other words, literature softens, veils, clothes what it exposes: the themes that it constitutes or borrows elsewhere", associating this with Freud's dictum, "[b]ut poetic treatment is impossible without softening and disguise"[13] (apud Rey 1982: 315-316). The verbs used by Rey also relate to Freud's recurrent terms, such as "Milderung" (*softening* or *mitigation*), "Ableitung" (*derivation*), "Verhüllung" (*disguising*) and "Verkleidung" (*clothing*). But we have to understand that this creative transformation does not allow us to confuse this type of knowledge or approach to such traumas with having intimate experience of them (and even less so with the artists themselves as individuals). I want to avoid the idea that "the best kind of text about trauma will therefore transmit trauma 'itself' rather than knowledge about it, [which] makes it possible for critics to embrace an aestheticized despair while construing that embrace as political wisdom" (Forter 2007: 282). This would seem a good opportunity to take into consideration Dominick LaCapra's notion of *empathy*, or *empathetic unsettlement*, an ethical responsibility when addressing trauma, which I will address later on.

I will not consider comics to be "the best form" of representing, discussing or opening up a path to address trauma, even though I agree with Hillary Chute that "[g]raphic narratives, on the whole, have the potential to be powerful precisely because they intervene against a culture of invisibility by taking what I think of as the risk of representation" (2016: 5). I would like to argue that despite the fact that historically developed and more widely socially accepted art forms such as cinema and literature have addressed trauma in many ways, the medium of comics is also a significant means to engage with, explore, and express *trauma*. No art form is intrinsically superior to any other art form.

And I also hope to show some diversity within this art form. We will come across examples of comics that are anti-linear, fragmented, self-reflexive, and which foreground materiality, and other tenets of post-modern textuality. But we will engage with more traditional forms as well, which manifest some degree of realism, and which follow causality and clearly ordered narrative arcs. I am not interested in a generalised discussion but rather in an analysis of a selection of texts that I feel may illuminate these issues. Generally speaking, comics are a hybrid form, bringing together in a same plane of expression fragmentary yet significant images and a sequential or fluid narrative state. Of course, the inherent manifold nature of comics complicates this account, but let us focus on that dichotomy for now. The convergence of images that should be read, verbal texts that should be integrated into the communicative aspect of comics, symbols that stand for specific actions, and several other elements of signification that may be used in the medium - expressive colours, structures and patterns, sound words/onomatopoeias, diagrams, leitmotivs, the principle of *tressage* (cf. Groensteen 1999), typologies of *mise en page*, panel transitions, and even the importance of formats and overall book design, etc. -, make comics a complex, multifaceted mode of expression through which may be played out the fragmentary, uncanny and unintegrated nature of trauma in a very telling way, a particular act of "visual witnessing... [that] can offer an absorptive intimacy with their narratives while defamiliarizing received images of history" (Chute 2016: 141-142).

And I am perfectly aware that any selectivity will bespeak of a specific history and that whatever history we create will be always selective (a Derridean "archive", as it were). Rather than creating an "alternative canon", which I understand is quite difficult anyway from such a perspective (untranslated Portuguese comics from small, "alternative" presses), I wish to discuss the intersection of trauma studies, comics representation, and politics around one of the many blind spots in comics scholarship in general.

I am not looking for a reified use of a particular nomenclature ("trauma", "traumatic", etc.), which would then be applied to the selected comics texts, as if it those words were already clearly understandable concepts with their closed characteristics, immediate formulations and structures, and so on. I realise that the spectrum of experiences represented or addressed by these comics are not psychologically overwhelming, but they might be illuminated by the instruments developed within critical trauma theory. This is not an issue of moral relativism, but rather hopefully the extension of Caruth's vision that "in a catastrophic age, trauma itself may provide the very link between cultures" (1995: 11).

Notes

1   Although Luckhurst's advice is "not to fetishise these technological origins" (24), for another appraisal on the invention of trauma as related to the medium of photography, see Ulrich Baer, *Spectral Evidence. The Photography of Trauma*, especially chapter 1 on Charcot's photographs, which enters into a dialogue with Georges Didi-Huberman's *Invention of Hysteria: Charcot and the Photographic Iconography of the Salpêtrière*.

2   In the same book, Luckhurst expounds in detail the opening up of the term: "The revised criteria in 1987 [of PTSD in the *DMS*] thus expanded the elements of re-experiencing to include intrusive recollections, recurrent dreams, 'sudden acting or feeling as if the traumatic even were recurring (includes a sense of reliving the experience, illusions, hallucinations, and associative [flashback] episodes, even those that occur upon awakening or when intoxicated)' and finally a new additional category of 'intense psychological distress at exposure to events that symbolize or resemble an aspect of the traumatic event'" (2008: 147).

3   Moreover, we cannot but stress that this short account does not give a complete picture of the diversity within each discipline. As Roger Luckhurst warns us, "it is valuable to be made aware that psychiatric discourse assumes a *plurality* of possible responses to traumatic impacts" (2008: 211, original emphasis).

4   I do not wish to engage in any kind of reductionism in relation to psychoanalysis here. I bear in mind the following words by Paul Antze: "As a matter of historical fact, psychoanalysis has always been something more than a clinical technique or a mental science. It is also a set of interpretative practices. In this

Chapter Two

latter guise its theories take on a different kind of importance; they are no longer simply models *of* reality but models *for* understanding" (2003: 100).

5 Proposed by Leys in her *Trauma: A Genealogy*. Blatantly polemical, Leys discusses the "anti-mimetic" genealogy of trauma as "a strict dichotomy between the autonomous subject and the external trauma" (2000: 9).

6 URL: http://kalital.com/Text/Worlds/index.html [last accessed March 2013].

7 The gender-laden used of "effeminate" opens up, as of course, the precise problems that have been addressed by some of the trauma theorists already mentioned.

8 See "Theses on the Philosophy of History", especially theses II and VI (2007: pp. 253-254 and 255).

9 Moreover, they existed in *comic book* format, which limited their circulation. See Gabillet 2005, especially pgs. 123 and ff.

10 Issues of gender also play a role, although work by Portuguese women artists will be conspicuously missing from this book, with the exception of that of Joana Figueiredo and Amanda Baeza. It is not that there is a total absence of feminine comic artists in Portugal, even though men outnumber women to a dismaying degree. A study of women artists in Portugal would deserve its own monograph, but unfortunately this is not the forum in which to have this discussion. However, I believe, with Jared Gardner, that there is an intimate relationship between the emergence of the autobiographical comics field (understood as widely as possible so that it would include auto-fiction and other borderline cases) with the feminist political and artistic movements of the 1960s-1970s (2008: 14). Whitlock, Chute, DeKoven, Chase are also good points of departure for such a study.

11 Precisely two authors who create a special space for the voice of "Others" not usually contemplated by mainstream comics. See the two "twin" essays Moura 2012a and Moura 2012b.

12 Perhaps even in the theatrical sense of the French word, *répétition*, "rehearsal".

13 The original German reads "Aber ohne Milderung und Verhüllung ist die poetische Bearbeitung nicht möglich".

Chapter 3

Marco Mendes and the ever-temporary rebuilding of the self

Marco Mendes (b. Coimbra, 1978) studied Design in Porto but has worked almost exclusively in drawing and comics as both a practitioner and a teacher, having taught both disciplines in Porto and Guimarães, and having founded in 2010, with fellow artists Sofia Barreira, Carlos Pinheiro and Nuno Sousa, the Clube do Desenho ("Drawing Club"), a successful non-profit teaching association dedicated to that art in the city of Porto.

The first phase of his comics work started in 2005, when Mendes, along with Miguel Carneiro, another fellow artist, founded the artistic-and-editorial duo A Mula [The Mule], which published a number of "classic" fanzines (xeroxed, stapled and folded A3 folios, mostly black and white). Their last project as a duo was the 2009 *Qu'Inferno*. This is an oversized heavy-paper-stock publication, with individually spray-coloured, silkscreen covers. A collection of comics and illustration, it was a veritable "who's who" of the Portuguese independent circles of the time. After this, both artists were involved in other collective projects, but A Mula was no more. Although this may not amount to a trend, it is remarkable that in Porto many artists have created editorial duos born out of personal relationships (colleagues at the university, roommates, partnerships, etc.). Apart from Mendes and Carneiro, Carlos Pinheiro and Nuno Sousa also had a zine called *O Senhorio* [The Landlord], Júlio Dolbeth and Rui Vitorino Santos founded the Dama Aflita gallery, and before them, but also within the same generation, Isabel Carvalho and Pedro Nora had various projects, from *ALíngua* [The Tongue] to *Stad* and *Satélite Internacional*. This background information is important in that it reveals the particularly localised strategies for creation and circulation of work in Porto, in specific networks made up of alternative record and bookstores, independent galleries or artist-run spaces (quite often the home of the artists themselves), fairs and so on. Of course, there are also collaborations with people from other cities and quite a lot of travelling, blog news and word-of-mouth.

Chapter Three

In any case, Mendes not only worked within these platforms, but also beyond them, participating in several exhibitions – in 2007 he had a solo show of his drawings, comics and paintings, *Uma Formiga na Saia do Universo* [An ant on the skirt of the universe] in Plumba gallery, Porto – creating murals, organising small press fairs and writing essays on comics and creation. Apart from his own editorial projects, his work can also be found in national anthologies, newspapers or projects such as *Mutate & Survive, Quadrado, Mundo Universitário, Efeméride, Crack On*, or international projects like *Stripburger* (Slovenia), *Jungle World* (Germany) and *Varsóvia* (Poland). A particularly important zine is the one he created with fellow Porto underground comics artists Janus, in 2007, *O projecto de fecundar a lua* [The project to fertilize the moon].

Mendes's oeuvre is composed mainly of autobiographical short pieces, although some of his stories are also informed by some degree of fantasy, delirium or self-fiction. They oscillate between a self-derisory humour and a profound inquiry into deep emotions, sometimes quite painful but seldom verbalised, whether related to lovers, family members or simply faced with the overwhelming anguish of life's uncertainties. Since 2005, Mendes has been working on a blog, *Diário Rasgado* [Torn Journal][1], first re-publishing his zine work, but quickly creating original work (both the autobiographical strips as well as self-standing drawings) that has contributed to his oeuvre. In fact, more often than not, these short stories[2] constitute an individual narrative unit, but there is an underlying principle that organises them, if not in a proper continuity, at least as a cohesive flow. These "units" that were first published in many zines and publications, as well as in the blog, were subsequently gathered into different formats, first into a soft-bound book (almost like a US comic book, with 32 pages) in English translation, *The Chinese Will Deliver the Pandas* (Plana Press: 2008), and then later, substantially reformulated (I will address below the changes in ordering, composition, rewriting, cleaning up, etc.) in the hardcover *Diário Rasgado* (Mundo Fantasma/Plana: 2012). In 2018, he began a daily collaboration with the Porto newspaper *Jornal de Notícias*, and once again he adapted his strips to that specific purpose, while allowing for them to be a reintegrated into his larger corpus. In 2019, these strips were collected in a hefty tome, *Tutti Fruti* (Mundo Fantasma). Unfortunately, this volume will be outside the purview of this chapter.

Serialisation does not mean for Marco Mendes, or any other Portuguese contemporary comics artist, the same thing as it did, for example, in Victorian times, an epoch and a market that allowed for profoundly significant developments in literary techniques, the massification of readership and the economic sustenance of its authors (Vann 1985: 2). On the one hand, it upholds some of the principles of Victorian serial fiction, concerning the possibility of rewriting before issuing the text in a "final" book format. Just as Victorian writers could either heavily revise their serialised texts, like Charles Reade, or adamantly decline to do so, like Dickens, so we can find in our corpus examples of profound revision (Miguel Rocha's first version of *Pombinhas*, as we will discuss in the next chapter), "simple" reordering (as Mendes does) or no transformation at all, apart from the obvious publishing format (the last chapter will discuss some examples), which in itself may contribute, however, to a radically different reading. But on the other hand, most authors today serialise their work on online platforms, from content-hosting services such as blogs or sites, social media like Facebook or Instagram, imageboards such as tumblr or 4chan, sites like Behance, or even digital publishing formats (issuu, cbr, pdf, epub, and so on). Where Portugal is concerned, blogs are still the most popular way of displaying work, although the tumblr community has grown in the last few years and Instagram has proved quite popular in the last couple of years. Moreover, most of these authors expect no payment whatsoever, and in the case of self-publishing, if the sold copies can cover the expenses of printing costs, so much the better. But that is not in itself a goal or a guarantee.

Unlike in "central" countries like France and the United States, autobiography is not a regular "genre" in Portugal, and only a handful of artists engage in it. There are artists who create an autobiographical page or two for zines, anthologies or commemorative or circumstantial publications, but not much more. People who make autobiographical comics in a more sustained fashion are very few. In that "narrower" sense, we may point to a travelogue by David Campos, a handful of short stories by Teresa Câmara Pestana, one or two projects by Amanda Baeza and Mosi, and more recently, by Francisco Sousa Lobo, in a complex mixture of fiction, auto-fiction and autobiography, but only Marcos Farrajota could be seen as a fully fledged "autobiographical comics artist", with an ongoing, consolidated project. Other traits could be emphasised, however, leading to different Portuguese-bound affiliations and groupings: an author who also explores deep emotions while avoiding melodrama is Paulo Monteiro; ironic distance is assured by Janus, Tiago Baptista and Miguel Carneiro; and the kind of formal questions we will find in Mendes are explored somewhat similarly by Carlos Pinheiro and Nuno Sousa. However, it is the convergence of all these traits that makes Mendes quite a singular author, whose work stands comparison with that of many other international names. The negotiation of these features in a single body of work produces an effect that Charlotte Pylyser has called "kaleidoscope humour", creating some distance but at the same time establishing bonds with a autobiographical comics-dominated scene, where "a confessional tone is readily associated with honesty and substance" (2013: 28).

It comes as no surprise, then, especially in view of Mendes's stunning graphics, that he occupies a very special position within the Portuguese scene, in an intelligent, genuine and artistically irreprehensible fashion. A virtuoso creator of academic-style, sight-size, realistic drawing, with his figurative, anatomically correct forms, Mendes nonetheless uses everyday non-fine materials (pencils, ballpoint pens, but also Indian ink, whiteout, Scotch tape), and also leaves plenty of the marks

Chapter Three

of the drawing process quite visible in the end result: corrections and alterations, pentimentos and erasures with lines overwritten on objects, dirt, graphic noise, almost illegible written notes, all of which become an intrinsic part of the expressive matter of his work. A figure may be perfectly delineated in its contours, but a shadow or an idea of colouring may be rendered by a seemingly rushed bunch of scribbles. This creates a paradoxical relationship with the reader, a contrast with what happens narratively and textually (in a narrower sense), given that this degree of visual or graphic noise, of dirtiness, augments the distance between narration and narratee.[3] Autobiography sometimes leads readers to believe that there is no distance between art and life, which consequently can lead to abusive interpretations or a false feeling of familiarity with the empirical author him- or herself. These marks of incompleteness and dirtiness, then, can act as a distance-inducing correction of such an attitude. If perhaps an illusion could be created "internally" (to the stories) that there is no frontier between tangible and perceptual everyday life and the life that solely emerges and is developed within a work of art, and that only can be expressed through it, these visual strategies of making its surface as visible as possible create an external side in relation to which there can be only a Brechtian *Verfremdungseffekt*. Over the last few years, Mendes has somewhat attenuated this "noisy" practice, and uses more noble materials, but our general description still holds.

From 2005 to 2006, no less than five A Mula-related fanzines were put out: *Paint Suck's*, *Lamb-Hãert* e *Hum, Hum! Estou a ver…*, *Estou careca e a minha cadela vai morrer!*, and *Cospe aqui*.[4] Following the freest path possible, these objects were solely guided by a "will to compile drawings, stories and other stuff that were 'lost' in the homes and studios of a few friends of ours", as the editors Mendes and Carneiro write in one of the presentation texts.[5] This has always been one of the possible functions of zines, to erect new monumental buildings out of ruins, something that links them with the work of Piranesi or Walter Benjamin, but at the same time they also present an active and outspoken critique triggered by "disenchantment with the local, national and international artistic milieu" (Mendes and Carneiro, idem). In this sense, the fanzines become a platform for the discussion of a world in which they may or may not be involved. In Portugal, a similar relationship between seemingly iconoclastic, cheaply produced comics publications and the visual arts circuit has an older reference, with the 1980s *A Vaca que veio do espaço* [The Cow that Came from Space] and *Facada mortal* [Deadly Knife Blow] by Alice Geirinhas, João Fonte Santa and Pedro Amaral, who would become the collective Sparring Partners, a group with many high-profile participations within the art world. To a certain extent, this sort of effort does not amount to much, given the fact that rarely, if ever, will their criticism reach the ears and eyes of the appointed recipients, but politically speaking this positioning is common to all of these works. And, in any case, whether considering the collection as a whole or solely each artist's individual contribution, these publications create "temporary autonomous zones", as the editors themselves write (in *Cospe aqui*), following Hakim Bey.

We can therefore do a double reading of Mendes' work, first as singular contributions, isolated and concentrated, and then as parts of a continuous text. In the pages of these first A Mula fanzines, Mendes participated mostly with singular sight-size drawings, in which not only is his virtuosity (influenced by the photo-based, highly realistic paintings of Arlindo Silva, a fairly well-known painter in Portugal, and Mendes's roommate at the time)[6] manifested, but the noisy traces of the drawing process are also visible. These scenes include speech balloons or written notes that try to capture snippets of real-life conversations, and although they may be organised according to a chronological or axiological order, that is to say, with the imposition of narrative or some other kind of sequentially,[7] they are always already, following Mendes's words in *Estou careca*, "pages of a comics journal in which at least one year of common life [with the portrayed people] is narrated". Although drastically different from Fabrice Neaud's *Journal* project, Mendes's work has presented from the start narratological, ethical and representational strategies that prompted comparisons with the French artist.

Quite often, we consider the publication of a "book" as a proof of maturity, especially if it presents a long-form story, or at least it will be viewed as the confirmation of a certain level of success, commercial, critical or otherwise.[8] In Portugal, however, the chance of being published, especially in commercially consolidated houses, is slender for comics, and if we considered solely "officially" published books, we would surely overlook many interesting things. In fact, it was only in 2011-2012, especially with the publication of *Diário Rasgado* in book form that Mendes gained a little more public attention, including from the specialised media, despite the fact that all the material in the book had been published before, albeit in different form and order. But to say that the author is publishing the "same" material in the zines, the blog, *The Chinese Will Deliver the Pandas* and *Diário Rasgado* is, on the one hand, a little deceptive, since they involve different textual arrangements, but on the other, implies ongoing work across all titles, with *Diário Rasgado* being the hypothetical general title. In fact, the case of Mendes is quite similar to that of an author such as Edmond Baudoin, all of whose books, no matter how different they may be from one another (fiction *versus* non-fiction, travelogue *versus* autobiography, childhood memoir *versus* diary, self-centred *versus* focused on specific family members, collaborative *versus* solo, adaptation *versus* graphic journal), gravitate around the same conceptual core, which we could name either "subjectivity", "memory", or "self", but which is always not only open to representation but also to revision and re-presentation.[9] What I have written elsewhere about Baudoin also applies to Mendes: it is as if his every work contributes to a "continuous poem" (Moura: 2018).[10]

If the word "diário" [diary or journal] offers a sort of "proof of effort", a rhythmic capacity for searching amongst many life events to identify their condition of

Chapter Three

writable or textural possibility, for seeing them as worthy of being transformed and transmitted, the adjective "rasgado" [torn or rent] forces us to rethink that view. These may be pages that, after all, are not worthy of being recuperated by memory. They are exceptions to that grace, thus they are torn off, taken from the larger corpus, sacrificed, thrown away. But we can also interpret such a title as a form of rescue: the diary itself being an inaccessible object, not only because it does not belong to us but because it has no body within the world, these are, then, the only pages that are granted legibility. The act of tearing pages, a somewhat violent manual movement, also puts into our minds the idea of a sheet of paper now made even more imperfect. For the adjective does not point to the actions of "cutting away", "detaching" or "separating" a page, but of "tearing" it away. One of the sides, the one attached to the quire, will end up in an asymmetrical shape, with irregular curves and spikes, perhaps a few of the sentences "incomplete", a few drawings "hurt". And imperfection is one of the characteristics of Mendes's pages, part of his exploration of slightly different styles and approaches to drawing, diverse degrees of completeness, corrected texts, and so on, as mentioned before. It is as if the difficult task of looking at ourselves every single day in the same manner was expressed through these internal differentiations, and the act of tearing ourselves away from ourselves, so that we can look at ourselves "from the outside" (a typical principle of comics autobiography), is made possible.

Like most autobiographical authors, Mendes represents himself as a character within the diegetic world, a character only slightly more central because he appears more often, because he is the centre of focalised attention and action, and also because we follow the extra-textual pact, i.e., that the "Marco" in the strips is representing the author himself. Now, although throughout the history of comics there are a handful of examples of stories told from the protagonist's visual perspective, so that we see practically what the character would see through his or her own eyes, the greatest majority of comics do not do that. First-personal *visual* perspective or internal ocularisation is not unheard of, but it is not common.[11] When it is used, however, what is given to be seen through those panels is a surprisingly narrower view than that accessible naturally to human binocular vision. The choice of representing the "inside" of the gaze is culturally inhabitual and becomes rather strange and uncomfortable.[12]

Most (autobiographical) authors simply depict themselves in the plane where the rest of their characters are located.

> A person cannot from within look at himself from outside: an ethical "short circuit" takes place, and the only way out of this is to create a special external point of view on oneself and the world which by definition cannot coincide with the "I-for-myself", to create, in other words, a literary hero (Barsht 2000: 25).

These words belong to Konstantin Barsht, in an investigation of Dostoievs-ki's creative process that not only studies the Russian author's writing, but also the notes and the schemas he drew as a scaffold to that phase. Barsht presents a dichotomy between the Russian words *lik* and *oblik*, the first one standing for a person's actual "face" and the second for its reflection, or "appearance", in a mirror. The writer gives the example of a beautiful woman putting on make-up in front of a mirror as equivalent to a writer working on a text. Although there are significant differences, both are setting up an external point of view and, according to what-ever aesthetic rules and norms they follow, are creating an ideal object, a face (for the woman as an end in itself, for the writer as a means to an end). According to Barsht, for Dostoievski, the face is the "personalised image of the idea": the "human facial image" (*chelovecheskii lik*, in Russian) is unique. More than that, it is "the unity of the internal (the idea) and the external (the face) in man" (2000: 23).

Hans Belting explains how "Through its many variations, the human custom of image creation translates, in addition, the many ways with which man considers his own body. The cultural history of images is thus reflected in a parallel history of the body" (2004: 35). These seemingly unrelated lines of thought converge in what concerns me here, a representational choice that I will call the *torsion* of self-rep-resentation (of one's own body, of the I). Belting adds that "[the representation] is, as a matter of fact, the *production* of a bodily image that immediately participates in the self-representation of the body (original emphases; idem: 123). This means that each artist creates a body that stands for his or her own but as if it were the body of an other. Unlike in written autobiographies, where there is an immediate use of the first-person pronoun, in visual media, especially pictorial/graphical media the *auto-biographiable I* is displaced from the base-I, both in time and space, into a I-as-s/he. The face of a person, in these circumstances, becomes closer to its Latin etymolog-ical root, the *persona*, as both the actuality of a form that exists on the positive, ideal, perfect plane (the *eidos*) and a more illusory and superficial form (the mask). In this transformation, we will consider both Marco Mendes's more or less straightforward autobiography project and, later on, Miguel Carneiro's avatars in his absurd narra-tive universe.

This *torsion* leads inevitably to a first degree of dissociation – after all, we don't see our own faces except indirectly through reflexes, and a drawing is a reflex that goes through more personalised filters and channels than, say, photography. But as I have already mentioned and will discuss again later, the way Mendes engages with numerous genres and tones allows for the creation of secondary dissociations within his autobiographical project. Catherine Mao talks of a "flottement identi-taire" [floating identity], and points to Jean-Christophe Menu and Manu Larcenet as examples (**Mao 2013**). However, this problematisation has been present ever since autobiographical comics emerged, if we accept a specific parentage (see Grove

Chapter Three

2004; Hatfield 2005: 128 and ff.; Chaney 2011, Refaie 2013). Robert Crumb, in "The Many faces of Robert Crumb" in *XYZ Comics* (1972), deals with the issue of subjectivisation, self-presentation and social masking in a few pages. Aline Kominsky's "The Bunch Plays with Herself" (published in *Arcade Comics* no. 3, Print Mint, 1975) can be considered a sort of nexus or origin point for the way the human body went on to be considered throughout most autobiographical comics, especially by women authors. The body is, after all, "perhaps the most awkward materiality of all" (Highmore: 119), so to explore it opens up quite affect-laden vistas of self-portraying, self-reflecting and self-constructing. Justin Green explores the same issues within a framework of the exploration of trauma, which allows for the presence of fantasy and non-realist strategies in autobiographical narratives (Moura 2015). And Harvey Pekar's entire oeuvre opens up the issue of style and representation.

But let us go back to the question of *torsion*. The figuration of the events and actions experienced or seen by the autobiographical protagonists is not, then, made through an ocular imitation of the empirical, human, visual perspective, a total "subjective gaze", as it were, but through a transformation or reduction of the protagonists into characters, similar to all others. We should also take into account that the imitation of these experiences has *less* to do with the Greek concept of *mimesis* - to a certain extent mirror-like, a simulacrum of something that is different from itself, and is outside of itself, save for the fact that it mimics its movements and, above all, its looks (in Peircean terms, it would be the equivalent of an *icon*) - but rather as something closer to the Christological *imitatio*, an *incarnation*, an irruption of the body's originary image. In the case of the Classical *imitatio*, it is Christ's body that becomes the resonant body that emerges from within the empirical body of the imitator; in the case of autobiographies, it is the fictive body in relation to the "real, empirical body" of the authors. What is more, it also creates a reflected body in the "inside" of the diegetic space, the space of representation (Didi-Huberman 2007: see especially chapter II)[13]. This is the first dismembering between the observing "I" and the observed "I": between subject and object, subject and predicate.

There is a supplementary reason for this creation as it relates to human memory, and the way in which memory itself is constituted, as something removed from time and space, a "vertical zenith" that unites two events, which, despite being disconnected causally and temporally, establish a sort of *figuram implere* relationship that ends up by bonding them together, the "former heralding and promising the latter, the latter realizing the former" (Auerbach 1968: 84). The two "Is" would correspond to those two instances, confounded with one another. The author creates a puppet to represent him or herself in order to revisit the memory he or she is retelling.

This torsion has an important narratological consequence. It relates not only to issues of identity (Lejeune's "autobiographical pact" confers nominal identity upon author, narrator and character) but also to narrative *function*: the instance that organises visual facts and the represented events (Bal 1991: 163 ff.; Lejeune 1975 and 1980). In a certain way, this displacement of the representation of the "I" allowed (if not obliged; see Fehrle 2011 for a riveting discussion about what feels "natural" or not in the comics medium, in contrast with literature) by comics is similar to Kaja Silverman's "heteropathic identification", which we have come across before. For Silverman, who bases her argument on Max Scheler's work, this identification takes place when "the subject identifies at a distance from his or her proprioceptive self" (Silverman 1996: pg. 23). So instead of identifying the Other as an "I", naturalising it and absorbing it, it is rather a going out of the self, an alienation of the self, as if it were an Other. Empathy, rather than sympathy, ensues, as we have seen following LaCapra's interpretation.

In turn, this little detour recalls the etymological development, discussed by Georges Didi-Huberman (who quotes from Edgard B. Tylor's *Primitive Culture* in 2002: 57), that has been traced between "witness" and "superstition". As in French, the Portuguese word for witness, "testemunha", is derived from the ancient Latin juridical term *testis, -is*, which refers to a third party that would intervene, disinterestedly, in a dispute between two parties. A synonym of *testis* was *superstes [superstō]*,[14] which was used to label anyone who had observed or experienced something from beginning to end, not very differently from our current generic use of the term "to witness" something. That verb literally means "to be" (*stare*) + "on top of" (*super*), but a more usual meaning was "to make something last", "to preserve" or "that which survives"[15]. In any case, it is the origin of the word *superstição* in Portuguese or *superstition* in English, and of cognate words in other modern European languages.[16] It is as if an observation based on experience (a *testemunho*, an act of witnessing) has necessarily to be transformed into something that could be doubted by someone else (a superstition). A space that would store everything that others may not believe in, not because it is fantastic or incredible, but because it is *outside* the experience of others. The authors I will refer to, especially those who use autobiography or something close to it (Mendes, Carneiro, Tiago Baptista), are not above what is told, but *outside* it, thus bringing a strong bond again between those two ancient words: on the one hand, by telling the reader about themselves, they draw themselves as if from the outside (*above themselves*) as a strategy that allows for those experiences, those observations, that retold life, to reappear in a calmer, more soothing way so that, on the other hand, they can be presented as if in a juridical case, disinterestedly, as if in a court (with *witnesses*). Finally, they become like a *third* party that testifies, talking about themselves as if about someone else: *here's what happened, ecce homo, you be the judge.* What was witnessed is shown in a way that will survive, will relive, through remembrance, through being read.

Theorists such as John Paul Eakin (2004) and Leigh Gilmore (2001), among others, help us to think of autobiography as a construction of the self, an imposition

Chapter Three

of form (and order and coherence) on an unstoppable, formless flow. Eakin writes:

> When we talk about ourselves, and even more when we fashion an I-character in an autobiography, we give a degree of permanence and narrative solidity - or 'body', we might say - to otherwise evanescent states of identity feeling. We get the satisfaction of seeming to see ourselves see, of seeming to see our selves. That is the psychological gratification of autobiography's reflexiveness, of its illusive teller-effect (Eakin 2004: 129).

Like many contemporary artists, Mendes is well aware of the tradition into which he is becoming integrated. We have discussed the generalised lack of memory of comics as a medium. However Mendes belongs to a generation more informed about the long development of comics as an art form, a generation of artists who work in alternative circuits and who are able to draw from the most diverse sources, both in geographical and historical terms as well as in relation to genres and styles. Therefore, it is not difficult to inscribe Mendes into a long "family" that includes the North American precursors of autobiographical comics such as Harvey Pekar and Justin Green, to all the contemporary artists working in that "genre", as well as the European line which started with Gotlib and Giraud-Moebius (a handful of stories of the late 1970s) and later reached Fabrice Neaud and David B. via Baudoin and many others. More specifically, Mendes's self-derision and occasional humour bring him closer to Joe Matt, especially when the author-as-character addresses his readers directly, "breaking the fourth wall" (making us respect forcefully the role of the encoded reader, Genette's narratee) in order to frankly expose all his faults (physical, economic, professional, sexual, in relationships, etc.). But where Joe Matt reaches an excessive humour, to the point of almost absurd caricature, towards which his highly stylised graphic approach, influenced by classical American "bigfoot" children's comics, contributes, so that according to the rhetorical rules of *captatio benevolentiae* we "forgive" those character imperfections, Mendes does not seem to demand that reaction from his readers. This does not mean that Mendes completely avoids excessive humour. He does use it. His work is quite often informed by visual clichés (the cover of the fanzine *Carlitos*, created in 2008 with then-girlfriend Lígia Paz,[17] shows him as a caveman, and *Chinese* as a BDSM "slave" to a dominatrix), and introduces several degrees of metamorphosis away from realism to escape the "real" weight of his confession. However, they are at the same time exceptional, as they offer an even more sincere, barer exposure of life that creates a certain distance from the supposed vicariousness or identification of the reader. Again, *empathy* is welcome but abusive *identification* is not. LaCapra, writing in a wholly different context (historiography), but one that connects with some of the notions presented above, understands empathy as "a form of virtual, not vicar-

Marco Mendes and the ever-temporary rebuilding of the self

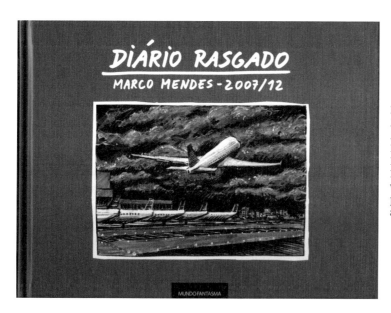

Figure 3.1: Marco Mendes (2012), *Diário Rasgado*. Porto: Mundo Fantasma; cover. Reproduced with the kind permission of the author.

ious, experience related to what Kaja Silverman has termed heteropathic identification, in which emotional response comes with respect for the other and the realisation that the experience of the other is not one's own" (2001: 40).

Mendes's mixture of "fiction lines", each one very different from the others, creates an undisrupted *basso continuo* in all his comics, which are quite melancholic.

If we look at the cover (Fig. 3.1), we can almost discern this elegiac tone. The moody colour scheme contributes immediately to this. Being a diary, it is expected to contain dates, of course, but the pairing of the name and a limited time span also imbues the cover with a gloomy tone, as if looking at a tombstone. Moreover, the picture is that of an aeroplane taking off, but it is not clear whether the protagonist or someone else is on board, or if it represents a departure or a return. Even if there is a confirmation within the diegesis, the feeling brought about by the cover is isolated from the matter within. In fact, we will discover that the plane is carrying Lili's, Marco's girlfriend, who is leaving for Barcelona to study, and that the book has their relationship as its centre, although it is not always the focus. The book even hints at a sort of structuring arc around the relationship. It opens with this girlfriend entering Marco's life, follows their passions and tensions, and finishes with their split and its consequences. The gravitational pull and pressure of this relationship seems to be felt in everything else in the book, even when there is no direct connection.

The "narrative heart" of *Diário Rasgado* is, arguably, this relationship, its central trauma, but the "small traumas" that are explored throughout its pages go beyond that love story. As I have mentioned, each "strip" can be read individually, as a singular unit. Many of them address other everyday problems: unemployment or

103

Chapter Three

low wages, lack of security for the future, a difficulty in dealing with overwhelming odds in relation to broader politics (expressed through exposure to news stories and comments on them), ageing and health, family life, and so on. Moreover, there is a constant melancholy portrait of daily life in Porto or elsewhere, with a particular emphasis on differences in the economic comfort of others, showing homelessness, hunger, poverty, quite often in comparison to Marco himself. There are moments when he and his friends complain about their lack of opportunity, but at other times he contrasts some of his lucky breaks in comparison to other people's misfortune (like when he drives past a man looking for food in trash bins). These "small traumas" are pervasive, constant and colour the whole ambience of the project, without being formed into a coherent nucleus that could be pinpointed as the "traumatic event" Mendes would "work through".

When referring to *Maus*, Ernst Van Alphen writes: "The cartoon medium is of course heavily invested with the marker of fictionality and imaginativeness" (1997: 22). However, we can surely accept the notion of an open-ended continuous gradient curve of those markers. That is to say, something akin to Scott McCloud's pyramid of the comic universe (1993: 50 ff.), with the difference that it would consider the inherent formal specificities and affordances of comics, and not solely the superficial, figurative, stylistic approach of the given artist. As is well known, one of *Maus*'s markers is the use of theriomorphic humans (and not anthropomorphised animals, as usually described), which points to the fact that "in the visual realm Spiegelman chooses multiple mediations, [but] in the aural, by contrast, he seems to seek absolute unmediated authenticity" (Hirsch 2011: 26). On the other hand, Marco Mendes seems to follow a realistic approach to drawing, but one that allows for fantastical representations, which have no relationship with the "documentary approach" that their visual style seems to promise.

Let us take a look at one particular image. The first page published in the *Diário Rasgado* (Fig. 3.2) book deserves a close reading of its own. It is a text-less, title-less full-page image. Let us remember that each of these pages were originally "units" with no particular order (except the chronological one of their publication on the blog), so it becomes quite significant that this one was chosen to open the book, which purportedly sets a more definitive reading order to the texts, or actually fuses them into *one text*. This image shows an interior scene, the living room of the protagonist's home. In it, we perceive three fragments of human (male) bodies: a hand entering the image at the upper left corner, holding a half-smoked cigarette, a leg that enters the lower part of the frame from the right and ends in a foot towards the middle, and, slightly hidden, the face of someone lying down on his side. On the one hand, taking in account the diegetic and visual information - whether gained from the blog or from later in the book - it is fairly easy to identify these body parts as belonging to the three men living in the house: Marco, Didi Vassi and Palas.

Figure 3.2: Marco Mendes (2012), *Diário Rasgado*. Porto: Mundo Fantasma; n.p. Reproduced with the kind permission of the author.

However, we also believe that there is a (even a blatant) intertextual reference, on the visual track, to Guido Buzzelli's *Zil Zelub*. In fact, the very first page of the Italian author's most famous book opens by showing the protagonist - himself a self-fiction avatar of Buzzelli - on a seemingly conventional page, with his body judiciously framed so that only parts or fragments appear, but making us believe that this is just a question of composition and angle choice (although the last panel seems awkward). Only when we turn this page do we discover that the previous pseudo-superficial physical fragmentation was actually literal (within the fiction), as Zelub's legs and arms are detached from his trunk, with a will of their own. So begins the story of *Zil Zelub*. Now, when we turn the pages of *Diário Rasgado*, we will not find any kind of diegetic confirmation of this, but could we still speak of the *fragmentation* of a single body? The fact that Mendes often uses, knowingly or not, intertextual references in the creation of some of his compositions (to which we will return later) allows us to pursue this thought. Even though such a fragmentation is not explored literally, imaginatively or diegetically in Mendes's book, it is present to some degree, for the disposition of the bodies, as I termed it, "judiciously framed" and showing a "superficial physical fragmentation", leads us to the idea that there is some exploration of the dissociation of the book's "Marco".[18]

In almost all comics' autobiographies there is a degree of *dédoublement*, a doubling of the empirical person into "author" and "protagonist", as we have seen with the notion of *torsion*. There is no difference in *Diário*, of course. On the one hand, obviously, this doubling is graphic, for authors more often than not represent themselves in a manner quite distinct from their empirical cognitive perceptions (the first-person perspective). On the other hand, and in relation to this book in particular, Mendes inserts a note at the back of the book stating that everything present

Chapter Three

in the book belongs to the world of fiction, but that is perhaps the biggest fiction of all. Even if we accept the fact that we are not looking at the most basic of autobiographies – there is no such thing, but let us postulate, for argument's sake, the existence of a *zero degree* – we will be in the presence of an auto-fiction, or an auto-fantasy, in the sense that the author creates a double of him- or herself, an avatar, a "fiction suit" that s/he employs then in the fictions that s/he creates, but in which all the elements have connections, even if not direct, point-by-point, to his or her lived reality. I have no wish to go down the unproductive road of considering every work of art as autobiographical, but I have no wish either to restrict my considerations to those texts where Lejeune's "pact" can be detected.

In the conclusion of her essay quoted above, Catherine Mao shows how autobiographical comics "solve" the questions posed by self-representation. Not by self-analysis, but by a movement towards the external, a double one moreover, first of all through a "uniform, that of the comics' character", and secondly through a third party: a muse, a lover, a relative, a landscape (2013: paragraph 33), in relation to which a dialogue ensues that focuses on the self-construction of the artist (idem: § 24 and ff.). Once again, Mendes's strategy in this last point is quite close to Baudoin's.

Mendes quite often uses panels with a subjective point of view, where the shot/reverse shot technique reveals who is the observer of the previous scenes. Although there are a few cases in which we see a framed scene as if from the character's own point of view, it is more usual to see the character's back, or the back part of the

Figure 3.3: Marco Mendes (2012), "Afrodite", in *Diário Rasgado*. Porto: Mundo Fantasma; n.p. Reproduced with the kind permission of the author.

head, etc., as if guiding us with the position of his body. According to Johannes Fehrle, Martin Schüwer calls this technique "half-subjective panels", drawing from Deleuze to characterize it. Fehrle explains further, quoting from Schüwer, that this is "[m]ore effective [as] a narrative technique in which 'the camera does not merge with the person or remain outside her, but is with her'. Thus we can see characters and relevant parts of their surrounding environment, while at the same time their feelings colour the scene. In other words, subjective and objective image merge" (Schüwer apud Fehrle 2010: 293). But this can be achieved in other ways.

A case of focalisation and a certain transmission of melancholy is found in the strip titled "Afrodite" (Fig. 3.3). This is one of the many strips that Mendes creates with no verbal text, which forces the reader to infer more profoundly and more personally the degree of emotion and experience that is expressed, in contrast with those cases where dialogues, captions, jokes, etc., can centre things in a more superficial communicability, that is to say, where much is surmised from what is said (and from little else, although this is extremely rare). We could attempt to describe this strip as fully as possible, engaging in an ekphrastic exercise, but it would be rather difficult to be wholly precise about the feeling of *desire* that is present in the fourth panel. The naked body of the model is depicted in the first three panels, although in the third indirectly (or even to the third degree, given the fact it shows a *drawing of a drawing*); in the fourth panel, the young woman, if it is the same character, is no longer "the model". Marco is acting like a drawing instructor, and all his actions, hypothetical words, gestures, and laid-back attitude in the studio show the power he has over both the students and the model. He is the focus of attention who "moulds" her body in the perception of the students. In the first panel he makes a broad gesture as if presenting her whole body, in the second he makes a framing gesture, and in the third it is his hand holding the pen, as if showing his student how to draw. In each of these panels non-natural, excessive, "energy" lines converge towards the central body of the woman, which is also represented chromatically in an underlying contrast (white against grey in the first panel, black with white contour highlights in the second, with thick contour lines in the third). Moreover, it is significant that in all three panels, Marco's look (or gaze) is never directed towards the model. In the fourth panel, there is an insurmountable distance: there is a clear distinction between inside and outside, the woman seems to protect herself and walks away towards the dark part of the panel, while Marco, apparently relaxed, smokes a cigarette leaning against the threshold, and follows her with his gaze. It is true that we cannot see his eyes, covered by the spectacles, shadows and distance, but the inclination of his body and head helps us to infer that. If these scenes can work in isolation as an exchange of gaze-lines, desire, representation, and the subjectivisation of masculine and feminine identity and agency, within the narrative economy and ordering of *Diário* (quite distinct from that presented in the blog posts), it also gains other meanings.

Chapter Three

Figure 3.4: Marco Mendes (2012), "Pesadelo", in *Diário Rasgado*. Porto: Mundo Fantasma; n.p. Reproduced with the kind permission of the author.

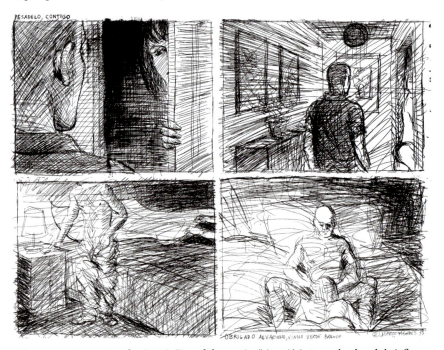

Figure 3.5: Marco Mendes (2012), "Pesadelo contigo", in *Diário Rasgado*. Sketch briefly published then deleted from URL: http://diariorasgado.blogspot.com/ Retrieved by and reproduced with the kind permission of the author.

The strip is found *after* Lili splits with Marco, and it is found *before* another strip called (and about a) "flirt", dealing with a new, different, love interest. But the immediate strip after "Afrodite" shows a story in which Marco pays a prostitute a visit, and has sex with her (Fig. 3.4). In the first panel we can barely see the face of the prostitute but it is very similar to that of Lili. This strip is called "Pesadelo" [Nightmare]. Furthermore, a first unpublished draft was entitled "Pesadelo contigo" [A nightmare with you] (Fig. 3.5). This was published in the blog, but removed a few days later (author, personal communication). So several complicated lines merge in each of these relationships between Marco and these different women. Is the female character with whom Marco "flirts" the model from the previous strip? What about the sexual nightmare? Is it a dream, a memory or a projection of desire? Or is it autobiographical fact, in some way?

The author does not focus upon the Marco-Lígia relationship in the same analytical or clinical vein that, say, Jeffrey Brown, Gabrielle Bell, Joe Matt and Chester Brown do in their respective works. He rather dilutes that relationship by immersing it in the rest of his life, as represented in *Diário rasgado* - sharing his flat with the roommates, his professional life, his family, his everyday. It is then the absence of Lígia/Lili that points towards a mourning that influences all subsequent scenes and episodes, including those that seem completely unrelated to that relationship (a few examples are the strips called "Águas passadas", "Domingo à noite", "Jantar", and, as we've seen, "Afrodite").

There is also another theme that could be taken to be the dislocated core of the book, and which is quite evident in "Saudade", and in a few other stories that were not included in the book. In fact, all Mendes's comics could be seen as a process of "curing", of transforming the memory of those relationships and all those moments into text. As soon as they exist as texts, they can be structured in such a way that they will have a narrative arc, a resolution, a closure.

Perhaps ironically, as if confirming a formula, and emphasising a conventional narrative arc, the book returns in the end to the opening scenes, with young men of a disillusioned generation, deprived of hope, sharing a low-rent flat, and abandoning themselves to the easy pleasures of drinking, smoking pot, going out at night, leering at the opposite sex and making cheap jokes (see Conclusion). This seemingly defeatist attitude, however, may arguably be a form of political resistance to the hypocritical seriousness of a hegemonic society, an attitude that constrains every discourse. Or to put it in another way, it is as if society made permission to have a dialogue conditional on submission to certain "rules", as if a right to have one's own voice came at the price of only speaking in a certain manner. So these disreputable and marginal behaviours would act counter to that hegemonic, normalised discourse. In this respect, it is quite important to understand also that the author never stands outside his own political-social context, even if he does not

Chapter Three

present an explicit discourse upon it (like, say, Neaud does). However, if we identify the moments when all the characters refer to their own jobs, their professional expectations, careers, economic and social situations, or when they comment (more or less judgementally, more or less humorously) about other people, who may be either representatives of a certain idea of social normalisation or of the pariahs the protagonists themselves stand for, in the end there is a certain politicised ambience, informed by left wing politics, unimpressed by the discourses of supposed "success", "compulsory entrepreneurship" or the "unavoidable economic conditions" that seem to typify capitalist contemporaneity. This ambiguity mirrors the pervasive social disenchantment of these characters - above all, the protagonist - and acts upon what Sianne Ngai calls "ugly feelings", which I will explore further in the last chapter.

It is valuable to look beyond the work published within the *Diário rasgado* book collection, and comprehend how every single image created by Marco Mendes contributes to this "Continuous poem" idea.

Marco Mendes made a colour illustration for the Portuguese Communist Party (PCP) newspaper, *Avante!* (issue no. 1953, May the 5th, 2011) (Fig. 3.6), as one of a group of comics and illustration artists who were invited to participate in this commemorative issue of May the 1st, by creating images on the theme of International Worker's Day or any form of resistance against the liberal policies that were increasingly making themselves felt, in the country (usually described as "inevitabilities", which is a polite way of saying that there is no room for their public discussion). One of the things that needs to be understood in order to read this image is that in the period immediately after the 25 de Abril, many, if not all the left wing parties (PCP included) created colourful murals scattered throughout the cities of Portugal. Some of them were maintained for decades, almost as unofficial monuments (that is to say, there were no active policies either to keep and restore them or to efface them) but, coincidentally or not, they began to be painted over around the late 2010s.[19] The author thought about them when he decided to create this image (private communication with the author), but there was one other "monument" probably in the back of his mind. Even if Mendes did not actively and explicitly mention it, there is an echo of Goya's *3 de Mayo de 1808* (1814). There are quite a number of similar elements in the composition, from the disposition of figure and ground and the objects in the visual plane, to the diagonal line that obliquely divides the field, the relationship between the walls and the half-hidden background, and the colour scheme, especially the bright, contrasting yellow. But the very atmosphere and the political lesson of Goya's famous painting also seems to resonate in Mendes's image.

Historically, May the 1st marks the 1886 Chicago Haymark affair, but as a commemorative date (as in other countries, it is a holiday in Portugal, although not until after the 1974 Revolution), it stands for the workers' ongoing struggle and

Marco Mendes and the ever-temporary rebuilding of the self

Figure 3.6: Marco Mendes (2011), untitled illustration, *Avante*. Lisbon: Edições Avante! Issued March 5th, n.p. Reproduced with the kind permission of the author.

resistance against capitalism, a struggle that seems to be increasingly questioned by the advances of late capitalist neoliberal policies as they are applied in countries such as Portugal, usually disguised as "necessary structural reforms", or whatever euphemism, doubletalk and jargon are used.[20] More often than not these words are vague, or at least indirect (as are "budget cuts", "dislocation", "tax rises", "subsidy termination", etc.), but they point to a problem currently felt, which is that it is more difficult now to even *imagine* that life might be better in the future. While the generations that lived through April the 25th actually saw political openness, and during the 1980s and 1990s witnessed European integration and a rise in material wealth, today even the prospects for graduates of, for instance, getting a job, moving to their own place, or even affording to have children, are not promising.

Goya's painting shows the massacre of the victims of Napoleon's imperial machine, and it had a groundbreaking role in European painting, in the way that it represented war. It has a close relationship with Goya's own engravings *Los desastres de la guerra* (1810-1820) and, through these, with Jacques Callot's *Les grandes misères de la guerre* (1633).[21] The connection between these lines, on the one hand artistic and on the other hand thematic-political, can be seen in Marco Mendes's own work: its continuity and its convergence - if we return to the idea of a "united poem", or

Chapter Three

"oeuvre" – are quite telling. For instance, it is not innocent that the "change" operated in Mendes's image turns the killer platoon into an abandoned, shattered car. The idea of the "April murals" gradually worn away not only by the weather and the years but also by neglect, political vandalism and the short memory of the Portuguese, is confirmed by the faded image on the wall. In the interior of this "fiction", is an actual mural, not a group of people holding a demonstration. But at the same time it is as if their insistent, surviving and confrontational presence creates the possibility of a resistance: in the materiality of the drawing itself, in the matter's own fictionality: these are actually paper people who are *still (or finally) demonstrating* in that space.

This divide can be read as corresponding to Jacques Rancière's distinction between "police" and "politics". For Rancière, the activity known as politics is not only an "exercise of power or the deciding of common affairs," but actually the pre-requisite that such a (notion of) the common exists, that the common is symbolised (2004b: 6). The two ways of symbolising the common are, on the one hand, the totalising, function-assigning and appropriateness-deciding powers of the police (in other words, politics as exercised by politicians and official mechanisms of power), and on the other hand, "politics" [*politique*] proper (for Rancière),

> which calls into question the divisions of common and private, visible and invisible, audible and inaudible. This calling into question presupposes the action of supplementary subjects, subjects that are not reducible to social groups or identities but are, rather, collectives of enunciation and demonstration surplus to the count of social groups" (idem).

The image thus complicates the agency of the characters depicted, who can be seen as both powerless (nothing but drawings on a crumbling, forgotten wall) and empowered (by being active *as drawing* in between the two separated spaces, that of privilege and that of the end result of capitalism's planned obsolescence).

Other elements also seem to concur with that phantasmatic notion that at the same time is already dissipating but also, albeit indistinctly, rising. The nocturnal scene presents two secondary colour areas, the brighter, electric blue of the "private condominiums" (whose replacement of Goya's church is not by chance, surely, as markers of property, privilege but also as potentially protective spaces that are denied to the people depicted) and the smudged green of the dilapidated car, as if we were presented with the life cycle of contemporary capitalism's goods – deftly inverted in terms of visual fields – and sectioned by the wall (also old, unfinished or damaged, but insistent), both primary colours imposing a sort of daylight upon the nocturnal scene. These effects are done by Mendes's method, which is not "clean" nor linear. Many of the "mistakes" or "first choices" are still visible in the final image, as well as the marks of materials such as grainy crayons, pastel pencils, and so on. This can also have a political reading: as Rancière writes, "In politics, subjects act to create a stage on which problems can *be made visible* - a scene with subjects and objects, in full view of a 'partner' who does not 'see' them" (my emphasis, 2004b: 7; also, see Miller 2017). By making these issues and the preparatory marks visible, as well as part of his own continuous text, which will still be read in general terms as an autobiography, Mendes is integrating these addresses to other people into his own subjectification process.

The formal choice to make this "graphic noise" visible and integrated into the final art implies that for Marco Mendes the need and the urgency of his creative gesture is oriented solely towards its mechanical reproducibility, as if that was the true and only life of the image, with no concern for the original art, or without even considering the original as an artwork in itself. Is this to be understood as a critical practice that hampers and contests the reification of the drawing itself as commodifiable and saleable? As usual, the author, who commingles and criss-crosses personal memory and collective history, autobiography and fantasy, positions his self-representating avatar is found right in the foreground of the mural. He is the bald, bespectacled man carrying the red international flag on the right, linking arms with the miner, which recalls the many graphical permutations that Portuguese graphic artist and painter João Abel Manta created during the Revolutionary period.

We could also argue, however, that Mendes-the-author does not wish for Mendes-the-character to occupy the same "moral place" as the victims in Goya's painting. In the fictitious mural, the place of the white-clad man of Goya's masterpiece is taken by Mendes's avatar, with his black turtleneck sweater and his horn-rimmed glasses, almost a caricature of the intellectual, somewhat dissimilar to the "proletarian masses" represented by the other characters. Nonetheless, he wants to be present as an ally of the struggle. In the mural, all the character's mouths are open, as if shouting. Although it is obvious that their medium and location are fragile and ephemeral (these are not the glorious and utopian masses of Delacroix' *La Liberté guidant le peuple*), their voices can still be heard. Again we resort to Ranciére:

> Politics is not some age of humanity which is to have been realised today. Politics is a local, precarious, contingent activity - an activity which is always on the point of disappearing, and thus perhaps also on the point of reappearing (2004b: 8).

As we can see, apart from the tradition of comics, we can also inscribe Marco Mendes into other visual art fields. Painting is one of them, and perhaps it is not too far-fetched to look at his work, especially in its social dimension, as connected to Courbet, who wanted to capture reality without resorting to any filters of ideali-

Chapter Three

sation and without beautifying it (which does not necessarily mean avoiding fictive elements). Situated in the 21ˢᵗ century, Mendes's post-modern discourse does not allow him to deal naively with reality.[22] As a matter of fact, his drawing approach, its stylistic structuring, his choice of a certain opaqueness of materiality, with visible traces of the process, the consequent manipulation of the meaningful structures of comics (even if these look like the most simple four-panel grids), are all deliberate gestures, concentrated, performed with conscious awareness of the transformation of his first "impressions of reality" into a wider texture with meanings of their own.

If reality is unattainable in itself (the numenon) it can be construed *through* the expressive and artistic tools available to the author, so that even Mendes's supposed "documentarist" approach, when it takes place, is filled with aesthetic meaning. Still, Mendes's created reality tries to give the impression, or mirror or reshape a certain idea of genuineness. His irony in relation to inhabited spaces, his choices of self-representation, no matter how filtered they are, the "material dirtiness" of his drawings (even when there is some digital clean-up that flattens the materiality of the original drawings, something debated in the book), and even the integration of fantasy elements into his "real life" are all factors that contribute towards that genuineness.

Let us take a closer look at the seemingly casual manner with which Mendes creates his approach to image making. We find corrections in the shape of lines scribbled on top of the words, contour lines for some characters redrawn on top of the first attempt, quick gestural lines to demarcate shadow patches or volume in certain objects, whiteout blots for the precise purpose of to marking a correction (for they could be used for other purposes, such as colouring or lightning effects), the uncleanness of the areas "outside" the panel borders, the presence of Scotch tape in a few corners, and so on. All of these marks, along with the images and drawings and borders are part of the author's specific expressive tools, but they add up to a certain quality that introduces some distance between Mendes and a certain classic, methodical and "clean" idea of how to create comics (an artistic method that prises above all the revisiting and remaking of the original material in order to reach a final reproductive result, *la ligne claire* being perhaps its highest, most famous exemplar), and, on the other hand, augment the feeling of authenticity. It recalls Walter Benjamin's powerful metaphor in "Die Erzahler" essay, when he talks of the mark of the storyteller on the story being similar to the "way the handprints of the potter cling to the clay vessel" (Benjamin 1969: 92).

It is necessary however, not to confuse "genuine" with "true", the noumenic quality, the reality of events and things. That would be a fruitless path to follow, which would lead only to dangerous, and unimportant, questions such as "did this *really* happened?" It is not by chance that the first story Mendes chose to open the book (after the initial, previously mentioned, fragmentary image), "Evereste", discusses the protagonist's fantasy desire of climbing that mythic mountain in order better to look at the world, like an isolated and heroic figure similar to the one represented in Caspar David Friedrich's famous painting, *The Wanderer Above the Mists* (1818). But the book as a whole actually reveals a ground level perspective, which is still able, however, to give us back an image of nature, the workings and the daily life of the world, and creates a certain *face,* that is to say, a ground-level, empathic access to experience.

This "noisiness" that we have referred to in relation to the author's materiality allows for a distancing effect. The visuality never becomes too familiar, transparent or naturalised. It does not become an illusory window into a hypothetical world, where truth could have a role to play. Quite the contrary, being in a constant mutation, its tactility, its incompleteness (from a classic perspective), its mish-mash of several visual approaches within the same page, or even the same panel, summon up another of Walter Benjamin's concepts. In 'Goethe's *Elective Affinities*", Benjamin argues that in "In the expressionless [*Ausdrucklose*], the sublime violence of the true appears" and, a little further on the philosopher adds that "[o]*nly the expressionless completes the work, by shattering it into a thing of shards, into a fragment of the true world, into the torso of a symbol"* (Benjamin 1996: 340). Of course, Benjamin is referring to Goethe's novel, which presents itself as a whole, coherent and with a crystal-clear structure. The fragmented nature of Diário rasgado is quite obvious, but it is not only related to certain contemporary conditions of production, as we have seen in the first chapter. That is in fact its creative context, and the author accepts it as it is, and he does not tries to hide it or disguise it. On the contrary, he flaunts it.

And in fact, another of the recurring traits of narratives such as these is that same fragmentary nature, its narrative disorder (in the specific sense that it does not obey strictly normative temporal and causal axes), its several types of (possible or realised) recombination, which invite the notion of circularity, and discordant rhythms. This is what E. Ann Kaplan would call "narration without narrativity" (*2005:* 65), which employs dream and fantasy scenes in its texture, in which the linear temporal flux is interrupted by flashbacks, often sudden. Mendes adds to these strategies his mode of humour, as well as the intersection with other comics genres.

The reconfiguration of the works is quite noticeable, whether we contrast the ordering in the book with that of the previous English anthology (*Pandas*) or with the dates of the publication of the first blog, or even their dates of production; which are scribbled in every strip (at the end of the volume there is also a date list). If we go through the "whole work", the "Continuous poem", the effective selection made out of the available material, we will come across some interesting ideas. For example, the absence of a strip such as "Pesadelo" from the economy that is constructed with the book is quite revealing.

Chapter Three

The point is that Mendes reuses or even repurposes some of his previous, "daily," singular strips as well as his first published zine pages and imposes an almost unbreakable formal rule upon them: the four-panel, 2 by 2 grid, as if he aimed for another sort of continuity and coherence to his production, and wished at the same time to create a dialogue with a specific and age-old tradition of the medium of comics, the newspaper humour strips à la Schulz, even if Mendes's own punch lines and ellipses deregulate comicality and melancholy. This formal stratagem bolsters the idea that more important than a supposed "truth" is the formation, the creation, the impression of the genuineness of this(these) character(s)' experiences, inspiring empathy, which in turn reserves and respects the place of both the reader and the subjects of the reading. An insurmountable difference, across which second hand experience can prove gratifying and enriching.

Marco Mendes, by working within an economy of genres and book-production that may be called "alternative", creates his *Diário* in a space for negotiation afforded by a tense balance between abdicating the "dominant fictions" (to use an expression by Kaja Silverman) and maintaining some elements of narrative coherence. There are recurrent characters, a space-time axis that brings some degree of cohesion to the diegesis, no matter how fragmented it is, is minimally identifiable, relationships between every single "fragment" are established in a way that allows for a continuous reading, and so on. Moreover, the very possibility of recombination suggests that an incessant search presides over the work - it could be re-launched again in a different order, for instance - and therefore that a constant process of rebuilding coherence is under way.

Notes

1   www.diariorasgado.blogspot.com.
2   Usually they consist of an oblong composition of four panels, distributed in a 2x2 grid, each of which has its own title, maintained in subsequent editions.
3   Not to mention issues of materiality and of making visible the dimension of artefactuality of comics.
4   The first title is in English originally, the second is a phonetic pun on "Lick you" in Portuguese, and the following are translatable as "Mm, mm, I see...", "I'm bald and my bitch is going to die!" and "Spit here".
5   *A minha cadela*, etc., n.p.
6   In fact, Silva's 2005 painting *Doi-doi* [Boo-boo] depicts Mendes himself, seemingly bleeding from the head and nose, an image for Halloween.
7   In fact, many of them were presented at an exhibition in Coimbra, and a book was published: *Anos Dourados* (Mundo Fantasma: 2013). Although in the blog there is no particular distinct strategy to present the "strips" and the "drawings", the inclusion of some in the *Diário Rasgado* book allows us to imagine

some possibility of integration into the continuous work, as discussed.

8 This endorses the distinction between graphic novels and comics that is proposed in some academic circles, and also draws attention to the blatant lack of criticism of works that, independently of their remarkable nature, are published in formats that fall "under the radar": fanzines, magazines, newspapers, some web-based platforms, etc.

9 In Baudoin's case, for instance, we can see this via the recurring leitmotiv of the child with the finger in his mouth: starting in *Passe le temps*, it will be found in *Derrière les fagots, Le premier voyage, Le voyage, Le chemin de Saint-Jean, Travesti, Villars sur Var* and *Éloge de la poussière*.

10 An image taken from Portuguese poet Herberto Helder, who considers (most) all of his books as part of one single, "Continuous poem". A heavily edited anthology of his work came out in 2001: *Ou o poema contínuo*.

11 We will not distinguish here fiction and non-fiction uses of this. A few examples are Windor McCay's February the 25th, 1905 strip *Dream of the Rarebit Fiend*, Will Eisner's *The Spirit* 1946 story "The Killer" (originally published in the insert dated December the 8th, 1946), Bob Powell's 1953 short story "Colorama" (originally in *Black Cat Mystery* # 45). Marco Mendes also has a few stories like this, which I will address later on.

12 As in the quoted Eisner's story, eerily showing the inside of the orbital bones.

13 It would be interesting to confront this with writer Grant Morrison's concept of a "fiction suit" (2011: 117).

14 In Festus' *Glossaria Latina* (394, 37) it is written "superstites testes præsentes significat". All of these etymological developments and sources are derived from entries for *superstō* and *testis* in A. Ernout and A. Meillet's *Dictionnaire Étymologique de la langue latine. Histoire des mots*. 4ª ed. Librairie C. Klincksieck: Paris 1960. Tome II: pgs. 653-654 and 689.

15 It is in Plutarch that the usage "being a survivor" appears.

16 This time around, it is in Cicero that this word assumes the meaning of something opposed to a religious vision, in the sense of "superfluous practices", even though it has roots in popular usage.

17 Although this may seem an unnecessary biographical information, it is in fact a in-text information. It is Paz the woman represented in the covers of both *Carlitos* and *Chinese*...

18 Evariste Blanchet, in his reading of the same scene in Buzzelli's book, describes how the "grotesque and extravagant character of the scene paradoxically calls into question our judgment about the last panel of the first page [which seemed to present an anatomically wrong drawing]: we are so far from an objectively observable physical reality that the absence of realism cannot be understood simply as an error of clumsiness" (2003: 44-45).

Chapter Three

19 See the site of the Centro de Documentação 25 de Abril of the Universidade de Coimbra, which has several exhibition nuclei, like for instance: http://www1.ci.uc.pt/cd25a/wikka.php?wakka=coleccaoConceicaoNeuparth. Last access April the 10th 2014.

20 Especially more so after Portugal received funds from the European Financial Stabilisation Mechanism in 2011, which lead to the draconian measures of the so-called "Troika" (the European Commission, the European Central Bank and the International Monetary Fund) agreement.

21 See Chute 2016 for a discussion of these engravings within a context of comics studies.

22 Which does not imply, of course, that Courbet was doing so.

Chapter 4
Miguel Rocha and working through the acting out of history

Before he turned to comics, Miguel Rocha (born in Lisbon, 1968) worked in the graphic arts industry, and was involved in publicity and publishing. He notably worked for the magazine *Selecções BD*, one of a number of comics anthology weeklies that tried to maintain the trend of *Cavaleiro Andante* and *Tintin* through the decline of the late 1980s and early 1990s, as discussed previously. In sharp contrast with most other Portuguese authors in contemporary times, whose first steps were taken in fanzines or collective publications, Miguel Rocha, after one brief venture onto that terrain, started his career with book-long projects. This brought him immediately up against the challenges and difficulties that working on a book implies, but it also instilled in him a rare capacity for regularity and perseverance. He has also created a children's illustrated book in collaboration with João Paulo Cotrim, and has created a number of posters, some for high profile events (such as UEFA's Euro 2004 football tournament, that took place in Portugal), and some in more intimate collaborations, such as the poster for Montemor-o-Novo's theatre production of *Hans, O Cavalo Inteligente*, written by Francisco Campos, which Rocha would later adapt to the comics medium. His involvement with a cultural association in Montemor-o-Novo, where he has been living for many years, has led him to playwriting as well.

Having published more than 10 books, Rocha has not only pursued a wide choice of strategies, both stylistic and narrative, but has also varied his projects between solo work, collaborative work and adaptations. From his many titles, we can mention *O enigma diabólico* [The diabolical mystery] (written by José Abrantes, in a sort of homage to Edgar P. Jacobs; Quadradinho: 1998), *Borda d'Água* ([Water's Edge] a slightly autobiographical work reminiscent of an early Baru, or Max Cabanes's *Colin Maillard*, for instances, and published as the 5th issue of the Lx Comics collection of the Bedeteca de Lisboa: 1999), *As pombinhas do Sr. Leitão* [Mr. Leitão's doves] (Baleiazul/Bedeteca de Lisboa: 1999), *Eduarda* (based on Georges Bataille's novella, *Madame Edwarda*; Polvo/Bedeteca de Lisboa: 2000); *Março* [March] (written with Alex

Chapter Four

Gozblau; Baleiazul/Bedeteca de Lisboa: 1999), *Beterraba – A vida numa colher* [Beetroot – Life in a spoon] (Polvo: 2003), *Os touros de Turlessos* [The Bulls of Tartessus] (written by José Carlos Fernandes; Junta de Andalucia: 2004), *Salazar, agora na hora da sua morte* [Salazar, now in the time of his death] (written by João Paulo Cotrim; Parceria A. M. Pereira: 2006), *A noiva que o rio disputa ao mar* [The bride that the river wrangles from the sea] (again with Cotrim; C.M. Portimão: 2009) and *Hans, o cavalo inteligente* [Hans, the intelligent horse] (based on the play by F. Campos quoted above; Polvo: 2010). He has also published a handful of shorter stories in anthologies, written by Cotrim, as well as João Ramalho Santos and João Miguel Lameiras, and one adaptation of a Miguel Torga short story ("Miura", in *Contos Contigo*; IPLB: 2002).

Risking oversimplification, we could argue that Rocha's graphic approach, within the medium of comics, has two distinct phases. A first phase could be called artisan-like or manual, in which the author tried his hand at many different styles and tools, colour palettes and visual effects, with outstanding and varied pictorial, even painterly, results. A second, starting with *Salazar*, took him into the world of digital tools, eschewing almost entirely ink on paper. This does not mean, however, that his own particular gestuality and figuration, his own *graphiation*, suffered any dramatic alteration. On the contrary, there are many distinct traits that unite these two phases even though the creative media employed are drastically different, as we shall see. Rocha painstakingly searches for the best possible path to create a coherent work, the best fit with the "story". He also permanently reveals an almost encyclopaedic knowledge of the varied tradition within the comics medium, not by employing direct quotes but through very subtle ways of integrating those same traditions within the mesh of his singular works. This is notable in the variety of *mise en page* choices, formats and the colouring approach, to name but a few of the dimensions.

Março, for instance, explores a radiantly varied rainbow of colours and drawing styles. Informed, I believe, by the work of Neil Gaiman and Dave McKean's collaborations (especially *Violent Cases, Signal to Noise* and *Mr. Punch*),[1] this book focus on an ongoing dialogue between a couple as they walk through the streets of Lisbon and visit secret places. It is a short yet epic journey by the two main characters through the perceptions of the five senses, in which each chapter has a dominant colour drawing techniques are varied in order to both underline the specific sense and the variety of human impressions. The book was written with Alex Gozblau, another comics artist, and it prepared the powerful colour *tour de force* that later sustained *Beterraba*.

This last title was not *drawn* but *painted*. Rocha applied acrylic paint directly onto coloured card stock. This leads to a wonderfully stark contrast between scenes of brilliant Apollonian days and eerie Dionysian nights. *Salazar*, on the other hand, was entirely made via computer: apart from a few pencil studies in the beginning, Rocha used what were then very novel interfaces such as a graphics tablet with a stylus, which allows for the artist to use precisely the same gestures as if drawing with a pen, pencil or brush on paper but to "translate" those same gestures immediately into digital information. He also used many variegated materials such as newspaper clips, photos and fonts, but the entire book is black and white with a few applications of a very light, dull yellow and a ghoulish, sickly greenish grey. This is quite important for the character of the book. *Hans*, also created wholly digitally, mocks the sort of almost passionless, documentary, black-and-white police record photography. In any case, all his works are unified by a noticeable preference for highly stylised figuration, with round shapes for the characters and an expressiveness that is conveyed by a very small repertoire of visual changes. Digital *sfumato*, heavy and complex patterns, broad areas with pure colours or solid whites or blacks, the use of symbols or even visual metaphors, recurrent images within a story, "silent" panels, and so on, are but a few of the traits we can find repeatedly throughout Rocha's books. Moreover, and as we will see in detail below, whether he is working by himself or adapting a text or working with a writer, he seems to have a particular penchant for characters who one way or the other become isolated from society at large: a decision the characters themselves have made, either because they were pushed into it for lack of love or understanding or because they make their way through the world with such a unique vision that they cannot find a place easily.

I will focus on two books: *Salazar* and *As pombinhas do Sr. Leitão*. The reason for this choice is rather simple. From all the books published by Rocha, these are the ones that address the recent historical past of Portugal. In contrast with the other books, they are related to collective experience and cultural memory based on a real context, instead of the literary, cultural imaginary, whether of Greek myth (*Tartessos*) or *maudit* literature (*Eduarda*). Although *Pombinhas* is fiction, it takes place in actual historical circumstances. *Salazar* on the other hand is a sort of symbolic biography about the man who held the reins of the Portuguese Empire for decades and left his particular stamp on Portuguese politics and *esprit* for the years that followed (one could even say, perhaps, *until today*).

Furthermore these books create a productive contrast on several counts. First of all, the fact that these books are dated from 1999 (*Pombinhas*) and 2006 (*Salazar*) gives us a good account of the artist's "development", "growth" or, more appropriately, his ever-changing yet incessant search for stylistic approaches according to the narrative project at hand. *Pombinhas* is a solo work and *Salazar* was written with João Paulo Cotrim. Moreover, while *Pombinhas* has the typical format of a Franco-Belgian styled *album* (a softcover, approx. 32 x 24 cm, 48 pages), *Salazar* is closer to the typical "book format" that has swept through the world of comics, i.e., the "graphic novel" format: it is approx. 24,5 x 17 cm, with 210 pages. I hope that these differences will also be productive in my close readings.

Chapter Four

As Pombinhas do Sr. Leitão

This is Rocha's first book (Fig. 4.1). The album comprises two stories, the first being announced by the book's title, and the second a shorter piece. Although I will refer to the second story briefly below, our main concern is *Pombinhas*.[2] A short synopsis may be helpful. The main protagonist is Mr. Leitão, a short, heavyset and balding man whose profession is not clear, despite people calling him "sub-chefe" ("sub-chief," perhaps a small administrative function). Leitão obsesses about other people's lives, lest they be Communists jeopardising society, and about sex. This obsession meets a new object of desire when he comes across an impoverished, mute, young woman – her body is emaciated, she has no shoes – who becomes the protégé of a local restaurant owner, where Leitão is an assiduous client. The owner, Mr. Mário, wants his nephew Tozé to settle down and marry the girl, but Leitão steps in and brings the girl to his house to become his housemaid. Despite the fact that his sexual obsession for the young woman grows, Leitão is totally oblivious to the fact that his wife has turned his home into a brothel (for the second time, we are led to believe). When Tozé tries to take the girl away from that life, Leitão interferes and, in an act of revenge, calls the police, denouncing Mário's restaurant as a "Communist burrow", and locks the girl, naked, in a room. She escapes, and Leitão follows, but Mário and Tozé catch him and are determined to beat him up. But he is saved at the last minute by the local priest. The priest throws corn kernels at Leitão, so pigeons fly down to eat it, and the priest uses this to create a distraction, shouting that what everyone is witnessing is a miracle. People gather around and, gullible, follow the priest's lead. Mário and Tozé have no other choice but to join the crowd, to avoid being arrested by the police, who have unsuccessfully raided the restaurant. But the police do not miss the chance of catching some prey, for the last image of the story shows them dragging the young woman away. The reason is briefly exposed by the police officers' dialogue: she has no shoes on.

Some explanation is needed here. In 1924 a Portuguese League for Social Preventive Healthcare was founded, which proved extremely influential in fighting against what were, in their minds, "anaesthetic and anti-hygienic" habits, such as walking barefoot. In 1928 a booklet was published, entitled, in my English translation, *Bare feet – A National Shame That Must be Eradicated*. This acted as a sort of rallying cry for this "fight", even though as early as August 1926 a law had been published ("Decreto-Lei [D.-L.] no. 12073") that prohibited people from walking with no shoes within any city limits (something more clearly determined by local authorities). In August 1947, another law ("D.-L. no 36448") reinforced this, but throughout the 1950s and 1960s there were still many people walking with no shoes on, including in the major cities, which led to many arrests. In other words, this was but one of the many forms that the Portuguese bourgeoisie found to fight against the poorer

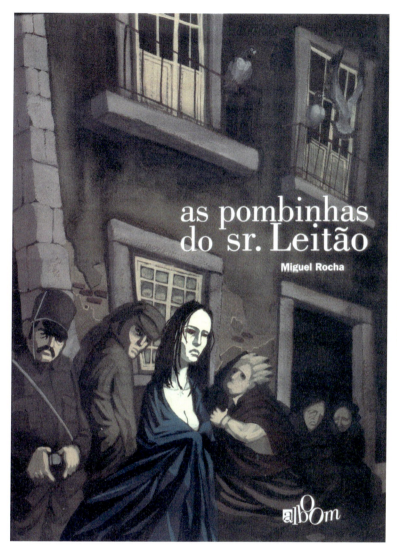

Figure 4.1: Miguel Rocha (1999), *As Pombinhas do Sr. Leitão*. Lisboa: Dalcia Azul; cover. Reproduced with the kind permission of the author.

classes, which had to be "put in their place" (preferably, away from the cities), and one of the reasons why there was popular (read, middle-to-upper-class) support of the new military, and later, the Salazar government.

The author decides not to identify in any decisive way where these actions take place. There is no verbal information (despite a non-identifiable "Santa Eulália police station") and the images are too generic. The reader can make an educated guess and imagine the diegesis taking place in one of the many popular *bairros* of the city of Lisbon, say Alfama, but it could also be set in any other smaller town across the country. The way people dress points to the period between the 1930s and the 1960s, and some of the advertisement pages clipped by Leitão help us to situate it around

Chapter Four

the 1950s. This nondescript mapping is, I believe, meaningful, in the sense that it can stand for the larger, symbolic "interval" that interrupted democracy between 1926 and 1974. If we consider the distinction between "acting-out" and "working-through" explained by Dominick LaCapra, and discussed in chapter one, we would say that *Pombinha* can be read not precisely as a specific recounting of a hypothetical historical event, but as an acting out of the cultural trauma of the oppressive nature of the decades under the Estado Novo regime. We will return to this below, specifically to the temporal consequences of this, in which "tenses implode" (LaCapra 2011: 21).

Leitão represents a whole class of people. Not those who held real, actual power, from the highest echelons of society or even in the Government, but those many middle men that exercised at all times, and to the largest extent as possible, whatever power they had. Leitão is an "informant", part of the unofficial yet (incredibly) large network of people who acted as spies for the regime's political police, the PIDE. They were not officially employed by the police, but as "concerned citizens" they were always on the prowl for dangers to the community (purportedly following Christian family values, respecting the State, and so on). At one moment well into the narrative, Leitão rings the police station and speaks to a sergeant introducing himself as "vigilant chief".

Portuguese historian Irene Flunser Pimentel, whose work has focused on the history of PIDE, has looked into how many people sought actively to become informants of this police force (2011). Not all were accepted, but the ones that were became extremely important in the mechanisms of the police - a sort of diluted Big Brother -a situation that created, among almost the entirety of the population, a permanent fear of being overheard or (wrongly) accused. This was an ongoing, pervasive emotion that informed the lives of the people who lived during Salazar's regime. Although Miguel Rocha is not analysing these issues directly, it is important to bear in mind that the book addresses the illusions of people who chose to act this way, people who created a fiction they would tell themselves that they were primarily concerned about certain values they wanted to uphold. But the truth is that they used that "little power" for their own selfish interests: in Leitão's case, his lust for the young woman. José Medeiros Ferreira (a historian and the ex-Minister of Foreign Affairs in the first Constitutional government, between 1976 and 1978), at the launch of Pimentel's book, spoke of an "everyday petty violence" that was felt back then, especially social class relations, which is precisely what is at stake in *Pombinhas*.[3]

In the opening scenes (Fig. 4.2), when Leitão is crossing a plaza, we see several characters in the image, each with their own descriptive caption. The author plays with ellipsis, but we can read those captions as pertaining to a sort of external, objective narrator. The caption near the woman who is searching for something in the garbage reads "hunger"; the two men by the tree have captions with "hiding" and "sacked from job"; and the one near the woman with the child reads "cold".

Figure 4.2: Miguel Rocha (1999), *As Pombinhas do Sr. Leitão*. Lisboa: Baleia Azul; n.p. Reproduced with the kind permission of the author.

Leitão utters a single word: "marginals", as if reducing all the social problems of these people to a social-ideological choice. If these people were poverty-stricken, it was not due to social conditions in general, but to their own "sinful" apathy and "lack of respect for authority". It was the role and mission of the bourgeoisie to "educate", if not "save", these unwashed masses.

But there is another important, retrospective, dimension to Pimentel's study. And that is the relatively smooth way in which the PIDE agents and their informants network were reabsorbed into the new democratic life of the country after the 1974 Revolution. Although in June 1974 a "Coordinating Service for the extinction of PIDE/DGS and LP" was created, these processes took too long, became consequently diluted in other institutions throughout the 1980s and ended with a whimper. Many of the PIDE agents themselves continued to hold administrative jobs related to the state, and many of the informants were never officially brought to court, although in the view of the democratic regime installed by the April the 25th coup and according to the subsequent Constitutional revision of 1982, the acts perpetrated by PIDE during the regime were considered criminal (and, under the 1976 Constitution, Estado Novo's crimes do not have a statute of limitations). Pimentel, in fact, reveals how surprised she was that the names of the informants are still kept secret today, more than forty years after the facts, in the official docu-

Chapter Four

ments housed in the archives of Torre do Tombo. One recurrent myth, a sort of white-washing of history, which emerges with the comparison of PIDE with other political police forces, holds that PIDE did not kill as many people or was not as violent as those from Spain, Germany or the USSR. Although numerically that may be true, the fact is that there *were* mortal victims - the candidate for President in the 1958 elections, Humberto Delgado, assassinated in 1965, is merely the best known case.

In fact, Pimentel, with Luís Farinha, wrote another book entitled, in translation, *Salazar's Victims. The Estado Novo and Political Violence* (2007), in which they explore the violence that actually came to pass. Maria da Conceição Ribeiro's *A Polícia Política no Estado Novo* [The Political Police of the Estado Novo] (1996, also in translation) is also an important tool for the comparison of the police forces that existed over several regimes in Portugal, and their respective legal structure and functioning. This force worked in parallel with the legal framework of the State. It had its own mode of operation, and although much is still understudied (Cerezales 2007), there are some known mechanisms. Not only did it censor newspapers and radio, as it also tapped telephone lines, violated the secrecy of personal correspondence, engaged in practices of denunciation and violent repression of strikes and demonstrations by workers and students, was instrumental in systematic election frauds, not to mention the imprisonment of people without any legal representation, and carried out actual torture, condemned people to exile, created prison camps, and so on. All this undermines significantly the idea still upheld today in certain sectors of society that "it was not all that violent". It is to counter this persistent myth, which for many people re-activates traumatising memories - in fact, Miguel Rocha's paternal grandfather was a political prisoner, tortured by PIDE (personal communication with the author) - that *Pombinhas* and *Salazar* act. This violence, perpetrated not only in Portugal's "continental" territory, but also in the colonies (from Angola to Macao), may have been "episodic" but that does not make it unreal or unimportant. The post-1974 democratic ambience favoured the severing of links with the old regime, especially in regard to these practices of repression, but this was a work of erasure, made to the detriment of a more effective work of *political mourning*. Perhaps it is the incompleteness of justice towards the acts of PIDE that allowed for the emergence of the notion of a milder police force when hyperbolically compared with other political polices from, say, Nazi Germany or Soviet Russia. Retrospectively, then, *Pombinhas* "acts out" that oppressive time and feeling. There is no "happy ending". On the contrary, not only is justice *not* done, but the innocent suffer even more.

This may remind us of Saul Friedlander's discussion about the need for historiography never to allow a sense of closure, but rather to leave some room for a *puncturing*, in his wording, to occur in an otherwise smooth, objective and rational narrative. Even though Friedlander is speaking specifically of the Nazi regime and the Holocaust, I believe that this holds some explanatory power over Rocha's books as well. Friedlander writes that:

whereas the historical narrative may have to stress the ordinary aspects of everyday life during most of the twelve years of the Nazi epoch, the 'voice-over' of the victims' memories may puncture such normality, at least at the level of commentary (1992: 53).

By focusing on the life of two individuals, the PIDE agent and the mute woman, Rocha performs a process of revisiting history that brings to the fore the voice of those individuals. Somewhat like Hillary Chute's corpus in *Disaster Drawn*, so too are Rocha's books "invested in a *narrative* elaboration of witnessing that unfolds conflicts and interpretations, and probes their particular human effects through soliciting testimony and communicating its dialogical contours" (2016: 30).

"*Working through*", writes Friendlander, "*means confronting the individual voice* in a field dominated by political decisions and administrative decrees which neutralize the concreteness of despair and death" (original emphasis; idem). And of course, when I write "the voice", I am being somewhat metaphorical. After all, the agent of PIDE's "voice" is present through his speech, but also his writing (the letters Leitão writes) and his clippings (of women bodies, discussed below), while the woman is mute (and no backstory is provided, reducing her almost to a symbolic level, although there is one enigmatic picture produced by Leitão himself on the first pages that may or may not be of the young woman), so we have to make inferences from the layered nature of the comic to interpret their character and their desires.

Even if the young woman and the young child in the "Alto da colina" short story included in the album are mute, and even if their actions ultimately fail, the *muteness* speaks of a political strength of comics themselves as an art form. Their muteness, but also their subversive roles, are made visible and that acts upon the narrative interpretative framework. The purpose is not to create a fantasy of empowerment but to create anew the space and time of the historical trauma that afflicted society. Under the influence of Maurice Blanchot, quoted previously, I would that say Rocha creates with *Pombinhas* the *site of disaster*: "Write in order not simply to destroy, in order not simply to conserve, in order not to transmit; write in the thrall of the impossible real, that share of disaster wherein every reality, safe and sound, sinks" (1986: 38).

Let me retrace a step, and ask again: in the light of trauma studies, is *Pombinhas* "working-through" or "acting-out" history? Dominick LaCapra institutes these two modes of making meaning from trauma by reworking Freud's own distinction between the labour of mourning and the state of melancholia, and displacing that distinction from psychoanalysis to history. I believe this may help us understand the role of Rocha's work within the panorama of Portuguese history. LaCapra is following Freud's notion of trauma, i.e., a breach of the protective shield (*Reizschutz*) that deflects overt and excessive stimuli. LaCapra distinguishes *acting-out,* which

Chapter Four

means having "a mimetic relation to the past which is regenerated or relived as if it were fully present rather than represented in memory and inscriptions" from *working-through*, which "involves introjection through a relation to the past that recognizes its difference from the present" (LaCapra 1998: 45). For LaCapra, who follows the psychoanalytical inflections of Laplanche and Pontalis, working-through does not "solve" the trauma, but it does create critical distance from the past, enabling the individual to distinguish the present from the past and therefore to break free from the repetition compulsion of acting-out.

Freud's notions about these twin processes were first presented in the 1917 essay "Mourning and Melancholia", as responses to loss that were opposed to each other. But he later revised his theories (like his ongoing reappraisal of his whole discipline), and in *The Ego and the Id* (1923) he redefined the identification process, previously covered by melancholia, as an integral part of the process of mourning (cf. Clewell 2004). If in the first essay, Freud considered that "mourning came to a decisive end", in his later, revised work "he suggests that the grief work may well be an interminable labor" (Clewell 2004: 61). LaCapra, of course, is interested less in the clinical dimension of psychoanalysis than in its transplantation to the field of history and culture, but he seems to follow the first Freud (LaCapra 2001: 65-66), creating a somewhat hierarchical, judgemental relationship between acting-out and working-through, which has as its basis Freud's distinction between a "pathological" melancholia and a clearer, more determined and socially more normalised and acceptable work of mourning. To be sure, LaCapra does not present an absolute binary, and there are various "modalities" of both acting-out and working-through (2011: 67), but in the interview with *Yad Vashem* included in *Writing History, Writing Trauma*, he is very clear when he declares: "it's via the working-through that one acquires the possibility of being an ethical agent" (144). He does, though, acknowledge that they "constitute a distinction, in that one may never be totally separate from the other, and the two may always mark or be implicated in each other" (150).

> Mourning, or working-through, allows the ego to let go, to give up the object of desire, through a declaration of its death or dissolution; acting-out is always a necessary step but consequently fated to be superseded. In the case it is not, and someone is possessed by the past and acting out a repetition compulsion, he or she may be incapable of ethically responsible behavior (2011: 70).

The absence of precise diegetic temporal and spatial markers in *Pombinhas*, the dilution of a clear-cut protagonist into both a "villain" (Leitão) and a "victim" (the mute young woman), the avoidance of a (formulaic) "happy end" and the choice *not* to have an explanatory, external narrative voice that could frame the events, lead us to read this book as looking at the past not to solve/absolve it, but to compulsorily repeat its crises. But I do not read its "acting-out" as an absence of ethical responsibility. Quite the contrary, and still in the light of LaCapra's lessons, I believe that that is Rocha's way of respecting history, calling his reader's attention to it and demanding an ethical response. The historian equates "structural trauma" (defined as "an anxiety-producing *condition of possibility* related to the potential for historical traumatization"; my emphasis, 2011: 82) to acting-out and "historical trauma" to working-through. In this relationship of trauma and history, it is worth quoting the author at length here:

> Historical trauma is specific, and not everyone is subject to it or entitled to the subject-position associated with it. It is dubious to identify with the victim to the point of making oneself a surrogate victim who has the right to the victim's voice or subject-position. *The role of empathy and empathic unsettlement* in the attentive secondary witness does not entail this identity; it involves a kind of virtual experience through which one outs oneself in the other's position while recognizing the difference of that position and hence not taking the other's place. (...) It places in jeopardy fetishized and totalizing narratives that deny the trauma that called them into existence by prematurely (re)turning to the pleasure principle, harmonizing events and often recuperating the past in terms of uplifting messages or optimistic, self-serving scenarios. (To some extent the film *Schindler's List* relies on such a fetishistic narrative.) (my italics, 78)

The term coined by Dominick LaCapra, *empathic unsettlement* ("a desirable affective dimension of inquiry" in historiography, 2011: 78) "is bound up with a transferential relation to the past, and it is arguably an affective aspect of understanding which both limits objectification and exposes the self to involvement or implication in the past, its actors, and victims". (102). Jill Bennett, in *Empathic Vision*, describes it as "the aesthetic experience of simultaneously *feeling for* another and becoming aware of a distinction between one's own perceptions and the experience of the other" (2005: 8). This is important in relation to *Pombinhas*, especially, considering that in *Salazar* things will work in a different manner, given its diverse diegetic economy. Rocha is not interested in creating a retrospective fantasy where the crimes of the past are avenged,[4] or where the characters would be granted some degree of justice that was not available to the people who have experienced *de facto* the oppressive violence of the Estado Novo. By re-creating the lack of justice (which is not necessarily a lack of "narrative closure"), Rocha forces the narrative of the book to act out that violence, so that it happens once again right before our eyes.

Where works of art are concerned, in contrast with historical witnessing processes, and where fictive paths become paramount, what is sought are less actual "objects of memory" that the *registration of a process*, "an *attempt to find a*

Chapter Four

language" (my emphasis, Bennett 2005: 31). This is an affective turn of the creative act, considering how, in the fiction of *Pombinhas*, "[r]ather than inhabiting a character, however, one inhabits - or is inhabited by - an embodied sensation" (idem: 34). In fact, for LaCapra the process of *empathic unsettlement* should "affect the mode of representation in different, nonlegislated ways (...), it is related to the performative dimensions of an account" (2011: 103). This in no way diminishes the force of the ethical position of the book. I follow Bennett in the consideration that:

> visual arts[5] presents trauma as a *political* rather than a subjective phenomenon. It does not offer us a privileged view of the inner subject; rather, by giving trauma extension in space or lived *place*, it invites an awareness of different modes of inhabitation (Bennett 2005: 12).

Pombinhas pays some attention to bodily sensations. These are not only evoked by the contrasting bodies of Leitão and the woman, or Leitão's appetite for salty food, which his seemingly phlegmatic wife does not provide and the young woman later is able to offer. More important are Leitão's obsessive sexual desires. These start as an abstract, fragmented construction. The story opens up with Leitão going through his daily routine of sitting at the restaurant, having lunch and coffee and cutting up all the images he finds in newspapers and magazines that depict women's body parts. Leitão is writing a letter, supposedly to a PIDE superior. In it, he reports on the life of all his neighbours, especially where the "adoption" of the unknown mute young woman is concerned. But the core of his letter has to do with social morality. Leitão is worried that the daily press is contributing actively to the "destabilisation of family harmony" by revealing "images of female anatomy details, introduced in an insidious fashion and wholly decontextualised" (*Pombinhas*: n.p. [4]).[6] But in fact, it is Leitão himself who is decontextualising these body parts, by cutting out clippings of photographs of sports, beauty pageants, cinema posters and even illustrated advertisements for kitchen utensils, some of which are presumably taken from feminine-oriented publications. Judiciously, women in bathing suits, various kinds of sports kit, revealing night gowns and so on, are cut away into details of legs and cleavage. Rocha makes this frenzy of Leitão's gaze visible by showing a two-page spread (Fig. 4.3), across which the clippings are interspersed with the panels depicting the man's daily life: some of these images act as the background of the panels while others take their place within the usual comics range of *mise en page*. However, this procedure rather complicates the normalised comics "protocols" or "trajectories of reading" (Chavanne: 229). The clippings should be seen instead as constant projections of the desire of Leitão (who even sleeps "amongst" them), and not as a diegetic access to his own scrap book, which, every time it is revealed within a panel, appears empty.

Miguel Rocha and working through the acting out of history

According to Renaud Chavanne's herculean study on comics' specific work of page composition (a term that in his optic should be substituted for *mise en page*), any change in "the principles of composition aims to create some sort of discourse, evoking a particular modality of the workings of the intellect" (2010: 257). In other words, each "reading protocol" necessarily implies a new cognitive disposition of the reader. In the case of these two pages, the reader is invited to share the permanent fantasies of Leitão, although we have a more critical access or a conscious understanding of that desire, whereas Leitão disguises, to himself, that desire as the actual upholding of good Christian, bourgeois, family values. In the right-hand page, the run-on letter caption reads "A knee here, the suggestion of a cleavage there, an ankle that makes us conjure up a perfect foot, the free-flowing hair of a young girl: thus are created the phantasms able to disrupt family harmony". Leitão is the one who creates these phantasms, it is he who "conjures up a perfect foot" from an ankle, and it is he who relishes in these verbal descriptions as well as the manual, thinly veiled, if displaced, masturbatory compulsion of snipping away these fragments. Leitão himself, in other words, through his cut-and-paste activities, engages with an "operative process for generating meaning" (Heesen 2004: 300).

The German scholar Anke te Heesen distinguishes the results of the clipping practice in the sciences and in the arts, considering the former case as "a notation system" and the latter as "montage and collage" (idem). This may seem to create a clear-cut dichotomy between the science-related emergence of "an order" that makes "sense out of formerly unrelated cuttings", while in contrast, within the purveyance of art, artists create "juxtapositions that [are] ruled not by the order of the former content but by the visual necessities of the new collage" (idem: 326). The fragmentary nature of clipping seems to be denied by the science-imbued practice, but Heesen herself points out to unexpected results and "contaminations" (her word), as for instance in Dada collage: "Unintended and unavoidable juxtapositions generated their own meanings and fantasies, as a result of the cutting practices, rather than those intended by the collector" (326-327). Leitão may mask the intent of his clippings with a mask of high morality, but what he does constitutes his own desire and sexual projections. By snipping away at women's body parts, Leitão creates an overall image of female desirability and object-making.

The very materiality of the clipping activity is made clear within Miguel Rocha's visual and material strategies. Heesen concludes by declaring that "(c)lipping collections were depots of reality that provided the material for their work, enabling them to rework this first layer of reality (as they called it) into a second, more focused version" (325).

Leitão's clippings, as I have mentioned, do not show up within the diegesis itself, within the panels, but rather create frames around them, surround Leitão and his archives, trickle down the sides of the pages, invade the background where the

Chapter Four

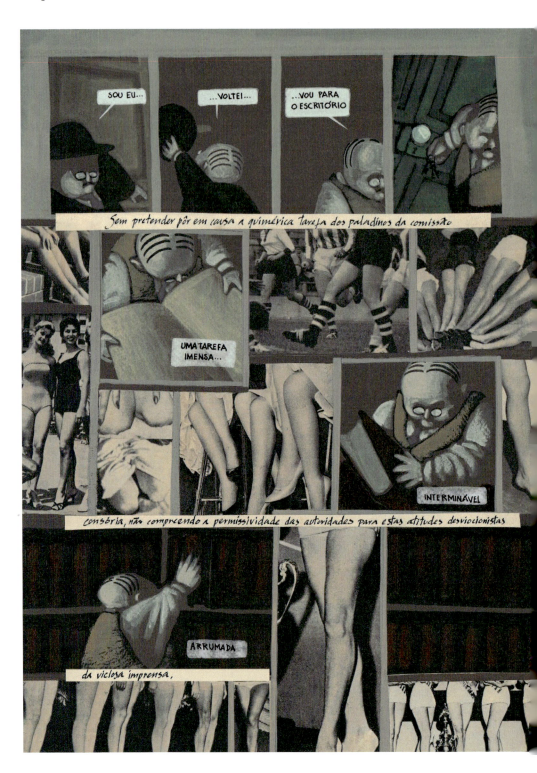

Miguel Rocha and working through the acting out of history

Figure 4.3: Miguel Rocha (1999), *As Pombinhas do Sr. Leitão*. Lisboa: Baleia Azul; n.p. Reproduced with the kind permission of the author.

Chapter Four

Figure 4.4: Miguel Rocha (1999), *As Pombinhas do Sr. Leitão*. Lisboa: Baleia Azul; n.p. Reproduced with the kind permission of the author.

panels rest, and take over considerable space from the diegetic scenes. It is not by chance that Leitão ends up by snoozing in these scenes, as if the separation between sleep and wakefulness, dream and vigil, tumultuous desire and social composure, had been snipped away as well.

These fantasies play out once again later, after the young woman has begun working in his home (Fig. 4.4). In his habitual reports, he starts by declaring his concern about the woman's hygiene, but his thoughts are disturbed by the verbal description of her taking a bath, which quickly gains a visual representation, first in the shape of an advertisement (one of the many Leitão clips), and then as an image that appears, naked or half-dressed in sensual underwear, as he traverses the city and buys several items of clothing items for her. Those projections make him paranoid. He runs and increasingly becomes out of breath.

There are also verbal puns involved in the title and beyond it, both literal and oblique, which mix these issues of body sensations, embodiment of desire and even animality. "Pombinhas" means "little doves" in Portuguese, in its feminine form, and they refer literally to the pigeons that fly onto Leitão's shoulder at the end of the story as much as to the "girls" that he fantasises about ("pombinhas" as an euphemism for young girls, with strong sexual connotations). Incidentally, Leitão, although a perfectly ordinary Portuguese family name, literally means "piglet". Finally, one common word used in Portuguese for informant, the equivalent to the English "rat," would be "bufo", which can either stand for a species of frog or of owl. At the same time, it is related to the verb "bufar", "blow" in Portuguese, standing either for a strong wind, or for the air a person can blow through the mouth but also through the anus (as in "breaking wind"). This concatenation of animal names underlines the base emotions and behaviours that inform the narrative. In fact, when Leitão discovers that his wife is employing the girl as a prostitute in his own home, he punishes his wife by forcing her to a sex act, making her to move on all fours and ordering her to "squeal like a pig".

By creating a narrative in such a confined space (Fig. 4.5) - the narrow streets of this city, the restaurant and the home - and with a small number of characters, *Pombinhas* feels more like a small stage play (an activity the author does engages with) than a historical epic. However, as we have seen, this concentration on individual characters de-neutralises the administrative, abstract discourse discussed by Friedlander. We cannot, in any way, discuss here all the comics works that, one way or the other, have addressed Portugal's history, but in recent times there have been a few titles that have focused on this same "interval" of time, such as Miguel Peres and Jihon/João Amaral's *Cinzas da Revolta* [Ashes of Rebellion], Asa 2012), Nuno Duarte's and Joana Afonso's *O Baile* [The Ball], Kingpin Books 2013) and Filipe Melo's and Juan Cavia's *Vampiros* [Vampires], Tinta da China 2016). However, these works seem to address that period solely to create a background onto which they project fantasies (the first involves a sort of American-style "rescue mission" adventure set in Angola during the Colonial Wars in the mid-1960s, which is also the setting of the third book, where a whole platoon is destroyed by dark, mysterious forces, quite possibly paranormal, while the *O Baile* is set just before the visit of Pope Paul VI to the Fátima sanctuary in 1967, and has a PIDE agent visiting a small fishing village to check on and repel a zombie attack). Apart from these fantasies and a number of "educational" books that re-enact the official, bland discourses about this era,

Figure 4.5: Miguel Rocha (1999), *As Pombinhas do Sr. Leitão. Lisboa*: Baleia Azul; n.p. Reproduced with the kind permission of the author.

Chapter Four

there is not much being produced by Portuguese artists[7] about this historical experience, and therefore *Pombinhas* stands out.

The book however, created in the 1990s, cannot be read solely as a *representation* of a "historical past", more or less authentic, more or less fictitious. It must be read in a Benjaminian sense, according to the German philosopher's view of the redemptive mission of history. Rocha is not *looking at the past*, but *reconfiguring* it, he is looking at the past through the present, as in Benjamin's famous metaphor from *Passagenwerk* and elsewhere.[8] In other words, *Pombinhas* is not so much a look at the past as an evaluation of its importance to contemporary readers. In "Thesis on the Philosophy of History", Benjamin declares:

> To articulate the past historically does not mean to recognize it 'the way it really was' (Ranke). It means to seize hold of a memory as it flashes up at a moment of danger. Historical materialism wishes to retain that image of the past which unexpectedly appears to man singled out by history at a moment of danger" (2007: 253).

Shoshana Felman construes from these words the idea that:

> Benjamin advances, thus, a theory of history as trauma - and a correlative theory of the historical conversion of trauma into insight. History consists of chains of traumatic interruptions rather than of sequences of rational causalities. But the traumatised - the subject of history - are deprived of a language in which to speak of their victimization. The relation between history and trauma is speechless" (1999: 213).

If the young woman is mute, she is able, however, to show some agency through the affordances of the comics medium itself - the way she gradually conquers her own fate and bodily movements, after being humiliated, stripped naked and reduced to an inert sexual object, even though her agency comes ultimately to naught, with her arrest at the close of the narrative. But perhaps it is precisely that ultimate defeat, her own "moment of danger", that illuminates the crimes and injustices perpetrated by the whole of the society and the period depicted obliquely in *Pombinhas*. Even though the conclusions of the stories seem not to provide us with a satisfactory and vindicatory happy ending, leaving instead what E. Ann Kaplan calls an "open wound" (2005), and their suffering characters are mute, we have nonetheless *witnessed* the events, so that we can judge the past. Once again, Walter Benjamin's redemptive role of history is present here, as when he writes that "we have been expected upon this earth" to redeem the voices of those that have not been heard until now.

In this book, but also in *Salazar*, Rocha uses images from external sources, such as photographs, postcards, clips from newspapers and magazines, as we have seen (diegetically, they are manipulated by Leitão). In spite of the actantial role that they play individually in each book, and in each scene into which they are integrated, we can read them in a overarching way by considering them to be props for memory. In fact, many comics artists who deal with autobiography, post-memory or historical trauma integrate into their practice actual or transformed props such as photographs, letters, maps, illustrations, other comics, and clippings. *Maus*'s use of photographs is famous, and has been particularly studied by Marianne Hirsch, and the objects integrated into Alison Bechdel's *Fun Home* (and the subsequent *Are You my Mother?*) have been the subject of papers by Ann Cvetkovich (2008), Robyn Warhol (2011) and Polly Mulda (2012). There is a permanent negotiation, especially in *Salazar*, between appropriated and transformed images, or in other words, collaged or reproduced work and drawn material. In the case of the former, Cvetkovich, drawing from Hirsch, speaks of such images as signs of an "unassimilable memory" (2008: 117). Gabriele Schwab, also extending Hirsch's work on the concept of postmemory and post-generational trauma, describes how later generations inherit "violent histories not only through the actual memories or stories of parents (postmemory) but also through the traces of affect, particularly affect that remains unintegrated and inassimilable" (Schwab 2010: 14). These affects make up precisely what Cvetkovich calls an "archive of feelings [that] carr[ies] the affective weight of the past" (2008: 120). Many of these objects, especially when not "translated" by the drawing technique or hand of the artist, as in the case of Bechdel, and reveal their original unalloyed materiality, open up this space of an *unassimilable, unintegrated* memory, perhaps even the irruption of the past "the way it really was" in the present of the *récit*. In *Pombinhas* they reflect the inner sexual phantasms of Leitão, expressed through the collage work.

In *Salazar*, as we shall see, they are used as part of a complicated negotiation with historical facts, official discourses and the utopian fantasies of the Estado Novo. The fact that Rocha always uses them in unbalanced, non-symmetrical and non-orthogonal constructions on the pages also points to their disruptive effect at the level of the specificities of narrative and representational structures in the comics medium.

As previously mentioned, the album *Pombinhas* has an additional story. In order to maximise profit, publishers work within standards of paper stock, paper size, page numbers, and so on. Small publishers work within larger constraints, so when confronted with "Pombinhas", the story itself, which was only 37 pages long, the editor-publisher asked the author to provide a few extra pages. Miguel Rocha produced two additional pieces. First, two illustrations that act as separators. Second, a shorter story entitled "... e no alto da colina, ao lado da igreja, a escola" [...and on the top of the hill, next to the church, the school]. This story has only six pages, and it has no connection with the main story, even though we can imagine that this would have taken place in the same village or city, and within the same historical period (maybe it is the hill seen at the end of the road in Fig. 4.5.?]. This story follows a single episode

Chapter Four

in the life of a young student who rebels against the oppressive, abusive regime of his teacher, who humiliates her students by keeping them in the classroom until one of the worst students correctly answers a complex history question. She also later forces them all to cut their hair off for "hygiene" reasons (with only the bourgeois boy being spared). The school is associated with the local church. In fact, the buildings are adjacent, so that the roles of Church and State are once again confounded: the priest acts as a supporter of the teacher's policies. The title itself points out, as is evident, the promiscuous roles of both church and school, or church and state, mimicking the power that stems from above (both from God and from the government). Although there are no direct elements that can either support or deny this idea, I believe that this short story can be illuminated by the socio-historical portrait of *Pombinhas* as well as by another story by Miguel Rocha, that I will not address, *Borda d'água* [Water's edge]. This last story focuses on the sexual initiation of a number of young teenagers, and according to some paratextual information, it could be read autobiographically. It went through several editions, including the original 1999 black-and-white version in the Bedeteca's Lx Comics book collection and another coloured version in the same year, issued every Sunday in the daily *Público*. In 2006 it was reissued (in black and white) by Polvo, with an additional story entitled "Um passeio no campo" [A stroll in the countryside]. In any case, "...e no alto da colina" could be read as a variation of the oppressive network of social relationships of *Pombinhas* from a child's perspective. The union of state and church, the humiliation of the poorer classes subject to the whims of the dominant middle classes, the subversive but ultimately powerless role of all the "violent acts" of the boy as a response to oppression echo the episodes of the wider story. The young protagonist refuses to have his and his brother's hair cut, he takes the ruler out of the teacher's hands and throws it out of the window and, after suffering physical punishment, hides the hair cutter. Even though he has learnt how to escape from the school, he ends up by staying instead of fleeing. Ultimately, this "little revolution", somewhat similar to that portrayed in Jean Vigo's *Zéro de conduite*, fails... just like the liberation of the mute young woman.

Although I will not pursue this train of thought, we could argue that by creating a comics narrative of this kind set in this former period, Rocha is also creating an alternative discourse on the comics that existed at the time, most of which were characterised by genre adventures or child-oriented educational stories that did not reflect or act upon the very real injustices that were taking place.[9]

Salazar. Agora, na hora da sua morte

This book was written with João Paulo Cotrim (Fig. 4.6). We have come across Cotrim before, when we mentioned *LX Comics* (the 1990s magazine) and the Bedeteca de Lisboa. Cotrim, as an editor, publisher, scholar, curator, and coordinator of many projects that involve many of the artists that compose the "comics scene" in Portugal, is a paramount figure in the national comics scene. To put it succinctly, Portuguese comics would be very different if it were not for Cotrim's political clout. It is impossible to assess his role in this text, but I would like to underline that he is also an outstanding author. As an active scriptwriter for comics (but also animation and illustrated books) he has created some of the most open-ended, poetic work within comics of the last twenty years. Having worked with a multitude of artists, he is able at the same time to strengthen the expressive characteristics of the image-creators but also to maintain his own poetic voice.

Allow me to list some of his recurrent traits. First of all, there

Figure 4.6: Miguel Rocha with João Paulo Cotrim (2006), *Salazar. Agora, na hora da sua morte*. Lisboa: Parceria A. M. Pereira; cover. Reproduced with the kind permission of the author.

is the elliptical nature of certain events that, despite being central to the plot, are represented obliquely, barely mentioned by a character. The attempt to multiply contradictory interventions with a large number of participating characters. The use of a "soundtrack voice" detached from the diegetic world, as if hovering a little above it in a running commentary. Unreliable narrators. Finally, more often than not, a use of language that relishes metaphors and irony (especially by imitating the flawed moral point of a character). Moving a little beyond the "literary" qualities of Cotrim's work, quite often we will find in his comics output the use of "parallel" relationships between words and images, according to Scott McCloud's typology in *Understanding Comics* (1993: 154 and ff.). All these traits of Cotrim's writing become particularly stressed in more personal projects or in collaborations with artists that allow room to explore the complex mechanisms of comics. *Salazar* was such an opportunity.

Curiously, *Pombinhas* and *Salazar* have been the subject of some of the few academic papers that mention Portuguese comics published in high-profile international books on comics studies available in more "central" languages. Lucía

Chapter Four

Miranda Morla wrote "Lisbonne en deuil, Portugal sans voix ou l'utopie de Salazar" [Lisbon in mourning, Portugal without a voice or Salazar's utopia], focusing on both books, in the context of a collection of essays on comics depicting armed conflicts, totalitarian regimes and ideological struggles throughout the world in modern times (Alary and Mitaine 2012). And as we have noticed earlier in chapter one, Mário Gomes and Jan Peuckert have written an article on *Salazar*. Although I do not agree with the broader view they have on Portuguese comics, issues I have already addressed, their close reading of João Paulo Cotrim and Rocha's book is remarkable.

It is unfeasible, and unwarranted, to include a biography of Salazar in this book, and to check, point by point, as it were, the accuracy or inaccuracy of the book. Although it is based "on historical fact", there is no desire here to create an educational text. In fact, both its fragmented, unordered temporal organisation and sophisticated and complex visual approach would be rather unappealing to younger readers in a school environment.[10] Suffice it to say that *Salazar. Agora, na hora da sua morte* (Salazar. Now, In the Hour of His Death), is less a biography than, to use Morla's apt description, an "autopsy" (270) of the regime that is confounded with his persona. In fact, this book cannot be used as a sort of easy-to-read, compact go-to biography, but on the contrary, a more intimate knowledge of the dictator's life would give better access to the poetical transformations that occur within it. And there are many sources available, considering that in the past few years there have been multiple works dedicated to his life, both private and public, both "objective" and "subjective", as well as new editions of his writings, photobiographies, and more or less fictitious depictions of his life and background in popular television series. However, it is not our goal to assess the representations of Salazar's life, which would bring us to a whole different territory and comparative field of transmedia *corpora*.[11] *Salazar* creates a texture around the life of the President of the Council of Ministers with the aim of providing us with a *reflection*, a portrait of the soul of the man.

In the book by G. Schwab referred above, *Haunting Legacies*, the author quotes Eric L. Santner and his notion of "narrative fetishism". This means:

> the construction and deployment of a narrative consciously or unconsciously designed to expunge the traces of the trauma or loss that called that narrative into being in the first place. The use of narrative may be contrasted with that rather different mode of symbolic behavior that Freud called *Trauerarbeit* or the "work of mourning." Both narrative fetishism and mourning are responses to loss, to a past that refuses to go away due to its traumatic impact (apud Schwab 2001: 10).

The goal of Cotrim and Rocha is to *slaughter the dragon*, as it were, once and for all, and perhaps even to "expunge the traces of trauma", but not through any kind of denial, whitewashing or downplaying the crimes of history. It is rather by pulling the mask off Salazar, by showing how despicable and petty he was both in his personal affairs and in the way that demeanour expressed or reflected the philosophy of the Estado Novo. The authors repeatedly show how his obsession for order focused both on national issues such as the economy, the relationship with the Church or the military powers that helped him achieve office, as well as mundane things, such as flowers that need watering or a small crochet table runner that needs straightening. By bringing to the fore his repeated affirmation that he desired no power for himself, but showing him controlling every little decision,[12] "failing" to find successors or solutions external to the machinery of state, they underscore his hypocrisy and exercise of disguised forms of power. In fact, Salazar is less a "charismatic leader" - using all the media propaganda powers within his reach - than a "strong dictator", "a master in the manipulation of a perverted rational-legal legitimacy" who employed a "scale of centralisation of decision in extension" (Pinto 2000: 2). Still, he carefully created an image of himself that was propagated by the State machinery (and is still used today by "saudosistas" i.e., people who point him out as a positive model of politics, people who "miss him"): a solitary, humble, celibate man, dressing in black and wearing old shoes, with little interest in personal wealth and power, abnegating personal benefits in the name of his mission to lead the country back to its past glory. "Politics is a necessary evil", he says.

And he is also an old man before his time, as it were, which is a recurring note in the book. There is one sentence in this book in which one of the characters says, "to remember is to grow older faster". João Paulo Cotrim plucked it from somewhere, perhaps Salazar coined it himself, and put it in the character's mouth. Miguel Rocha typed it and produced the drawings that go with it.

But perhaps both the characters and the authors are mistaken. Memory, as soon as it is committed to paper, or any other recording surface that turns it into *text*, is a sort of treason to the very life of memory. "We are made of memories", writes Edward Casey (quoted by Radstone and Hodgkin, 2003: 3). Death is part and parcel of human existence, so we write things down in order to spare them from being annihilated along with ourselves. However, the very act of writing it down, or drawing it, for that matter, fixates it in a formula, a crystallised form, a document or, worse still, a *monument*. And as we've known since Pierre Nora (1984), but also Alois Riegl (1982), monuments make true memory disappear and leave in its place a "lieu de mémoire", that is to say, a fabricated discourse informed by the political and circumstantial contours of the collective memory of the time.

Then again, memory is always already a "material social practice rather than mental faculty," "social to the extent that it functions as the site of transformation of such norms", according to Constantina Papoulias (Radstone-Hodgkin 2003: 116). This same author quotes J. Boyarin in the following: "Memory cannot be strictly

Chapter Four

individual, inasmuch as it is symbolic and hence intersubjective. Nor can it be literally collective, since it is not superorganic but embodied" (apud 117). *Salazar* brings many of these both individual and collective lines together, creating a complex mesh. Although the "voice" most heard throughout the book is undoubtedly that of Salazar's character (based partially on official, historical discourses and writings), it somewhat fluctuates in and out of an embodied, personalised point of departure. The title page begins after a few pages (in fact, it is the eighth page) that act like a prologue. The first spread shows what seems to be a large room cluttered with all kinds of chairs: regular wooden dining chairs, some more decorated than others, some with high backs, some of the Cheltenham variety, armchairs, settees, one beach deckchair. This set of chairs will become, in a way, a recurrent leitmotif (see Fig. 4.7 for a montage of multiple spreads). Several black captions are scattered across the spread, with sentences in the first person and others in the second person. One of these reads: "Resist, António,[13] for God's grace never failed you", and the next, immediately, "To whom does this voice belong?"

But we could also ask: to whom does this last sentence belong? Is it Salazar's own, asking who pronounced the previous sentence? Or does it belong to an external narrator? And what about the sentence in the second person? This could well be Salazar too, addressing himself. This doubtful attribution will cross the entire book, but we could also imagine it as a sort of polyphony of voices, all circling around Salazar's life. This ambivalence opens up an issue of narratorial authority, to quote Kai Mikkonen (2008: 315). Through a complex combination of narrative levels, effects of text, layout design and the image itself, one that will be presented several times in small variations, as we will see below, it contributes to what Lisa Zunshine called "levels of mind-reading complexity" or "sociocognitive complexity" (2011). By going back and forth in their use of the first and second person, the authors stay at an indiscernible level, and never move into a historical register that would be naturalised by the use of the third person. In this, *Salazar* follows a complex "attribution, re-attribution, and re-interpretation of mental states" (Zunshine 2011: 132). Even allowing for the problematisation of a neat division of homo- and heterodiegetic narrators by the comics medium, the very textual-verbal track of *Salazar* zigzags between those possibilities.

On the one hand, there are black captions with white seriffed and round typewritten fonts that belong to a sort of disembodied running commentary by Salazar about the events and people surrounding his life. More often than not, they are in the first person, but with a quality to them that disconnects them from the diegetic level. There are recurrent sentences, such as the one asking if someone will water the flowers, and sometimes questions addressed to a never-identified second person, yet another disembodied "you". Sometimes the first person is plural, and there are instances of a royal "we" - as when Salazar refers to his policies and options -as well

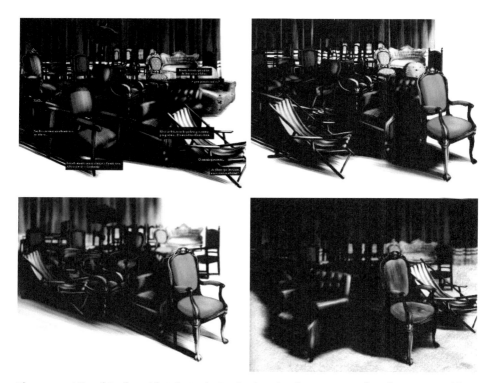

Figure 4.7: Miguel Rocha with João Paulo Cotrim (2006), *Salazar. Agora, na hora da sua morte.* Lisboa: Parceria A. M. Pereira. Montage of 4 original spreads.

as instances in which it is Portugal that is embodied by that pronoun, especially when referring to historical, past glories or to contemporary political relationships with other states. But there are also moments when those captions refer elliptically to Salazar in the third person, especially when the intent is to underline his putative humility:

> This man that was Government, did not wish to be Government. It was given to him, he did not take it... This regime which some call Dictatorship is as serene as our habits, as modest as the Nation's own life, and a friend of labour and the people (n.p.).

But on the other hand, there are also dialogues within the diegesis, presented in black italicised letters on a white background, sometimes "boxed" in contrast to the colours sparsely used in some of the scenes. And the dialogues are presented with dashes. Still, there is not much naturalisation or normality in these, as the language used by the characters seeks less to give an impression of reality than to be a stage for the maxims and philosophising of Salazar and his entourage.

Chapter Four

Considering that what opens the book is the accident that marked Salazar's decline and what closes it is his death, we could read the entirety of the narrative as a sort of hallucination played out within Salazar's failing, dying mind. It is as if the trauma of death splits the narrator into a *narrating superego* - the black captions - and a *narrated ego* - everything else that happens at the diegetic level - following Susannah Radstone's controversial take on trauma theory, and the way it developed through Freud's theories on subject-formation. We will return to Radstone's article in the last chapter, especially where her focus on the diffusiveness of authority in contemporary post-industrial, capitalist Western society is concerned, and it is quite telling that in *Salazar* what we have is actually an incredibly centralised, if not personalised and embodied, authority. But it is this paradoxical disembodiment or progressive dissemination of Salazar's own voice that is the most profound political gesture of Cotrim and Rocha's book, perhaps. Most of the book is focalised via the figure of Salazar, and we could say that the story is told by him from an indiscernible point in his life, perhaps even a transhistorical limbo that he inhabits after his death.[14]

As previously mentioned, the immediate next six pages - presented before the title page - show the accident he suffered in Estoril, in August 1968. According to the most common accounts (even though other versions circulate today), Salazar fell from a deckchair and hit his head against the stone slabs, suffering either an intracranial hematoma or a cerebral thrombosis. He went through surgery shortly afterwards but never recovered. In September of the same year, he was discreetly replaced by Marcelo Caetano but for some years he continued to receive the visits of ministers and other members of the Government, as well as signed dispatches and to be sent reports, as if he was still reigning over the destiny of the country. The prologue, then, functions as the site of a promised death, so that the whole pseudo-biographical reminiscence that follows can be seen as the proverbial "life before one's eyes"[15].

Although there was a botched attempt on his life in 1937, purportedly by anarchists (also shown in the book), his rule was thus brought to an end by a somewhat anticlimactic, ridiculous, domestic accident. One of the first short stories by the Portuguese José Saramago, Nobel laureate for Literature in 1998, is "The Chair" (found in *Objecto Quase*, lit. "Almost Object", from 1978, but translated into English as *The Lives of Things*), in which the hero is an anobium, a wood-eating beetle. Anonymous and almost invisible, it eats away the wood of the chair of a dictator until this "throne" collapses. A humorous take on the end of Salazar, it can nonetheless also be read metaphorically in relation to the whole country, understanding it as "rotten" on the inside and ready to be eaten up by bugs... And although "salazarento" is an irregular and not totally official anthroponym, many people use it informally to depict something that is old, mouldy and politically reactionary or suspicious. It is precisely this strange, almost biological malady that is at the centre of Rocha and Cotrim's "autopsy".

Moreover, the fact that the book is created via snippets of Salazar's life and elliptical representation emphasises the fact that the beginning of the end - the accident - is treated as a mere "anecdote" with "grotesque effect", as Gomes and Peuckert put it (2010: 118). According to these authors, whose main thesis is that "temporality is renounced" in *Salazar* (119), it is death that informs the whole structure of the narrative. In fact, there is no page numbering, which may also give the book a certain degree of narrative fluidity. Despite some degree of linearity - the "episodes" of Salazar's life are presented chronologically - the accident-event itself, represented twice as bookends, and ominously re-presented also across the book in the shape of the many chairs that "interrupt" the narrative flow (double-page spreads that I will discuss shortly), becomes a sort of motif, reinforcing the *tressage* work of the book. Gomes and Peuckert speak of a "thematic nexus with the central motif of death" (119). These authors discuss the use of images that bleed off the page, which they relate to Scott McCloud's description of the same visual strategy, in an exploration of the suspension of time. I am not arguing that there is not a suspension of temporality in *Salazar*. I agree that there is, and Gomes and Peuckert's analysis of the text is sound and well argued. But this suspension must be considered in coordination with other elements of the text, not only in general terms. In this I am following Brian Richardson's caveat about the "need to look less for dubious schematizations that apply to all texts than for specific structures that individually create alternative realms within the text" (1987: 308).

According to Neil Cohn, "[i]mages are just significations made meaningful through cognitively based concepts, while 'time' is a mental extraction from the causation/change between them" (2010: 134). This suggests that the reader's comprehension of a sequence of images splits into two separate systems, one concerning navigation through the layout and another the comprehension of the images themselves (idem: 137). So, for Cohn, there is not an almost automatic equation of panels and moments in time. Instead, there is a convergence between navigation and the interpretation of all other concepts that helps to create the perception of time. In many aspects, *Salazar* works less as a dynamic sequence of action-dominated panels/moments than as a procession of representations, objects and symbolic constructions. More than "an autopsy", this book acts also like a funeral procession of sorts, and every single factor works towards this impression.

The whole book is treated with bleakness in its colour schemes, mentioned before as the "ghoulish, sickly greenish grey". In a way, this is part of Cotrim and Rocha's strategy in denying Salazar, *post mortem*, any sort of justification for his actions and political decisions, or even fantasies, although it could be argued that some of the images, such as the Portugal-as-farmland images that appear recurrently, stem from his own mind. Perhaps the authors are even denying him human traits. A significant moment arrives with the scenes of Salazar's childhood. The "little boy António" is

Chapter Four

Figure 4.8: Miguel Rocha with João Paulo Cotrim (2006), *Salazar. Agora, na hora da sua morte. Lisboa*: Parceria A. M. Pereira; n.p. Reproduced with the kind permission of the author.

visually represented, in fact, as a child with the old man's face, Salazar's (later) iconic profile.[16] Later on, there is the silent laugh of Christine Garnier.

Garnier, a French journalist who enjoyed some intimacy with Salazar, which led her to publish her 1952 book, Vacances avec Salazar, was said to have had an affair with him. For our reading, it is quite unimportant if this is fact or gossip. But the authors show her in a restaurant being asked about this possibility, and her reaction is to laugh, quite amused and unabashedly (although there is no speech balloon or onomatopoeia to convey its sound). In a sort of diegetic foreshortening, and in a quite symbolical way, we see Salazar sitting at another table, with a less charming-looking, yet also young, blonde woman. The authors, by refusing a sexual connection with Garnier, are denying, perhaps not that subtly, the possibility of seeing Salazar as sexualised, of even as human.

One of Fernando Pessoa's most famous verses (from *Mensagem*) is the one that typifies human beings as a "postponed corpses". But Miguel Rocha represents his characters in *Salazar*, especially the protagonist, with a wax-like blankness to their skins, undynamic poses, sunken shoulders and vacant stares (irises are never drawn, only a dark smudge where the eyes are supposed to be) and so creates the illusion that we are looking at "corpses *in* life", mere gloomy puppets between inertia and dissolution.

As we have seen, *Salazar* was created exclusively via digital tools. Lucía Morla argues in her paper that the use of digital tools necessarily implies a "distance from the subject" ("mettre à distance le sujet"; 2012: 271). I disagree with the overarching idea that digital tools create such a distance, for this sort of generalisation and essentialisation of the creative tools does not help us to read the work. There is nothing essential about digital tools, as related to comics making, that allows us to say this. If there is a creative distance, or strangeness in *Salazar,* it is due more to the figuration and composition choices of the artist, as well as the fragmented nature of the narrative, its unreliable narrator, the transit between voices and characters, and the constant "interruption" via collages and the double-page spreads, "symbolic" images.

If some of the earliest experiments with digital tools in comics making did create a rather mechanised look that was explored precisely to survey the purported aloofness of post-industrial societies (say, Mike Saenz' 1988 *Iron Man: Crash* or Pepe Moreno's 1990 *Batman: Digital Justice*), subsequent work that includes or is entirely created with digital tools has created a rather complex layering of memory and affect (say, Dave McKean's art for the 1995 *Mr. Punch*, with Neil Gaiman) or has manifested no difference from the artist's usual output with ink on paper (as is the case of Bastien Vivès et al.'s recent work for the *Last Man* saga, 2013-2019). The same can be said about Rocha's art. After *Salazar* he has created at least two comics projects with digital tools: *A noiva que o rio disputa ao mar* [The bride that the river wrangles from the sea], also written by Cotrim, Câmara Municipal de Portimão: 2010) and *Hans, o cavalo inteligente*, already mentioned. By comparing and contrasting these works, we can see that Rocha uses these tools in very different ways, not only to reach different, if not radically contrastive, aesthetic results but also to explore varying degrees of emotionality, proximity with the characters and an overall colour-coded affective ambience.

One of the strategies afforded by digital means - but not exclusively, as collage or distinct drawing styles within the same work have been staples of comics-making since their inception (Smolderen 2009) - is the possibility of using actual documents within the *récit*, without the need to "transcribe" them or "translate" them through the artist's own style. In the case of *Salazar*, which produces complex non-orthogonal compositions across double spreads, this creates a space not only for a referential effect but also for a direct dialogue with historiography, collective memory and the work itself. Morla refers to "links of an almost sensorial order" (271).

These many "explosions" of collaged documents (Fig. 4.8) - newspaper front pages or clippings, photographs, postcards, pamphlets, prayer cards, maps, title pages of books, etc. - can be read at once as a free-association exercise of the Estado Novo imaginary and as memories that swirl inside the protagonist's mind. Rocha often uses emblematic spreads throughout the book. More often than not, "splash

Chapter Four

pages" or "double splash pages" are used within the medium of comics for spectacular or dramatic effects (hence their denomination). Will Eisner and Jack Kirby offer notable examples in North American comics. However, Rocha uses them less for spectacular effect than as time-suspending and symbolic devices. In fact, some of these images are used to interrupt the narrative.

There are least three images (two one-panel pages, the other a double-page spread) with the cartographic outline of Portugal depicted as a small farm, divided up into small parcels where several rural folk, all Salazar lookalikes, toil away to grow their modest produce (Fig. 4.9 presents a combination of several images shaping this illusion). In many respects, these are but the main fantasies of the *pax ruris* (Medina 1993) desired by the Estado Novo, the perfect idea of a backward, humble, yet proud Portugal.

The Estado Novo's attachment to a utopian notion of the land, evoked by Salazar's words about his pleasure in walking and working on his gardens and farm, is emphasised by the last two spreads showing a chair abandoned in the garden.

There is also a gloomy yet beautiful diaporama showing the works of Duarte Pacheco (twice Minister in Salazar governments, president of the Lisbon City Hall,

Figure 4.9: Miguel Rocha with João Paulo Cotrim (2006), *Salazar. Agora, na hora da sua morte*. Lisboa: Parceria A. M. Pereira; collage with several original pages. Reproduced with the kind permission of the author.

Miguel Rocha and working through the acting out of history

Figure 4.10: Miguel Rocha with João Paulo Cotrim (2006), *Salazar. Agora, na hora da sua morte*. Lisboa: Parceria A. M. Pereira; n.p. Reproduced with the kind permission of the author.

and visionary engineer throughout the 1930s and 1940s) put together in a sort of Piranesian construction (Fig. 4.10): the Tejo bridge (baptised "Ponte Salazar" and later rechristened "Ponte 25 de Abril"), the statues of the Fonte Monumental, known as "Fonte Luminosa" in Alameda, Lisbon, the viaduct that bears Pacheco's name and is situated on the highway near Monsanto-Alcântara, some of his buildings and, to the right, the Padrão dos Descobrimentos, which, although designed by Cottinelli Telmo (as we have seen in the first chapter, an architect, film-maker and comics artist), was integrated into the 1940 Exposição do Mundo Português, a project that had the signature of Pacheco and for which the Padrão can be seen as a metonym (as well as the compass rose on the ground in front of it). Placed right after the announcement of his death (in a car accident in 1943), the black sky and surroundings once again gather these objects as a sort of grim museum and cenotaph to one of the many names that emerged during the life and regime of Salazar. Acting as a contrast to the rural images, it nonetheless confirms the dichotomies defended by the dictator's speeches.

And, of course, there is the recurrent image of the room cluttered with chairs that we mentioned at the beginning of this section. It appears in a total of four double-page spreads, of which only the first includes words. All the other are "mute". This seems like an eerie game of musical chairs but with no music and no people: all that remains is the troubling idea of commutable absences.

Chapter Four

Miguel Rocha and working through the acting out of history

Figure 4.11: Miguel Rocha with João Paulo Cotrim (2006), *Salazar. Agora, na hora da sua morte*. Lisboa: Parceria A. M. Pereira; n.p. Reproduced with the kind permission of the author.

Chapter Four

But apart from these "interrupting" spreads, there is another "section" halfway through the book, twenty pages long, which brings about a more complicated passage between narrative levels.

There are many moments of visual intertextuality in *Salazar*. Not only where the use of "props" is concerned, of course, but in direct quotations from more or less well-known images or critical appropriations. By the former, we mean the moments when some of the compositions or panels remind the reader of other images related to Salazar. One of the initial scenes in the book, which shows Salazar's nurses (transformed in four panels into old widows) helping him wave to the crowds from the windows of the palace (Fig. 4.11), is a re-creation of a very famous three-panel sequence cartoon by João Abel Manta. An incredibly influential artist, Manta is a painter, illustrator and caricaturist who worked both during the dictatorship and after it, and created some of the most iconic – and also some of the most virulent – images surrounding the post-25 April era. According to one contemporary Portuguese comics artist and researcher, Francisco Sousa Lobo, in Manta "the epic and the popular meet in a kind of flat transcendence" (2014: n.p.). In 1978 Manta published *Caricaturas Portuguesas* [Portuguese Caricatures], which can be seen as a sort of Goyaesque[17] take on the 48 years of the dictatorship, sparing no aspect of how life was under the defunct regime. This association is quite significant and obvious in the following two pages.

But the most important and resonant transmutation is the one operated on the "A lição de Salazar" lithographs. This demands some expansion.

In 1938, a series of seven lithograph posters was commissioned to signal the ten years of Salazar's government. Entitled *A lição de Salazar* [Salazar's lesson], these were distributed widely throughout the country's primary schools as an indoctrination tool showing the conquests of the regime, on several fronts, contrasting them with the failures of the democratic-liberal governments that succeeded one another between 1910 (the end of monarchy and the implementation of the Republican state) and 1926 (the military coup that ended that cycle of troubled and short-lived governments). It is worth remembering that schools had one sole textbook, and that every single policy issued by the Ministry of Education was unfailingly followed across the country. One single lesson was being taught all over Portugal. And these lithographs were just one part of the project of homogeneity.

A basic analysis of the semiotic strategies employed in the posters would reveal the clear agenda of showing the superiority of Salazar's policies: the Republican era is shown in a smaller, partially hidden image, in subdued colours, and always with chaotically placed elements, while the Estado Novo is presented in larger scenes, colourful, organised and clearly read. The lesson is clear-cut: "a comparison between the present of order, progress and development, and a past characterised by disorder (especially financially) and social conflicts" (Samara-Baptista 2010: 14). The accompanying text underlines the efficacy of the policies of the state's corporatist ideology: financial organisation, an ordering of social progress, the construction of new and better roads and ports, a defence of Christian, national values, and so on.

Cotrim and Rocha use them all, cropping only the parts of the images that reflect the present situation of the Estado Novo, but they use them as an establishing shot for episodes that take place after the depicted scenes and that subvert the lesson or the utopian, limited scope that they present.

The first image to appear in *Salazar* is actually the last in the original series (Fig. 4.12). "Deus, Pátria, Família: a trilogia da educação nacional" [God, Fatherland, Family: the trilogy of national education] is the synthesis and crown of the poster set's project and goal. Here we have the perfect home: Christian, patriarchal, rural, and quite probably illiterate and poor. The rural utopia was always presented as a better moral and social model than urban life, seen as a cesspool of vice. The image shows no hint that this family owns a radio or that they even have electricity in their home. The wife is fulfilling her patriarchy-appointed domestic tasks, taking care of the dinner and the children, while the man is returning from a day of toiling in the fields. In spite of that, not surprisingly in this fantasy, he is clean, proper and sober. The table is set with an immaculate white linen sheet, as well as clean plates, cutlery and glasses. Moreover, the table shows the humblest but most important

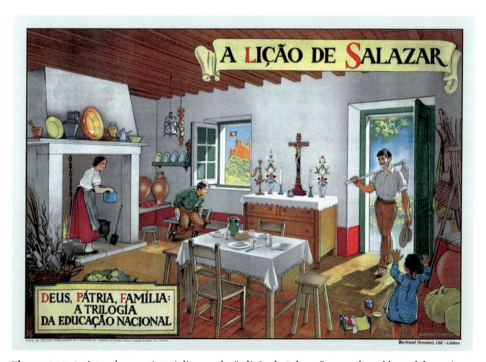

Figure 4.12: Artist unknown (1938), litographs "A lição de Salazar", seventh and last of the series.

Chapter Four

Figure 4.13: Miguel Rocha with João Paulo Cotrim (2006), *Salazar. Agora, na hora da sua morte*. Lisboa: Parceria A. M. Pereira; n.p. Reproduced with the kind permission of the author.

items of an honest, hard-working family's meal: bread and wine. That these are also the symbols of the Eucharist would not be lost to its public.[18] Through the window, we can see an old castle with the Republican flag flying in the wind. In one composite relationship, we can see both the symbol of contemporary Portugal and its glorious history. And conspicuously at the top of the table, in between the openings of the house that leads towards the state and allows the father to return, the Cross.

L. Morla makes a close reading of Cotrim and Rocha's play upon this lithograph in her paper, as they perform what she calls a "deconstruction of the Salazar ideal" (2012: 77). And in fact, this single page of *Salazar* not only acts as the heart of the matter of the book, it also creates a veritable *tour de force* of comics specificities (Fig. 4.13). The obvious contrast between the lithograph (originally very colourful) included at the top of the page and the "close-ups" below creates a focus on the harsh reality beyond the idealistic image. The "trilogy" of God, fatherland and family (see how the Portuguese flag on top of the castle's tower, seen through the window, the cross and the father's head are approximately in a line, all at the same height), which creates a united space and body in the lithograph, is shattered in the comics treatment, with the characters isolated from each other. God is absent below and the father, although he is also the point of convergence as in the original image – all other characters' sightlines are directed towards him, and he is entering the space – becomes a source of fear. No character's eyes can be seen, despite the fact that we are "closer"; their eyes are covered with shadows. The father does not seem to be carrying his hoe, which would be a symbol for a day's hard and honest work in the fields, from which he is returning in search of his just reward: a healthy meal at home with the family.

154

Neither does the father seem to have the happy demeanour of a contented labourer in the "deconstructed" version. In fact, he seems to bring back the reality and misery barely hidden by the consumption of alcohol. Morla writes:

> The patriarchal figure is no longer the representation of the respected and beloved leader, but the symbol of violence and of the aggressive and repressive authority that ill-treats his own children. The utopian print that the dictatorship proposed is quickly deconstructed by the images that contradict the routine, reassuring life extolled by Salazar's propaganda (idem: 277).

The scene that follows shows the woman begging the man to stop drinking, the man hitting her and then taking the son for a spanking.

The next few pages work along the same lines. Using the original lithographs as establishing shots, the authors then present a scene in which all the expected good behaviour of the population is undermined by reality, moved by both political desire or economic need. Instead of a group of respectful people gathering in the village centre, and acquiescing to the local powers, workers who disagree with despotic decisions are accused of Communism. The new roads are not shown as paths to social mobility, but simply as quicker ways for the PIDE agents to reach their targets. The image that shows the glorious industrial construction of naval ships and aeroplanes gives way to prostitution-ridden taverns. In contrast to the piles of riches of the state, we're guided through the shanty towns where people live in squalid conditions and children are forced to beg (Fig. 4.14).

The visual references evoked by the series of integrated lithographs not only work to provide a referential framework, as if they were "memory props", or contextualising markers but also trigger, from a cognitive narratological perspective, "prefiguration codes", creating a framework for reader inferences - in this case, "entering" a visual representation of the world as imagined by Salazar's propaganda - and consequently enabling the reader, through the detours operated by the authors, to engage with the "textual effect of subversion" (Kukkonen 2013: 42).

An important narratological consequence of these scenes is, of course, to move away from the level of Salazar's purportedly own thoughts and mental states and look beyond it, reaching the authors' own critical intervention. Although there is never any sentence from a present-day narrator that would contextualise Salazar's biography in the historical distance, the image deconstruction strategies act upon the utopian images, re-purposing them or extracting from them a subversive reading, which could not be attributed to Salazar himself, of course. He is, in this scene, elevated to a more-than-human power, personifying, as it did and still does, the Estado Novo. However, in a sense, this moment of attribution of power confirming his statute above the human level can be read both positively, as the

Chapter Four

Figure 4.14: Miguel Rocha with João Paulo Cotrim (2006), *Salazar. Agora, na hora da sua morte*. Lisboa: Parceria A. M. Pereira; n.p. Reproduced with the kind permission of the author.

confirmation of his overwhelming, state-personifying/embodying power, and negatively, once again denying his humanity.

This "educational" sequence is found, in the narrative, after some moments of pondering. First, we have Salazar sitting in front of the radio, amidst the portraits of Mussolini, Franco and Hitler, and thinking about Portugal's role throughout World War II. He is listening to a concert, and after that he hears the announcement of the end of the War. Yet another spread with the empty chairs follows, and then there is a jumbled collage composed of sheet music, handwritten letters, hymns and a Catholic missal, as well as a picture of Mussolini's body hanging at the Piazzale Loreto. In the bottom right-hand corner, Salazar stands beneath one of his *mottos*: "Study with doubt, realise with faith". If the images abstracted from the lithographs may be seen as an extension of Salazar's voice and desire, proclaiming a sort of rural utopia impervious to what happens in the rest of the world, everything else - the deconstruction itself - is at a different, autonomous level. After this, we return once again to the "mundane" life of the dictator, namely the episode with Christine Garnier (in 1951).

The sequence we have just described is therefore a powerful instance of authorial intervention in *Salazar.* After all, if Salazar, the character, is the focaliser of the narrative - we do not need to have a first-person ocular perspective (rarely used in comics, as mentioned in the previous chapter) confused with that of the narrator - these images do not correspond to Salazar's own mental states (dreams, projections, desires). The lithographs are used as an already existing visual translation of the Estado Novo's philosophy, and the visual deconstruction is the inquiry, the critical transformation operated by the authors, at a moment when they are unlinked, as it were, from Salazar. What takes place here is precisely a failure of a "sustained continuing-consciousness frame" (Mikkonen: 316), which reinforces the specificity of narratological categories of comics as opposed to their literary use.

As mentioned, Gomes and Peuckert insist on, and study in detail, the suspension of time that is the major theme of *Salazar.* Not only where the figuration of the dictator himself is concerned, but in other visual tropes, many of the represented events, sentences spoken by characters and even the way that the *mise en page* is conceived, whether through double-page spreads, the bleeding of many panels, the collage or appropriation of heterogeneous visual material and the fragmentary nature of the pages, even when they seem to be composed following more regular grids (most of them actually "semi-regular", in Renaud Chavanne's parlance). The researchers analyse the fatalistic tone of the book and conclude that comics are a privileged means of representing the stasis of Salazar's regime and the melancholic mentality of the Portuguese, although they risk essentialising comics, which they see as "constituted by dead images", given that the "dynamic suggested in comics is necessarily built on static corpses" (2010: 126). In the case of *Salazar*, and in contrast to *Pombinhas*, Rocha chooses to represent most of the visual planes from a more or

Chapter Four

less frontal, proximate perspective. Of course, his highly stylised approach does not allow us to describe it using notions that stem from more naturalistic or classical styles of comics, but it is not wholly absurd to say that there are fewer bird's-eye and worm's-eye shots in *Salazar*, as well as fewer dynamic poses of the bodies. Even explosions or acts of violence, such as Duarte Pacheco's accident, the bombs in Lisbon or Salazar's assassination attempt, are represented in an almost symbolic way, with a jumble of very fine straight lines meshed together in a white mass that seems to jump off the images.

Can we provide any general reading of *Salazar*? How does it relate to comics production in Portugal and what place does it have in relation to the texture of history? In terms of the "comics scene" in Portugal, we can say, without exaggeration, that there are not many books that can be compared to it, given the fact that most of the comics projects that involve depictions of the historical past engage with naturalising strategies, both at the level of narrative and image representation. In other words, " largely a public, often official, and narrowly political memory" (Confino 1997: 1394). Their purpose is, more often than not, pedagogical. Not that there is anything wrong with pedagogy, of course, but I am conflating this term with the simplifying and often non-confrontational, official discourses of Portuguese identity. After all, still today the "brandos costumes" [serene customs] is a myth repeatedly propagated, almost erasing the violence that characterised the Civil War (rarely named as such but instead referred to euphemismistically as "The Liberal Wars" or "The Miguelist War") of 1828-34, the conflicts under the First Republic and, of course, the Colonial Wars, fought "away from the eyes, away from the heart", to quote a Portuguese proverb.[19] Historian Oliveira Marques and comics artist Filipe Abranches also produced another book that, despite superficially catering to the pedagogical need for a "comic book" about the history of a city or an important personage, avoids the usual format of a compendium or a simplified account of the facts. *A História de Lisboa* (2 vols, Assírio & Alvim: 1998-2000) is also created from impressions and intensities, a composition of apparently dispersed fragments, which nonetheless follows a red thread: a thread, however, whose goal is not to sew the many mythological veils that cover Portuguese identity and self-knowledge back in shape but paradoxically to rend them.

Bringing back history not in the crystal form of a "lesson", but a lived reality, even if as tinted by the shapes and shadows of death as *Salazar*, in this sense, Cotrim, aided by Rocha, is a twin soul of Spanish comics writer Filipe Hernandéz Cava, whose oeuvre would lend itself to an interesting transnational comparison on how comics address history on the margins of official discourses and school programmes. Other artists could be brought to mind, from Alberto Breccia to David Vandermeulen, Kyle Baker or Jacques Tardi.

The authors are addressing an idea of *heritage* that is seldom thought of critically, but accepted as fact, an eternal and even commodified truth. Cotrim and Rocha are not looking for a commodification of Salazar's biography. By centring their attention on the man, and not on the socio-economic conditions of his claim to power, by not investigating the causes and consequences of the regime, nor even exposing the complicated relationships of other people with the dictator's figure (from the world of industry, the military, politics, etc.), the authors are underlining the subjectivity of the comic. They are at once accepting the power that Salazar holds as an icon, but re-using and re-interpreting it in a different manner. Cultural historian D. C. Harvey affirms "how concepts of heritage have always developed and changed according to the contemporary societal context of transforming power relationships and emerging nascent national (and other) identities" (2001: 327-335). At a time when representative democracy and free speech is possible in Portugal, but a more diversified, critical discussion of the historical past, especially the close one, and issues of identity is lacking, *Salazar* uses almost exclusively "objective" facts and affirmations by Salazar himself and the Estado Novo in an edifice that demonstrates its obvious limitations through a strategy of proximity to the individual and, as in the sequence of lithographs, focusing on their mundane consequences. In a way, the authors are paying attention to the following *caveat* of Alon Confino: "by sanctifying the political while underplaying the social, and by sacrificing the cultural to the political, we transform memory into a 'natural' corollary of political development and interests" (Confino 1997: 1394; for the issue of the individuality of memory, see also Crane 1997).

It should not be forgotten that Salazar himself contributed significantly to this so-called "fate-ridden" mentality, to a discourse that still holds sway today. One of his sentences quoted in the book reads "The ancient peoples are sad or cynical. We Portuguese were fated to be sad. A sentence set in stone, and with it I refuse the cynicism with which some wish to portrait me". Many thinkers have contributed to this identity, alongside the role played by popular culture,[20] and through it an idea of subjection to fate is enmeshed with the developments of history. Portuguese philosopher Eduardo Lourenço, in the essay entitled "Europa ou o Diálogo que nos Falta" [Europe, or, The Dialogue that we are Missing] (1987), speaks of Portugal's (last) four centuries as an "existência crepuscular" [twilight existence] (1987: 7). Once it has been repeated so many times, it becomes truth. We must be aware however, that historiography does not exist in a pure state distinct and separate from heritage, which would imply:

> that, firstly, there is something called 'correct' historical narrative that heritage is busily destroying and, extending from this, that until very recently, all history, historical narrative and other relationships with the past are somehow more genuine and authentic than they have now become (Harvey 2001: 325).

There is no "pure" memory, as Confino argues, that is not always already an intersection of several negotiations. Memory can be seen or described as "the ways in

Chapter Four

which people construct a sense of the past", "the memory of people who actually experienced a given event", and "the representation of the past and the making of it into a shared cultural knowledge" (1997: 1386). Singular and collective memories, experienced and historical memories, vernacular and official memories, instead of being seen as dichotomies, actually merge (idem: 1401-1402), and must be historicised. *Salazar*, however, seems to work in a different direction. By showing consistently and repeatedly dates and "memory props" that point to an effective historiography, Salazar not so much de-*historicises* as it de-*temporalises* its narrative structure, as Gomes and Peuckert have also argued.

One of the tenets of trauma theory is that the "overcoming or mastery of trauma must involve processes of 'integration' and 'assimilation'" (Elsaesser, 2001: 196). This seems to be a point on which Cathy Caruth and Ruth Leys would agree, especially when the latter maintains that in "[p]sychotherapy ... the goal of recounting the trauma story is integration, not exorcism" (Leys 1996: 123). Moreover, Leys discusses the collective and political importance of personal testimony of the past, and how in its narrative act, "the trauma becomes a testimony" (idem). In that sense, Rocha creates two more or less fictional books that are anchored in historical reality, and that a*ct out* the traumas of the recent past in the history of Portugal. But by that very act - the repetition of fears and injustices, and the exposure of the pettiness of Salazar - he transforms it into a manageable object, a textual object. Elsaesser, discussing Caruth's theory, explains how from those "processes (or 'techniques') of integration" one of the most important "would be narrative and the ability to tell a (one's) story, where the narrator is fully present to him- or herself in the act of telling" (2001: 196). In fact, Salazar is not wholly present to himself in his act of telling; quite the contrary, he is in a process of self-dissolution.

Although this is obvious, we must underline that neither of these books is a biography proper, but a work of fiction (*Pombinhas*) and a highly stylised biography (*Salazar*). Thomas Elsaesser, referring to the presence of trauma and its representation in the (contemporary) media of cinema and television, explains how "[t]his double role [that is, of "the power of immediacy inherent in the moving image" and "cinema's capacity to 'fake' such authenticity through the stylistic-narrational techniques of editing sounds and images"] has 'traumatized' both documentary and feature filmmaking" (2001: 197). Although with very different tools, such as narrative ellipses, visual metaphors, "exploded" *mise en page*, fluctuating narrative voices, and the subversion of the "memory props", the comics work of *Salazar* and *Pombinhas* also achieves a specific "traumatisation" of comics. They do not constitute a "talking cure" for a subject, but a space of negotiation where a collective trauma can be "acted out" as a necessary step for its "working through." Allow me to quote Elsaesser once again at some length:

> "If ['obsessive repetition [is] in fact the media's (and popular culture's) most 'authentic temporality and time-regime'], then repetition becomes part of creating in the spectator not just 'prosthetic memory' but prosthetic trauma, deliberately or inadvertently setting up a gap between the (visual, somatic) impact of an event or image and the (media's) ability to make sense of it, in order to make it enter into the order of the comprehensible and translating it into discourse." (2001: 197)

To a certain extent, it may seem that the mediation afforded by television, cinema and, by extension, comics, can lead to a dangerous situation, a situation that would bypass LaCapra's "empathic unsettlement" and lead one to naturalising, simplifying and overarching fantasies of rewritten history. However, on an individual, psychoanalytical basis, this always already takes place:

> Yet *Nachträglichkeit* is itself an aspect of a wider epistemological issue, the subject's need to invoke - or invent - an origin or absent cause in order to explain how one knows what one knows, in relation to an event or a course of action, but also in relation to the subject's self-awareness of his or her identity. It is in this sense that Lacan speaks of the *après-coup* as the act of the subject filling a void or a gap in his/her identity, by providing a causal-chronological sequence or a chain of signifiers, to assure him/herself of a spatio-temporal consistency and a place in the symbolic order. (...) But to the degree that the culture is generating and circulating new forms of media memory, the subject "invents" or invokes temporal and spatial markers (for example, the shifters "now" and "me") for her/his own memory, body-based and somatic, which is to say, she/he fantasizes history in the form of trauma (Elsaesser 2001: 198)

Elsaesser argues that trauma allows for a referentiality that is at once able to "place history discursively" but no longer with a specific spatio-temporal location: it "suspends the categories of true and false, being in some sense performative" (idem: 199), a referentiality that must go beyond the aporias of "objective history" but also beyond the relativism of deconstruction. *Interpretation* is the key word, but also key are the ethical implications of that interpretation, considering how history, following LaCapra, contributes to "a cognitively and ethically responsible public sphere" (2011: 91).

In a not wholly different context, Ernst Van Alphen discusses how some visual art works by second-generation of Holocaust survivors create "playacting" that opens the way to "felt knowledge". He points out how these works emphasise:

> the most powerful and socially constructive function that art as thought can fulfill in a world that cannot thrive without the "thick" thought offered by imaginative, imaging experiments. From the critical function of exposing, through

Chapter Four

the intervention and reorientation of rewriting, this function of working through history clutches the case for art as thought. But thought itself, thanks to art's experimenting with its limits, is now no longer "just" intellectual. It is now, in the strongest possible sense of the word, aesthetic - binding the senses through an indelible bond forged between the subject and the world it tries so hard to inhabit (2005: xx-xxi).

Rocha's narratives do not open up familiar paths. They do not allow for familiarity with the traumas that they address. Instead of contributing towards "self-conscious, deliberate attempts to preserve memory in historical ways", as Susan Crane defines Pierre Nora's *lieux de mémoire* (1997: 1379), Rocha tries to and manages to re-ignite the functioning of memory, even if a fleeting, dying one. *Pombinhas* and *Salazar* do not solve or absolve history, they make sure it is not forgotten. But by *acting out* the traumas that took place, and by *not* offering a formulaic framework that would allow for an ethically irresponsible identification with the victims (or with the major perpetrator in the figure of Salazar), he provides a remarkable stepping stone to a process of *working them through*.

Notes

1   None of which had been published in Portuguese at the time Rocha's book came out, which shows, once again, how Portuguese artists have to be active in their search and learning of contemporary currents beyond what is offered by the "local market". At the time of this writing, only *Mr. Punch* came out in Portuguese through VitaminaBD in 2007.

2   For the sake of simplicity I will always refer to the story itself in italics.

3   "Violência mesquinha quotidiana." See URL: http://noticias.sapo.pt/lusa/artigo/ll7oBGpXtN2Rqo%2B6jqD9gg.html [last access May, 21st 2014].

4   Playing into what Peter C. Luebke and Rachel DiNitto call "revanchist fantasy" (2013). This in an article on Suehiro Maruo's short story "Planet of the Jap", originally published in 1985, and translated into English in 1996. In this story, the Japanese use an atomic bomb in Los Angeles, so an annexation of the US ensues. Mark Waid's and J. G. Jones's short series *Strange Fruit*, which can be summed as "Black Superman fights segregation in the U.S. South", plays awkwardly into this category as well. In cinema, two famous examples are Quentin Tarantino's *Inglourious Basterds* (2009) and *Django Unchained* (2012).

5   Bennett never quotes comics as part of this broader area, but I think we can include comics in this category, if not socially at least aesthetically.

6   Although pages are not numbered, I will provide page numbers in brackets, considering solely the actual *planches*.

7   Perhaps we should mention that, unsurprisingly, a few years ago a comic book

was published by an Italian author, Giorgio Fratini, who lived for a while in Lisbon, entitled *As paredes têm ouvidos. Sonno Elefante* [The Walls Have Ears. I'm an elephant], with the second part of the title in Italian; Campo das Letras: Lisboa 2008). This book is basically about the famous building where the direction of PIDE/DGS was located, and a group of people around it, from employees to tortured prisoners. More recently, Nicolas Barral put out a book that takes place in 1960s Lisbon, with a Pide-centred plot, *Sur un air de Fado* (Dargaud 2021).

8 In a letter to Werner Kraft (dated December 27, 1935), referring to his *Work of Art* essay, Benjamin writes: "I am busy pointing my telescope through the bloody mist at a mirage of the nineteenth century that I am attempting to reproduce based on the characteristics it will manifest in a future state of the world, liberated from magic" (1994: 516. And section N of *Das Passagen-Werk* includes the small note: "telescoping of the past through the present" (2002: 471; [N7a,3]).

9 For a specific history of Portuguese children's comics of the time, see Ferro 1987; especially pps. 150 and ff.

10 Personally, I think that it would be rather interesting to use such a book, but considering the rather conservative stance of programmes both in relation to comics as well as non-established narrative formulas, I believe that its integration would not be easy. However, it is not impossible that individual teachers may have used it, as they are free to do so within the flexibility of the programmes.

11 One that would include a study of why Salazar was elected "The greatest Portuguese in History" in a popular television contest in 2007.

12 The text presenting the "Arquivo Salazar", or originally "The Archives of His Excellency the President of the Coincil [of Ministers]," in the Torre do Tombo National Archives, for instance, explains how these collections of documents - correspondence with Ministers, the Public Administration, the President of the Republic, but also details of his personal expenses and finances, etc. - are a "decisive instrument for the exercise of António de Oliveira Salazar's political power", showing how such power is "constituted, structured, concentrated and is uninterruptedly prolonged for more than forty years. Through the Archive, Salazar controls everything that directly or indirectly interferes in the political functions he commands". URL: http://digitarq.dgarq.gov.pt/details?id=3886687 (last access: May the 27th 2014).

13 Salazar's full name was António de Oliveira Salazar.

14 Although this would warrant a little more elaboration, I believe there are some points in common with Herman Broch's *The Death of Virgil* in this negotiation between the protagonist's conscience in life and in death.

15 Yet another literary reference that could be of interest, resulting in a comparative study, would be Gabriel García Marquez's *Chronicle of a Death Foretold*, given the centrality of the protagonist's death in informing every single other event de-

picted in the novel, the complicated narrator's voice in relation to the diegesis, the seeming lack of frontiers between dream and vigil, present and past, life and death.

16 One of the best-known icons of the Estado Novo's years is the Guimarães statue of King Afonso Henriques, or Afonso I, the first king of Portugal, created by Augusto Tomás, in which the head is superimposed with that of Salazar. Although this was a non-official postcard that circulated briefly in the 1930s, created by Monarchist sympathisers of Salazar, and immediately forbidden by the regime, the authors present it as being conceived by António Ferro, Minister of Propaganda, and accepted officially. This image was "recuperated" after April 1974, and retrospectively became one of the regime's best-known images. This sort of projection into historical, crusader figures also occurred with Franco and Hitler. One other known bizarre permutation is the identification of a very similar face to the dictator's in the *Panels of Saint Vincent*, a polyptich from the late 1400s attributed to painter Nuno Gonçalves. The authors will play intertextually with this known "icon" in their many avatars and possibilities of permutation, which is typical in politically radical discourses (for instance, there were a number of images mixing Salazar's face with that of the Pedro Passos Coelho, the Prime Minister between 2011-2015).

17 Something that has been repeated time and again, this was probably first pointed out by writer Mário Dionísio right at the outset, in his review of the book in "Um outro Goya e algo mais" [Another Goya and beyond], *O Jornal*, December 29, 1978). In it, he calls Manta a "post-Picasso Goya" and explains how these images "don't make us laugh. They make us think").

18 One of the most famous songs of the era, later immortalised by Amália Rodrigues, is "Uma casa portuguesa" [A Portuguese home]. Written in 1953, with lyrics by Reinaldo Ferreira, its core lesson is quite close to Salazar's view, and was disseminated significantly among the lower classes. It is also a perfect example of what C. Murray calls *popaganda*: "With the boundary between propaganda/official discourse and popular culture thoroughly breached it becomes misleading and meaningless to distinguish between them as separate categories. Instead the interaction between these two *apparently* separate discourses should be characterised as *pop*aganda" (original emphases, 2000: 142). Here are some of the lines from its first verse: "In a Portuguese home it is good to find/bread and wine on the table./When someone knocks on the door, humbly,/they sit down at the table with us./.../The happiness of poverty/is found in this richness/of giving, and be happy for it."

19 Which of course corresponds to the English "out of sight, out of mind".

20 Especially through music, above all the complicated Estado Novo's appropriation of the city-bound Fado song as a political, cultural and indoctrinating tool for the construction of a national identity.

Chapter 5
Minor comics and atomised responses to small traumas

This last analytical chapter will not deal with an individual artist or a single work but rather with various shorter texts penned by different artists. The reason is twofold.

First, I wish to operate a sort of social shift in the perspective so far: it is my belief that by considering solely formats such as albums, books or graphic novels we are being constricted precisely by certain commodification choices and commercial categories *against* which the works central to this chapter act. Ever since the transformation of comics from mostly press-related formats to book-related forms, and the subsequent "literary turn", throughout the 1970s and 1980s, especially in Europe and the United States, the comics medium has gained not only a new impetus, but a new life, with a new understanding of its own history and even cultural validation (Lesage: 2011 and 2015). But this renders quite a significant number of comics invisible. The privilege that most comics studies give to conventional book formats (whether collections of comic book series, stand-alone graphic novels, Franco-Belgian albums, and so on) creates an illusion that comics have always been produced in book-related forms, or that it is in those formats that we find the comics that most warrant academic attention. As we know, the medium's history and present diversity are far more complicated than that, and criticism should aim to cover a wider field.[1] If we pay attention to certain examples of what may be called "wild publication" (drawing from Jacques Dubois's lessons in 2005), objects that are marginal in relation to literary institutions and distribution models, we widen the scope of our definition of comics, both socially and aesthetically.

Consequently, in some instances, I will only refer to a single title by a single artist, while in others I may refer to a larger group of works. Amassing such different productions in one chapter, however, as will hopefully become clear, mirrors the "collective" nature of these comics, and the way in which they contribute to a certain image of the pervasiveness of traumatogenic social situations in contemporary Portugal, as seen by comics. Hillary Chute pointed to the "cross-discursive form of comics" as being singularly "apt for expressing [the] difficult register [of trauma]"

Chapter Five

(2010: 2), which as I have emphasized in the introduction, I do not wish to overplay to the point of considering it superior to any other art form. The shift of attention in this chapter is intended to show that such approach can be achieved not only through the most habitual, dramatic techniques but also through low-pitched, experimental work, which may defy "that habituation of trauma into numbing and domesticating cultural conventions", as Roger Luckhurst puts it (2008: 89). This will open up a "narrative *possibility*" (idem, original emphasis), going against the grain of some of the central tenets of trauma studies, especially the declaration by some theorists of the very impossibility of narrating the event. Jenny Edkins makes this as clear as possible:

> Traumas, by definition, are events that are incapable of, or at the very least resist, narration or integration into linear narratives or, in other words, into homogeneous linear time. Trauma is not experienced in linear time; there are no words, no language, through which such an experience could take place. A traumatic event cannot be integrated into our symbolic universe, the very universe that has been called into question by the trauma. It cannot be narrated (Edkins 2014: 132).

But can one narrate through any other means? Indeed, and this is the second point of the different nature of this chapter, many of the works that I will cite do not follow the usual narrative or structural protocols of conventional comics. One way or another, they try out experimental approaches. We are entering what Portuguese comics critic Domingos Isabelinho has called the "expanded field" of comics, as previously quoted. We will argue that these comics forms are *minor* forms, in the strict Deleuzian-Guattarian sense of that word, which can provide yet another important inflection in our understanding of ways to express small traumas.

As we have seen before, Dominick LaCapra makes a distinction between, on the one hand, *ontological* or *structural* trauma, which relates to individuals and is addressed by psychoanalysis, and, on the other hand, *historical* trauma, which:

> is specific, and not everyone is subject to it or entitled to the subject-position associated with it. It is dubious to identify with the victim to the point of making oneself a surrogate victim who has the right to the victim's voice or subject-position (2001: 78).

Karyn Ball, discussing this very distinction, brings the point home when she writes that historical trauma "is triggered by an actual loss rather than an unconscious absence" (2007: xxxii-xxxiii). What this allows, and taking into consideration the issue of art, is that an empathetic *distance* is accorded to the reading. Still following Ball, what happens is that the spectator is prevented from assuming a pious identification with victims that cultural theorist Susannah Radstone associated with Manichean constructions of testimony. Rather the viewer is implicated by the camera as a voyeur in the perpetration of the crime and in the lag between its perception and the action that might bring the perpetrators to justice (2007: xxxix).

This is precisely what we have seen in *Pombinhas* by Miguel Rocha. But according to LaCapra, *empathic unsettlement* should "affect the mode of representation in different, nonlegislated ways... it is related to the performative dimensions of an account" (2001: 103). And some of the "nonlegislated ways" afforded by comics are the ones we are about to engage with in this chapter.

In the interview with Yad Vashem included at the end of *Writing History, Writing Trauma*, LaCapra further discusses these distinctions, and raises an important question:

> How do you affirm a democratic politics if you don't have some notion of working-through that is not identical to full transcendence, and yet is distinguishable from, and acts as a countervailing force to, endless repetition of the past or being implicated in the trauma, or continually validating the trauma? (2001: 153)

The answer may be in minor comics addressing small traumas.

The concept of *minority* in its literary-philosophical sense was coined by Gilles Deleuze and Félix Guattari in their short book, *Kafka. Pour une littérature mineure* (1975). The chapter entitled "What is Minor Literature?" (2003: 38 and ff.) is very clear in pointing out what the authors see as its three main characteristics. Firstly, in it, "language is affected with a high coefficient of deterritorialisation". Second, "everything in them is political". Lastly, "everything takes on a collective value". We will go through each trait in the following paragraphs, splicing them with other sources relevant to our subject matter. Naturally, Deleuze and Guattari pursue these notions in relation to Kafka's writing, following the particular specificities of a Jewish Czech writer writing in a bureaucratically styled German, so we must try to understand how they can be understood in relation to a territory as different as comics.

As far as I can tell, Jan Baetens was the first person to attempt an approach to the comics medium through the lens of this particular concept. He did so in two articles, both from 2008. The first is "North and South in Belgian Comics", which summarises the characteristics of specifically Belgian comics and then points, quite briefly, to the French philosophers' concept as a promising analytical tool in what the comics scholar deems "cultural semiotics" (2008a). The second occurrence is "Of Graphic Novels and Minor Cultures: The Fréon Collective", which displaces the discussion from a national/linguistic context to a wider one, namely, the

Chapter Five

place of comics as a specific art form within larger cultural units. Those cultural contexts are, in the first instance, the "graphic novel field" in both the United States and Europe, although mainly France and Belgium, drawing largely from material expounded in French in Baetens's groundbreaking *Formes et Politiques de la Bande Dessinée* (1998), and, and in a second level, the so-called "intermedial turn" (2008a).

Each of the components of *minorité* – its deterritorialised nature, and its political and collective force – is imbricated and influences the others. Although I will discuss these components or, as Simon O'Sullivan calls them in an article on photography, "modalities", separately, it should be borne in mind that each one includes theoretical consequences of the other two.

The first characteristic or trait of this minority nature is that of *deterritorialisation*. This has to do with an intensive, affective quality of the language employed, which in the case of comics includes the specific structures of comics making (from panels to the multiframe, from braiding to significant format choices). It can be considered from a topographical or even a national point of view. After all, the present book is discussing a group of comics works that are brought together first and foremost because they seem to belong to the same cultural, social and political unity. One of Jan Baetens's arguments about the characterisation of the specifically Francophone Belgian comics he addresses in one of the aforementioned articles is precisely the fact that they are devoid of local characteristics, preferring to aim for slightly more diluted features, which could be accepted, first and foremost, by French audiences. Baetens refers to such equilibrium as "something between absence and irony" (2008a: 118). Despite the fact that Miguel Carneiro, Marco Mendes, Carlos Pinheiro, Nuno Sousa, or other Porto authors, and Joana Figueiredo, Daniel Seabra Lopes, José Feitor, or other Lisbon authors, all of whom I will study presently, do not use local speech as a shortcut to local culture, they do use real spaces and references in order to create a social cartography where their stories become anchored, rooted, somewhat localised.

Deterritorialisation, however, should be understood as a profound quasi-metamorphosis, an ongoing process of becoming, that may end up reterritorialised or not. It is, according to O'Sullivan, the emergence of:

> noise – or glitches as we might call them – that free language from itself, at least, from its signifying self... an experimentation with, and from within, language. A rupturing of representation. A breaking of the habit of 'making sense', of 'being human' (2012: 6).

The narrative and figurative choices of authors such as Marco Mendes and Miguel Rocha, for instance, are integrated into clear representation strategies. No matter how fragmented they may be, the stories of these authors manifest distinct plots, definitive characters with psychological attributes, organised sequences of events, a more or less clearly evolving timeline and so on. But Joana Figueiredo, José Feitor, Daniel Seabra Lopes and Miguel Carneiro, on the contrary, explore other kinds of organisation of scenes and presentation of characters. They accentuate rupture.

O'Sullivan refers to forms of figuration as "narration and illustration, which is to say representation" (2012: 13). For O'Sullivan, figuration is one of the "wrong positions" of the *figural*, the other one being the "*absolute* deterritorialization of the figure (the move to total abstraction)" (idem). What this means is that even in the case of pure or geometric abstraction, the shapes will find a *code*, that is to say, they will *pass through the brain*, instead of directly impacting the nervous system (2012: 16). A reader of this sort of abstract work will always integrate it into pre-existing categories. That is to say that such work will become re-territorialised. Take Lewis Trondheim's *Bleu* (L'Association 2003), for example. This small booklet comprises nothing but colourful blots and abstract shapes against a blue background. There is no text, no frame borders, or other typical comics structures. However, we can rapidly interpret the "movements" of each shape or the "interrelations" between the various shapes as "consuming", "digesting", "turning", "fusing", "splitting" and so on. We are projecting animal behaviours and even human-like will onto these shapes, which partially defeats the initial abstraction.

In this sense, we can see the experiments of some abstract comics or, even more patently, the Oubapo project's many comics, as falling into that second "wrong" position. They too pass through the brain. As soon as one "reads", "interprets" or "gets" the method, there is nothing else to see or be affected by. This is something quite different from the minor, stuttering and stammering comics I want to address.

It is also important to underline once more that most of the texts I will deal with in this chapter have been published either as or in fanzines, small press publications, or have been presented as art objects. In any case, they can be categorised as pre-existing formulas or formats. They can be seen as "independent comics," even if there is always the danger of using such word as a catch-all term for incredibly varied productions. For the time being I want to consider this output as being part of the world of micro-editions, in which absolutely free self-expression is possible, and as something marked by the "angry idealism" with which Stephen Duncombe characterised post-punk fanzines from the 1970s (1997: 3), which were extremely influential for years to come, not only, but particularly in the comics medium. Ann Poletti also reinforces the idea that the seemingly simple materiality of these objects bolsters the many forms of self-constructedness, through "their unique status as homemade texts to practice a particularly complex set of representational strategies" (2008: 86). Contrary to standardised books, where choices (paper stock, binding, covers, fonts, etc.) are usually limited in terms of materiality or following cost-effectiveness criteria, rendering most of the "choices" practically invisible or

Chapter Five

at least transparent, in editions of this type "the text-object has a distinctive phys-ical presence which is constitutive of the modes of signification the form makes possible" (idem: 88). We will address oversized magazines, photocopied booklets, comics made out of post-it notes, and so on, where those material traces become part of the self-reflexivity of the texts.

A *minor* literature – or cinema, or comics – is one that operates an act of *deter-ritorialisation*, using the usual elements of the (major) art form so differently that we are forced us to look at that form in a completely new way. It has nothing to do with numbers, with "marginality" from a commercial or reception point of view. What takes place is rather an active distancing from whatever traits characterise the dominant discourse. That is why Deleuze and Guattari say, as clearly as possible, that one of its main characteristics (the second of three) is that everything in it is "political", in the sense that whatever gesture, small trait, or connection it manages to make, on its small scale, connects immediately to other issues that bring about a value judgement (2003: 39 ff.). We will return to this aspect shortly, with a small detour through Rancière, in order to expand what can be done with "politics".

Within the aesthetic-experimental plane, deterritorialisation works to under-mine a major structure from within. We may come across a comic that seems to be following the usual characteristics of the medium, the existence of characters, a spatial-temporal organised axis, causality, and so on, but presents those very same elements in a radically different structure. Through this disruption, the very oper-ation of deterritorialisation, instead of turning the text into a "failed" one, rather brings into crisis the very need for those conventional structures in the first place.

The final aspect of minority, in accordance to Deleuze and Guattari, is its *collec-tive nature*. This refers to the position of the speakers working within a major, domi-nant culture. Instead of pretending to be universal in their discourse, they are self-conscious about the specificity of the group within which they speak and to whom they speak. Small presses, fanzines and independent publications have quite a distinguished community dimension to them (Duncombe, 1997). More often than not, there are social events intrinsically related to them, from fairs to exhibi-tions, meetings and even specific practices of trading or sales. This is no different in Portugal for these authors and the small publishers they belong to or work with. The networks of diffusion are rather different from more commercial productions, namely bookstores, but that does not mean that there are no examples of crossover. Marco Mendes, for instance, despite having had most of his first work published in quite simple A4 photocopied fanzines with low runs, managed to collect many of his strips into wide-circulating books.

If, following Jacques Dubois, we imagine a normative comics institution, these objects would be at the margins of it. They would be what the Belgian theorist has called "wild publishing" (2005). Based on a marginal economy, with rare examples of state support or funds, their goal is not profit. Affiliated in a complex mesh of sub- and counter-cultures, these are contra-institutional comics, which mirror the output of other creative circles, with "specific material conditions and relations of production, and embodied in the prismatic network created by independent and nonprofit presses, small-press distribution centres, reading series, poet talks, and list serve discussions" (Ngai, 2005: 303).

As Deleuze and Guattari write in *Kafka*, "[minor literature's] cramped space forces each individual intrigue to connect immediately to politics" (2003: 39). It is as if the confined space and span of the minor text, precisely because it stands out against the cultural landscape, has political consequences merely by expressing itself. This trait directly involves its "collective" side, since even when referring to seemingly individual subject matter, its actions and consequences have to do with the struggles of a group. Currently, Portugal has a varied, even if small, comics market, which I have presented and contextualised. Most, if not all, the works featured in this chapter work against the grain of publications that wish to reach a wide, popular audience. Although we cannot say that this 'indie' market has an extensive reach, as it does in countries such as France, Belgium, the UK, the United States or even Spain, these are works that nonetheless create what one could call, with Gertrude Stein, "little resistances" (apud Ngai: 294). Moreover, and underlining their collective aspect, they do so always within specific networks of collaboration. Most of the authors publish their own work, but also publish, and sometimes are published by, others. The work of a given artist can be found across several publications from different publishing collectives. The commutations are endless. Finally, they use formats that receive a more limited, perhaps more obscure, circulation but one that demands or allows for proximity between producers and readers (for instance, the publication is bought from the artist him- or herself at a fair, or ordered online from their site or blog, etc.). Of course, this has important repercussions along the political dimension.

Indeed, the final trait of minor literature that we have to address relates to politics. "The political domain has contaminated every statement", write Deleuze and Guattari (2003: 40). I will take a longer time discussing this trait, as I wish to inflect it through Jacques Rancière's understanding of the word.

Nonconsensual Politics

Many of the works that will be addressed within this chapter have been the subject of a previous treatment, as they were part of the selection that was presented as an exhibition entitled *SemConsenso. Banda Desenhada, Ilustração e Política* [SansConsensus. Comics, Illustration and Politics], which was held at the Museu do Neo-Realismo in Vila Franca de Xira, Portugal, between 2015 October 31 and 2016

Chapter Five

March 20. This show was curated by the current author, and it attempted a strong dialogue with the literary, cinematographic, musical and visual art production associated with the wide-ranging and long-lived Neo Realism movement in Portugal, from the late 1920s up until the 1980s. The exhibition became an opportunity, in fact, to see how pertinent was the possibility of thinking about many of these small-press and self-published fanzines and printed objects in the context of the then contemporary economic crisis and political tension in Portugal over the last few years.

These works have been created in a social context that has become increasingly extreme, in which one of the poles, more often than not the representatives of right-wing governments and capitalist forces, presents itself as the "correct one", in relation to which everything else is "on the outside", and, therefore, undervalued if not completely ignored. To such a point that even when a dialogue seems possible, it is conducted according to strict rules established by those in power. So that if those "outside" wish to dialogue, they must abide by the rules established by those "inside".

One of the typical defence mechanisms of a hegemony is to present its solutions and paths as "objective", "realistic", "necessary", "unavoidable" and so on. And anything else that is different, that is to say, any sort of *dissent*, will be seen as "blinded by ideological principles", in clear contrast with the hegemony, which, of course, affirms itself to be ideology-free. This is repeated *ad nauseam* as if we were not living in post-Althusserian times, and we had not learnt how a whole complex of systems of representation is expressed through material forms, which in turn, shape individuals into social subjects. We should remember Karl Mannheim famous dictum from *Ideology and Utopia*, "A society is possible in the last analysis because the individuals in it carry around in their heads some sort of picture of that society" (1997: xxv). Mannheim's idea, and even his wording, recall Benedict Anderson's "imagined community", which prompts us to ask: what if we imagined something different?

Unlike the relatively concentrated practice of Marco Mendes and Miguel Rocha, even with the latter's different stylistic approaches, the heterogeneity of the artists of the present chapter should be quite clear. It would be difficult to find overarching common traits where visual styles, work methods, process materials, communication strategies and text distribution techniques are concerned in order to consider them a coherent "school" or even a tendency. We can neither group them together according to genres, types of humour, nor even the social role of their work. Even though they may publish in the same publications, participate in the same events, share any given set of circumstances or even formally share an organisation structure (an association, for instance), the "collective" side of their minor production emerges from the work itself, not from a conscious collaboration. There are a few cases where a convergence is possible, but we cannot just subsume them to a comprehensive vision. What they share is a concern for a new *distribution of the sensible*, to use a turn of phrase by Rancière.

Minor comics and atomised responses to small traumas

For the French philosopher, there is a clear distinction between politics as performed by the class of people that are involved in parties, who are elected, hold office and exercise power institutionally, and politics as manifested in everyday life and decisions. For the first, Rancière sometimes uses the term *la police*. This has to do with the acquisition, maintenance and exercise of power. The second he sees as *la politique* proper, which is related to the conquest of the right of expression by those who do not possess it. It is an emancipatory drive that brings into question the sense of collective (established) values.

In *La Mésentente*, Rancière explains how politics proper takes place when those who are usually unheard and unseen, or whose voice is considered purely as "noise", are able to occupy a space that was up until then out of their reach, forbidden by the rules and power of the *police* (1995: 43 and ff.).

An example that plays an important role in some of the work that follows may help bring this closer to home. In Porto city, more precisely in the Alto da Fontinha, a socially depressed part of the city, inhabited by poorer working classes, there was a primary school that had been disused since 2006, although it continued to be property of the City Council. A group of citizens and activists decided to occupy it in April 2011, in order to "return it to the community", serving not only the children of that area, but also teenagers and older people. This group of "occupiers" cleaned up the place, refurbished it, brought new materials and shared equipment into it, and created a series of courses for the local community, from drawing and reading workshops to music, bike repair, yoga and capoeira classes, but also introductory and practical courses on documentary cinema, for instance.

This group came to be known as Es.Col.A (which is the acronym for "Auto-Managed Collective Space" but also a pun using the Portuguese word for "school"). Needless to say, and despite the fact that some of the articles of the Portuguese Constitution defend "popular actions" for the preservation and usage of municipal property, these were, strictly speaking, illegal actions. And despite the attempt of Es.Col.A to become organised institutionally as an association, which would open a (remote) possibility of dialogue with the City Council, and even to apply for financial funding, things very quickly went awry. In May 2011 they were evicted for the first time (and seven members of the movement arrested). There was an attempt to solve this situation legally, but bureaucracy became an insurmountable hurdle. On April 19 2012 they were evicted once again, but this time there was a suspiciously strong presence of the police at the premises. Furthermore, through the complicity of certain media (Porto newspapers and television chains), the whole operation was highly publicised, with the occupiers framed as criminals and drug-addicts who had ransacked the place, a venue now "rescued" by the forces of authority.

The story is, of course, extremely complex, and we will make just two final comments. On April 25 2012 (the day on which Portugal commemorates the 1974

Chapter Five

Figure 5.1: AAVV (2012), *Buraco* issues 1 to 4. Porto: Buraco; covers. Picture by PM. Reproduced with the kind permission of the authors.

Democratic Revolution) people re-occupied the school in a festive ambiance (hundreds of people, among them both locals and activists, were present) but Es.Col.A was not able to resume its activities. And despite the apparent intervention

Minor comics and atomised responses to small traumas

of municipal employees at the site, there was no transformation whatsoever. The Alto da Fontinha primary school remained, years after the "occupation", abandoned.

I am describing this situation at some length because *Buraco* [Hole], which published comics-related material, whose contributors included many of the artists featured in this chapter, made the dramatic decision to create a fourth issue completely dedicated to Es.Col.A (Fig. 5.1). Moreover, many of the artists were involved in the demonstrations in support of the project, as they had common acquaintances or shared the same principles and were often working in other non-profit cultural associations in the city. *Buraco* started at the end of 2011 with the format of a tabloid newspaper, publishing comics and illustrations. The number of pages in each subsequent issue grew, from sixteen (issue 1) to twenty-four (issue 3), with mostly black-and-white printed pages, but with a two-colour cover and central spread. The magazine had a fixed roster of artists, all living and working in Porto, including Marco Mendes, whom I have discussed in the first chapter, and Miguel Carneiro, Bruno Borges, Carlos Pinheiro and Nuno Sousa, who will be central for this chapter. Each issue had guest artists, including Joana "Jucifer" Figueiredo and José Feitor, on whom we will also focus. The work in the first three issues already dealt with various social realities, tied to particular circumstances either of the city of Porto or of the country in general.

Marco Mendes continued his exploration in short melancholy humour strips, while other artists worked more elliptically. Nuno Sousa, for instance, presented a one-page story (Fig. 5.2). A man who seems to be homeless is sleeping in a park bench. He wakes up and asks a passing young man what time it is. The young man tells him the time, 8h05, and the homeless man seems quite worried, and leaves the bench hurriedly, as if late for an appointment. The title, translatable as "living above one's means" plays upon an often-repeated sentence stated by many politicians, including the then President of the Republic, Cavaco Silva, in order to justify the draconian measures that the austerity governments of the time, as well as the joint decisions of the International Monetary Fund, the European Central Bank and the European Commission, informally known as the "Troika", had brought into effect in order to curtail the financial crisis in Portugal. The awkward humour, of course, is to show how these measures were particularly affecting a very large working class, or underclass below it, which had never had the chance to even comprehend what living "above one's means" would be. Right after this short piece by Sousa, Jucifer presented a two-page story, with only six panels, in which two characters talk in an elliptical way about jobs, pay and welfare cuts, a typical discussion among an ever-increasing class of young people with precarious employment situations.

The sentences found on the covers of the publication, a self-description of the project, point out this ironical take. "We hit rock bottom. So we dug a deeper hole", reads the cover of issue 1. "The sky's the limit", proclaims issue 2, with a drawing

Chapter Five

Figure 5.2: Nuno Sousa (2012), "A vida acima das suas possibilidades", *Buraco* # 4. Porto: Buraco; n.p. Reproduced with the kind permission of the author.

of the feet of a probably hanged man. "A door is closed. A window is opened", states the cover of issue 3 over the contrasting images of a walled-up door that has been breached again, the back cover presenting the endless horizon over a sea in a canted image (check the cover at the right bottom corner of (Fig. 5.1).

Issue 4 changed drastically, exploding both its format, its participants and the nature of the pieces. With more than 100 pages, printed on cheaper newspaper stock, it presented itself as a "satirical and pro-lyrical newspaper"[2] and sported two covers. On one side, there is a representation of Bordalo Pinheiro's Zé Povinho character, discussed in the introduction, and superimposed on it, a Jolly Roger (the skull-and-bones pirate flag). On the other side, a portrait of the then President of the City Hall, Rui Rio, but with his face totally covered by a black circle. These covers were based on silkscreen posters that were issued by Oficina Arara (to which Miguel Carneiro belongs) and distributed all over the city of Porto during the April 25 demonstrations in defence of Es.Col.A (with many variations, which allow identification of Rui Rio), in more public *détournement* actions.

This is an issue that declares itself part of the "União Fontinha". Collecting newspaper clippings, documents from the Es.Col.A movement and the City Hall, statements from participants, photos from the project and the demonstrations, articles, ironic texts, short comics, illustrations and caricatures, essays, collages and games, *Buraco* 4 acts as a sort of deterritorialised archive and response to the situation explained above. It is both an opportunity for the people who participated in the Es.Col.A movement to explain and share their experience and the chance to respond to the dominance of the "politique politicienne". There are texts about "communities under construction" and short reportage pieces about other "Occupy" movements, such as the one in Tower David in Caracas. José Smith Vargas, a younger artist who had been creating many short journalistic comics pieces for a small-print-run anarchist newspaper called *Mapa*, participated with a ten-page (three of which actually show two half-sized pages) piece covering the police-conducted eviction of April 11, the demonstration of April 25, as well as declarations by both sympathisers and (politician) critics of the movement lifted from other media. By re-appropriating statements from politicians, such as Paulo Rios'[3] concern that "[Es.Col.A's] behavior may be altruistic but it is wrong. Can you imagine what would happen if others followed suit...?", and by visually expounding the bureaucratic nightmare the association had to go through and the police violence of the eviction, Vargas shows the absurdity of the disproportionate power relations but also the individuality of each participant, including the local inhabitants who welcomed the project into their lives.

Most of the comics and illustration artists use either humour as a defiant stance against those who hold political power, or celebrate the events throughout the issue. Contributors include Teresa Câmara Pestana, André Lemos, Bruno Borges, Carlos

Chapter Five

Pinheiro (none of the pages are signed, and there is no index either, but one can recognise the *graphic signatures*). All in all, therefore, this collective effort upholds the principles proclaimed by the movement. By showing solidarity through the publication of a themed newspaper, *Buraco* is directly engaged in a local movement, an engagement that brings about a new dimension to the movement itself, which, despite having a blog, makes an effort *not* to address the media.

But there are slightly different tones at work, however, which reveal the proverbial crack in the wall. Nuno Sousa offers a fragmented story in which passersby do not stop to help what seems to be a dead man in the street and a group of students involved in a humiliating and very public "praxe" [hazing]. Marco Mendes, perhaps unsurprisingly, turns this celebration on its head to reveal the inefficacy of these popular movements when acting against established powers. His participation in *Buraco* 4 presents a four-panel strip (Fig. 5.3), in which three panels show throngs of people marching the streets of Porto supporting Es.Col.A (the banners read: "No one stops the people's actions!", "Let's occupy a dream" or "The school is for everyone"). But the last one shows a close up of the school gates bolted shut with a heavy lock. The view embraces the empty patio, filled with debris and wilted flowers (probably the carnations used on April 25, the "flower of the Revolution"), while a single shadow of a policeman stands guard over the emptied out space.

Figure 5.3: Marco Mendes (2012), untitled, *Buraco* # 4. Porto: Buraco; n.p. Reproduced with the kind permission of the author.

Minor comics and atomised responses to small traumas

Buraco continued as a title, but it became a totally different graphic project, exploring political criticism but eschewing comics altogether, situating it outside the purview of this chapter.[4]

Following Jill Bennett, in *Empathic Vision*, we can look at *Buraco*, as an overall project, as engaging with a "sense of the political as a mode of thought embedded in a particular set of practices" (2005: 150). If we can read the particular works as political texts, as direct dialogues with, responses to, or interventions into the events that took place in the city of Porto, it is more interesting and revealing to note how, as an organised project, it contributes decisively to what Arjun Appadurai has called "landscapes of group identity" (apud Bennet, idem) and, before him, what Anderson called "imagined communities". Here the sense of community construction is quite strong, active and conscious, even if it is a community - at least for my purposes - that solely exists between the covers of the publication. Nevertheless, issue 4 seems to underscore Jill Bennett's argument:

> Giving testimony is thus the occasion for a face-to-face encounter in the sense evoked by Gayatri Spivak (and elaborated on by her commentator Sara Ahmed) when she argues that what is important in the politics of resistance or liberation is not simply the act of speaking but the *possibility of being heard.* (...) a politics of listening, predicated on the listener's willingness to enter into such *an encounter with another* (2005: 105, my emphasis).

Buraco 4 was, then, both a homage to the Es.Col.A project and an alternative information media outlet. It re-published items from mainstream news outlets with notes "correcting" them, and provided many documents, from official communication with the City Council to manifestos and photographs. There are a number of comics reportage on the "despejo" [eviction], poems, interviews with the people who live in the occupied school's *bairro*, opinion articles and essays with historical, political and philosophical assessments of people's resistance, the right to demonstrate and the absurdity of the law. In relation to this last point, perhaps the following example will suffice. After the violent action of the "despejo", three men were arrested and sentenced to... do community service. A rather strange punishment for people who were dedicating themselves to community service in the first place...

One other artist took on a similar cultural-political project. Here was yet another "occupy"-like movement in the city of Porto, although not directly related to the Es.Col.A movement. The Portuguese-Chilean artist Amanda Baeza used it as a basis to create, in early 2013, a small booklet. *Our Library* (published by the Latvian publisher kuš!) (Fig. 5.4) depicts in few pages and not many words the story of a library constructed by the people and then destroyed by a seemingly militaristic power, but creating the hope of a future utopian return. Whereas the booklet

Chapter Five

Figure 5.4: Amanda Baeza (2013), mini kuš! #13: *Our Library*. Riga: kuš!; cover and page (n.p.), collage. Reproduced with the kind permission of the author.

indicates that *Our Library* is "[b]ased on a true story", there is no further paratextual information about the events. However, for those who might catch the reference, events depicted seem to mirror what happened to the Biblioteca Popular do Marquês. This "Popular Library" was a small construction erected in 1946 at the Jardim do Marquês, at the heart of the city of Porto. As a "popular library", its goal was to provide the local inhabitants, comprised of the poorer working classes, with some of the tools that could lead to intellectual, cultural and even moral and civic improvement. The library remained opened and served the local population, especially children, by organising public readings, poetry writing contests, and the like, up until 2001. Closed by the City council, the facility remained abandoned for a whole decade. On June 16 2012, a group of people took it upon themselves to reopen the space and not only filled it with books and brought back activities, free of charge, but also did some improvement work on the structure. Sadly, three days later City Council officials and policemen boarded up the space once again and threw all the materials they found into the garbage, ensuring, in their outlook, the impediment of criminal activities and most especially the occupation of private property.

This is not the forum in which to criticise this action or go into further details about it, but *Our Library* seems to correspond to Amanda Baeza's need to address such an unjust event by creating a short, fictional story about a similarly interrupted project. The book points out, however, that despite the destruction of the library and death of its hero, it was not a "failed" project. As its pages declare: "Sometimes our heroes are killed//that doesn't mean they have failed/they simply put into motion//...the change we want to see in the world/and that work isn't finished yet" (Baeza 2013: n.p.). The last scene of the book shows a new structure erected on the site of the former library, illuminated at night, and inviting new readers in. This is all drawn in a very geometric, stylised fashion, with very bright, contrasting colours, eschewing realism proper in favour of strongly symbolic compositions and figuration, a highly dynamic look (reminiscent of New Wave authors such as Mark Beyer, whose unique high-stylised approach was deployed in stories about urban decadence, dark and paranoid fantasies).

Other artists responded to social issues as well, even if in an oblique manner. Bruno Borges, for instance, published a one-page story, with 6 regular panels, in *Buraco* no. 5 (Fig. 5.5). The only thing we see is a list of meat for sale ("one kilo of pork chops", "4 hamburgers", and so on). It is an almost impenetrable, non-narrative experimental comic. But it is in fact a commentary on a commercial promotion gone awry. A supermarket chain, Pingo Doce, engaging with so-called "dumping practices", lowered the prices of all products below 50% on May 1 2014, which is a holiday, specifically in order to celebrate workers' movements. As a result, a massive torrent of people visited their establishments, especially in urban centres, which led to conflicts, petty violence and awkward episodes of frenzied buying. This was repeatedly shown on the news, commented on and discussed. While debates about Pingo Doce's dumping practices (they were fined for it), labour practices in general and consumer culture are quite appropriate on International Workers' Day, what should have been a day of celebration of workers was hijacked by the spectacle of violence and desperation by people who suddenly gained access to arguably superfluous goods usually beyond their means. Borges's short comic, with no commentary, becomes in itself a reification of the piled-up supplies of meat. Borges' minimalist, slipshod-looking drawings seem to show a human body in a prone position, a wall, a crucifix, combining perhaps the idea of animal meat ready for consumption and the decay of human flesh, or impending death. On the other hand, more simply, there might be an identification of body parts corresponding to the labelled meat - the last panel is the easiest to identify, as we look upon a man's legs and read "2 legs of free-range chicken".

Other artists created longer pieces that addressed the state of the nation, whether culturally, economically or politically. Pepedelrey (Pedro Pereira) created a six-page story entitled "Recuar!" [Backing up!] in 2014 (Fig. 5.6). This was supposed to come out in an anthology of Portuguese comics associated with an exhibition at the Italian Treviso festival, *Quadradinhos*, but for undisclosed reasons the piece was not accepted. The author provided the publisher with another story, but proceeded to publish the rejected piece on his blog, along with articles from the Portuguese

Figure 5.5: Bruno Borges (2012), untitled, *Buraco* # 5. Porto: Buraco; n.p. Reproduced with the kind permission of the author.

Figure 5.6: Pepedelrey (2014), "Recuar!", published at URL: https://lifeofpepe.blogspot.com/search?q=censura [last view: December 20th 2021]. Reproduced with the kind permission of the author.

Constitution, declaring that his story had been censored.[5] The story presents a meandering commentary by an outsider narrator and shows different scenes that in one way or another mirror the alienated quality of contemporary Portuguese society. A seemingly 19th century-styled woman stands before an ATM machine proclaiming our modernity. A bullfighting scene shows how "we confuse barbarity with tradition" (bullfights, including the public killing of the bull, are legal in some parts of the country). Another scene shows a man sitting in front of a TV set hooked to an IV drip, but with a football instead of a drip-bag. Against a background that seems to be dripping with blood, a map of Portugal crossed by the dollar sign is presented sideways, with men hanging from it. This last scene reads: "This Portugal is dead, run and managed by well-organised criminals".

Critical reception of these works in Portugal is very limited, if it happens at all. Some of the criticism that has been levelled against these works (although in informal circles, which will come across here as "hearsay") is that they may be considered, where their political dimension is concerned, as poorly articulated, and even ineffective. This seems to mirror some criticism towards similar literary trends (see Giglioli 2001). The reasons for such criticism lies mostly in the fact that these works do not actually expose the contexts they emerge from in a sustained manner (using concrete names, data, etc., in a journalistic or essayistic fashion), nor

Chapter Five

do they engage with whatever dimensions they find faults with in the situations supposedly represented, and even less do they provide a clear answer or alternative to the problems. Furthermore, the very form of criticism that these works articulate seems to be rather vague or clichéd. Social inequalities and crises seem to be addressed, but not in clear terms, and there are no solutions for redress articulated.

But it is precisely by trying to deal with overwhelmingly powerful odds - a dominant City Council, a coercive company, the widespread economic, political and social instability in the country - that the authors create these oblique, original comments that make an alternative to the "police" discourse visible. Within a psychoanalytic context, Susannah Radstone engages with the problem of addressing these responses: "...in a society where authority is diffuse, incomprehensible, or even incoherent, aggressivity *toward* that authority is less easily managed, since that authority is harder to identify and thus less available for incorporative fantasy" (original emphasis; 2001: 116).

Who should be blamed for the state of society? Whereas it is easy to perceive that the responsibility is shared by the members of successive governments, public bodies, workers' unions, political parties, private companies, supra-national institutions, it is very difficult to blame *one* particular problem - people's alienation, bureaucratic decisions, a lack of general interest in civic movements - on any one particular agent. The proper authority is always elusive, diffuse, ungraspable, if there is one. By denying the sanctioned, normative discourse about how one should address these crises, these authors are proposing a discourse of *dissent*.

Quite often, the word "consensus" is employed by the political classes in its habitual, common sense, as a synonym for the "the accepted way" of expressing opinions or engaging with practices within democracy. No matter how much responsibility the consequences becomes diffused. However, just as with other words turned into mantras in the liberal context of today, such as "the inevitability" of "austerity", the sacrosanct "entrepreneurship" and the "governmental axis" (that is to say, the idea that only the parties that have had enough clout to become part of governments, namely the Portuguese Socialist party (PS), and the Portuguese Social-Democrat party (PSD), are qualified to speak with balance about finding solutions for the governability of the State), the usage of this term has contracted perspectives on what can be part of the democratic equation. Consensus, therefore, is not a sign of open and active participation, but rather a means of reducing who can participate, and a narrowing down of the space of possible action. It is a narrow "distribution of the sensible", which Rancière explains as: "the system of self-evident facts of sense perception that simultaneously discloses the existence of something in common and the delimitations that define the respective parts and positions within it". (2004: 12)

This is what permits us to look at *dissensus* as "the demonstration of a gap in the sensible itself. Political demonstration makes visible that which had no reason to be seen" (2010: 28). Dissensus is emancipatory, that is to say that it creates more room for democracy, more agents involved in democratic discourses, it elicits more democracy. The very existence of comics enables the pursuit of such a goal, for as Chute stresses, drawing from Jean-Luc Nancy, "representation is not just a copy of the thing but makes the thing observable; it exposes with insistence" (2016: 101). The relationship between art (in which we can include comics) and politics can be seen not as a crossing between a fictional territory and reality, but as two manners of producing fiction, according to Rancière (see 2009). The dominant form of consensus is itself a fiction, which pretends to be non-fictive: it is the "inevitable way" of doing things, the "realistic way", the only way, the objective way, or other suchlike expressions. But there is another way, the creation of new fictions, which allow for: "the dismantling of the old distribution of what could be seen, thought and done [*du visible, du pensable et du faisable*] (2009: 47).

Political art, thus, does not have to be necessarily structured according to pedagogical or propagandist principles. There is no reason to believe that there is a divorce between experimentation and political expression, given the fact that "... formal innovation has quite often been thought of as being on the side of political change but also, and above all, because political change has always been disserved by poor aesthetic choices" (Baetens 1998: 108). Creating new distributions of the sensible can be done without recourse to immediately legible social realism and can sometimes even integrate strangely genre-bound stories, with seeming fantasy tropes and apparent escapism, with no morality whatsoever, as is the case of Daniel Seabra Lopes's work, that I will read presently.

True Trauma, Unbound Fiction

> When the critical imperative is driven by a demand for testimony in a legalistic sense, the trauma memoir is instantly put on trial and must verify its conformity to a strict pact: verisimilitude; identity of author, narrator and character. Yet, as has been consistently observed, trauma is not necessarily a stable or straightforwardly evidential or narratable event, but might be mobile, subject to all kinds of transformation and revision. This might be well the defining element of a traumatic memory, and *what makes it particularly amenable to fictional narrative instead* (Luckhurst, 2008: 137, my emphasis)

In 2012, the independent publishing house Chili Com Carne issued a volume entitled *Futuro Primitivo* ("Primitive Future"). The editor, Marcos Farrajota, invited forty-five Portuguese and international artists to provide him with material that he could edit at will, under the wide-reaching theme of the "post-apocalyptic". The artists responded in the most diverse ways, of course, some of them following more or less expected clichés from adventure and science fiction genres, others simply showing scenes of everyday life, as if stating that we are already living in the end of days.

Chapter Five

Minor comics and atomised responses to small traumas

Figure 5.7: Daniel Seabra Lopes (2012), untitled. Published in remixed form in *Futuro Primitivo*. Cascais: Chili Com Carne; n.p. Reproduced with the kind permission of the author.

Chapter Five

Despite the fact that the artists sent in either straightforward, coherent stories, loose visual material or *cadavre exquis* collaborations, *Futuro Primitivo* is not a mere anthology. The result is a 160-page so-called "remix comix" where each artist's contribution was intercalated with those of the others in diverse ways. The reader can either try to look for the material from one single author or, more easily in purely physical terms, read it in one go, trying to come up with the necessary associations of meaning between one piece and another, sometimes mingled panel by panel, or page by page, or with short sections from the same hand followed bysections from a different hand, etc. (Fig. 5.8) Within the material that was sent, the on-and-off comics author Daniel Seabra Lopes provided Farrajota with an untitled fifteen-panel series. These panels were published in the book amidst many other submissions. I will refer to it, however, as a self-standing piece, as I had the opportunity to manipulate it myself in order to present it within the *SemConsenso* exhibition.

The opening panel shows the smoking craters of several volcanoes (Fig. 5.7). The following six panels show scenes (two of the panels are sub-divided) from a futuristic, yet familiar cityscape, filled with smoke and dead people lying on the ground in the streets, railway platforms, a parliament, households and offices. From the eighth panel onwards, we follow what seems to be a trio of characters who escape the lethal, billowing smoke using skis, then a powerboat and finally individual hot air balloons. These could be scenes from a Stephen King meets Jules Verne-like novel of an unexplainable catastrophe, either man-made or ecological, but there seems to be no connection to the reader's own reality.

However, I believe that unlike artists such as Amanda Baeza, Bruno Borges or Pepedelrey, who created critical commentaries in different ways based on real events from contemporary Portuguese society, Daniel Seabra Lopes, along with Joana Figueiredo, José Feitor and others, incorporates violent fantasies and enacts them in his comics. Unable to challenge authority, too diffuse in its forms, or to provide a more articulated discussion about the social-economical crisis in Portugal, these authors create these small fictions in order to mirror certain violent, *ugly feelings* (Ngai 2005) in relation to what one may call the impeding doom within Portugal (rampaging inflation, growing unemployment rates and disparagement of the unemployed, the debasing of the value of education, the lack of critical attention towards the arts, especially "low forms" like comics and illustration, and so on). These artists bring about what Radstone calls "complex identifications in play in post memorial testimonial scenarios" (2001: 122), where there is always the possibility not only of identification with the victims but also an identification with the perpetrators. Famously, Art Spiegelman employed the Nazi metaphorical representations of Jewish people as vermin in *Maus*. And as we've seen, Miguel Rocha stages re-enactments of violence, silence and propaganda both in *Pombinhas* and *Salazar*. Instead of choosing, as it were, the role of "good guy" (hero or sufferer), these artists

Minor comics and atomised responses to small traumas

Figure 5.8: Miguel Carneiro (2009), "Espera o pior e nunca ficarás desiludido!", *Qu'inferno*. Porto: A Mula; n.p. [original postcard series, 2008]. Reproduced with the kind permission of the author.

explore the expression of the "bad guy": the violence and meanness, or the apathy, the indifference, towards the suffering of others.

Miguel Carneiro embraces this "low form" in order to mirror the problematic of a diffuse authority. Carneiro is also a painter, from Porto, but has worked as a comics and a silkscreen artist. We have already referred to his early comics production, when we discussed the early fanzines with Marco Mendes, under the duo A Mula. While still at the university of Porto, Carneiro put out a number of fanzines with Mendes, always with shifting titles. Throughout these publications, Miguel Carneiro presented short stories with disparate styles, but always with the same main character and supporting cast. Using the name of the protagonist, we will refer to this body of work as "Monsieur Pignon".

Each Pignon story is presented as a self-standing unit (Fig. 5.8), more often than not as one-page gags. Nonetheless, we can look at it as both individual pages *and* as an ongoing text, either within a single publication (where sometimes there are common visual characteristics shared by the pages) or in its entirety. Carneiro emphasises in varying ways a sentence at the top of each page, whether it is a piece of dialogue or not, which works as a title for that specific page (in exhibitions, for instance, it is quite usual to identify each individual page by that "title"). Carneiro

Chapter Five

uses English and French sentences amidst the Portuguese, sometimes quotes from songs (such as Bob Dylan's verse, "There must be some kinda way out of here" from *All along the watchtower*) to literal, bad translations of Portuguese into other languages or fixed expressions (e.g., "aussitôt dit, aussitôt fait").

Monsieur Pignon[6] is a moustachioed, hat-wearing character who traverses several urban and not-so-urban landscapes sharing reminiscences, commenting upon life in general or engaging in absurd dialogues with other characters. Pignon, to be sure, is not Carneiro. This is not an autobiographical character, nor are these auto-fictive stories. However, there are moments when a somewhat autobiographical streak can be understood in some of the events that befall the character. It is important to realise that the A Mula fanzines published autobiographical material by Marco Mendes, as well as realist paintings and drawings by people such as Arlindo Silva, André Sousa, João Marrucho, João Marçal and a non-artist collaborator, Didi Vassi. The recurrence of these people's faces in each other's work created a sense of family or of a small universe of friends within the publication, as in the publications of Toronto artists Seth, Chester Brown and Joe Matt in the early 1990s, for example.

In one of the aforementioned magazines (*Estou careca...*), Didi Vassi represents Miguel Carneiro under two different guises: the "usual" Carneiro and the "Pignon" Carneiro. Vassi is not a comics artist. But, as a friend and (then) room-mate of Carneiro and Mendes, not only does he appear once in a while as a character in *Diário Rasgado*, for instance (as does Carneiro, incidentally), but he also participates in the fanzines with amateur-looking drawings. Lacking drawing skills, he portrays Carneiro variously with curly or straight hair, black-inked or with a simple outline, etc. Still, he can be identified from the black-rimmed glasses, for instance.

Apart from that, Pignon is also physically similar to a sort of caricature of the poet Fernando Pessoa, who has already become a cultural icon overshadowing the historical character. Both the stylistic and behavioural transformations that the character undergoes, thanks to the multiplicity of approaches taken by Carneiro, imply that Pignon himself, like Pessoa, is able to tap into what Portuguese philosopher Eduardo Lourenço has called a "multidimensional universe of contemporary interiority" (1987: 9). But Pignon's interior musings, presented verbally in his monologues and thought balloons, are often met with brutal interruptions. It is very telling that in one particular scene Didi Vassi chooses to depict a philosophising Carneiro drawn as his usual daily self, and another Carneiro, similar to Pignon, simply declaring his wish to go to bed early.

In fact, many of the stories starring Pignon "philosophise" to a certain extent. Either Pignon himself or other characters speak about life in general, death, the future, economic uncertainty, relationships, and so on. However, these themes are either disguised or curtailed with frankly bad puns or cut short with some sort of vulgar expletive. At the beginning, the jokes are rather pornographic and sexist, or

Minor comics and atomised responses to small traumas

just plainly imbecile, toilet humour. To a certain extent, Carneiro is exploring tropes and styles similar to those found in cheap cartoon magazines from the late 1970s. José Gil calls these tropes *grosseria*, Portuguese for *vulgarity*:

> Today, with the expansion to planetary scale of kitsch as a universal genre of taste, it was inevitable that *grosseria* [*vulgarity, coarseness, loutishness*] would become accentuated in our archaic country, so close to postmodernism.
> What is vulgarity? It is the result of effort and the impossibility of giving shape to a formless visceral background... To some piece of refined wit, someone answers back with an obscenity: but far from producing a Rabelaisian effect (in which the background is brought up, in its own shape, to sublime forms, or to a parody of the sublime), vulgarity destroys the refinement and cultivation of the irony, smashing it into a viscous and repugnant ooze (2004: 106).

To Gil this means a weakening of the mind, of the spirit. It connects consciousness directly to the body and its visceral spasms. This also helps us understand why there are so many permutations between bodies in Pignon. Miguel Carneiro is dexterous in his drawing skills, exploring multiple styles, changing not only materials but also aesthetic approaches. Some of the stories are obviously drawn with cheap ball-point pens and markers on restaurant paper towels, other are less crude and use China ink and detailed cross-hatching. Pignon's body is also very elastic, sometimes displaying hands as big as his whole body, at other times respecting some anatomical and proportion rules. Other characters, like a chicken-headed character or the Coconino County-like mutating landscape point to this permanent metamorphosis. The obsession with certain violent, even though cartoonish, actions, bodily fluids and sexual exploits are so exaggerated that they become ridiculous.

To a certain extent, this sort of regression to a non-conforming body or societal behaviour can be seen as deterritorialisation, breaking what was expected to assume a normative form into restless, uncontrollable bits and pieces, each with its own independent behaviour. This is an exercise in minorisation, not only expressed in the conduct of the character but the multitude of material forms of Pignon's stories. If we consider culture to provide "a space of (serious) play, a transitional mode where knowledge and meaning can be constantly disarticulated and reassembled", as Isobel Armstrong argues (apud Luckhurst 2008: 79), then Carneiro embodies this playfulness by refusing to take seriously discussions about themes that nevertheless become apparent and present in these short stories. In *Qu'Inferno*, Pignon stars in a 9-page story entitled "Histórias de merda cheiram mal..." [Shitty stories stink...]. Pignon is walking along a street while seemingly sharing advice with his reader. The advice is about bowel movements, but then he starts to explain the consequences of this discipline:

Chapter Five

> You'll see. It's a brave new world! Not only will you feel lighter, relaxed, as you'll contribute to reduce the effects of authoritarianism and hypocrisy...//which steal innocence throughout the world, inducing fear and stupidification! You don't have to be fucked in the arse to shit better anymore!

The diatribe continues, linking emptying the bowels to "enlightenment" and "enviable lucidity", until Pignon declares that he is thirsty from talking so much, and enters a tavern to drink. But this textual mechanism is recurrent in many of the strips. While it seems that the character is referring to something vulgar, the wording seems to imply a more profound, general, social sense. It is as if the character (and the author through it) wished to discuss important themes but, lest he ends up by pontificating, he prefers to disguise it with crude manners and language, expecting nonetheless that the shock may make his listeners or readers to "wake up". To a certain extent, it almost reads like a typical zen koan, where the master farts or slaps his student towards enlightenment.

Smallness

As we can surmise from many of these examples, we are not talking about huge commotions or overwhelming events within Portuguese society, but everyday occurrences and obstacles to small groups' civic liberties that do not elicit outrageous responses from the general public, but mainly indifference, or worse, acceptance of the point of view of the authorities. Which comes as no surprise, since whenever any mainstream media attention is given to the struggle of these groups, they are depicted as "malcontents", "permanently dissatisfied", "naysayers", "dissenters", "feminist killjoys", "lawbreakers" and so on. Once again we see how trauma is a keyword in this context, allowing for a wider spectrum than usually thought of. As Dorothea Olkowski argues, and especially within the contemporary European world, many are the "sufferings brought on by society, by our fellow human beings" that are much more prevalent than the "big issues", which directly affect a statiscally small number of people, even if they serve to intimate others. Olkowski continues, explaining that these are:

> sufferings that range from the great to the small: from war, poverty, oppressive governments, and families to excessive and diverse cruelties and insults, panics and shames. Here size and spread are insignificant since the latter, the *small sufferings*, can ruin a life as easily as worldwide traumas (my emphasis; 2007: 47-48).

I would like to introduce here the notion of *micro-narratives*. This term has nothing to do here with the simple size of the story. As Pierre Alferi writes, "Brevity is never reducible to shortness" (2016: 159). The very idea of *shortness* can be approached from either a stylistic/rhetorical or a theoretical perspective. In the first sense, it does not imply a value judgment but rather the choices made by authors in offering too little or too much of their story, which will lead to a certain effect in the reader (Schlanger 2016), whether euphoria or sheer boredom (Schneider 2016). It is a textual strategy. The second perspective demands a shift to a (tentative) consideration of micro-narratives as, necessarily, different from narrative in general, albeit without being *anti-narrative*, for "...the difficulty of narrativization should not be equated with the absence of narrativity" (Baetens 2001: 96). There is still the possibility of describing these micro-narratives by referring to narratological categories.

If *narrative* is understood as the combination of a story (the occurrence of events) and a narrative discourse that conveys it (its mediation), it can be said that within a micronarrative we can identify the events themselves but not their order, and even less so their causal relationships. Causality is not synonymous with order, but nevertheless causality imposes itself as the teleology of order. Still following Alfcri, one should consider them less as a "figure of speech" than a "figure of temporal and causal thoughts" (2016: 162). We are not referring, then, to one-page comics or the publication formats known as "mini-comics" but to textual strategies that question typical narrative structures such as causality, the moralistic role of heroism and naturalism (Alferi 2016: 179), temporal order, the relationship between identifiable parts, between any characters who appear, and even the characterisation of the figures in the story. It leads to a postponement of the story's finality (Alferi 2016), to "...a refraction effect of novelistic singularity" (Schlanger 2016: 15).

In principle, the atomised piece I will discuss presently by Joana Figueiredo would be considered a non-narrative piece, perhaps even a non-comics piece from a more classic perspective, but it does involve many of the categories usually present in comics production. The interrupted cycle by Seabra Lopes would be considered a non-textual entity, and José Feitor's zine (more of which later) would be seen solely as a collection of illustrations with short captions. However, not only does each of them exist as "a distinct entity able to produce effects, perhaps even pleasure?" (Schlanger 2016: 115) but they also "open up a breach in narrative prose" (Alferi 2016: 167). Once again, my aim is not to create hierarchies of judgment, but to open up a space (*la bréche*) to discuss things usually overlooked when considering comics in broader terms.

Joana Figueiredo is an artist who has participated since the late 1990s in a number of fanzines, whether solo or in collaboration with other artists, or even collective anthologies. Some of her most successful fanzine series were *Na verdade tenho 60 anos* [Actually I'm 60 years old] and *Osso da Pilinha* [Penis bone], which she co-created with Marcos Farrajota, about their relationship. She has also created a large number of images for book covers, concerts, fairs and posters for meetings, making her a sort of underground superstar. Some of her solo publications were printed under the name of

Chapter Five

Figure 5.9: Joana "Jucifer" Figueiredo (2008), *Post-Shit* exhibition display (photo by PM). Reproduced with the kind permission of the author.

"Crime Creme" and she has also signed a number of works as "Jucifer". However, the use of her pen name or her pseudonym is not continuous or systematic.

The piece I would like to concentrate on is called *Post-Shit*. In late January, 2008, a small art gallery (which has since closed down) organised an exhibition called *Quadradinhos, Histórias Postadas* [Little squares (yet another name for *comics* in Portuguese) Posted Stories]. Seven artists were invited to create comics-related stories by employing an unusual, then new, format of 3M post-it adhesive notes, which would

Minor comics and atomised responses to small traumas

be attached to the walls of the exhibition. The main goal was not only to create new pieces, of course, but to generate new ways of thinking about the presentation of comics in art-related spaces, three-dimensional environments, the division or porosity between artistic disciplines, and so on.

Most of the artists simply created their stories by using each individual post-it note as a panel, and most "compositions" (i.e. their arrangement in a particular shape) of these panels on the wall followed the habitual grid or linear presentation of the stories as if on a printed page (at least one author later re-published his story in a conventional publication, where the original specificity was completely eradicated). But, unlike the majority, Joana "Jucifer" Figueiredo took full advantage of the open-ended nature of these objects. Figueiredo created 60-plus images that were seemingly randomly put up on the wall, for people to move around and re-glue as they saw fit (Fig. 5.9). The images show a multitude of characters in varied situations without any coherent links between them.

The artist presented this piece on two other occasions in other comics-related exhibition contexts,[7] but without the opportunity for the public to manipulate the notes. In that same year of 2008, she also collected the images in a small booklet with a very low print run, giving the piece its name, *Post Shit*. Of course, this publication restricted the freedom of the original project, but turned it into a printed, published object instead of a unique art object.

What we see in the images is organisable into specific spaces or categories: a class room, a hospital, a war drill, meeting rooms, industrial machinery, a command centre, and so on. Apart from the uniformity of the drawing style in which figures that seem to be something between human and pig-faced people are presented, the characters have a few other common traits, such as a symbol on armbands or hats (a Greek cross on a white circle on black background, recalling both the Red Cross and the Nazi symbol, a deliberate ambiguity), or the professional uniforms they wear - military, medical, overalls, etc. But there are also characters in casual attire, with or without the symbol (Fig. 5.10). Moreover, because some situations seem close to one another, we may imagine that there are recurrent characters. There are many scenes that portray army-related activities; others take place in hospi-

Figure 5.10: Joana "Jucifer" Figueiredo (2008), One of the *Post-Shit* images. Reproduced with the kind permission of the author.

Chapter Five

tals, business meetings, an industrial plant floor, an art class, a kindergarten, and so on. There is only one instance of a double panel, with two post-it notes making up a continuous image of two soldiers carrying what seems to be a religious-themed painting. But it is impossible to say that these are "the same places" or that these are "the same characters". This is not an Oubapian exercise from which a reader could surmise a multitude of linear, perceivable and therefore naturalisable combinations (a re-territorialised image, to return to Deleuze-Guattari's terms).

Some of the images contain text in speech balloons, but they do not enhance understanding of the hypothetical narrative situations, as they probably would in a one-panel cartoon. Three apparently young men with long canine or feline ears and with casual t-shirts depicting goat-like creatures raise their right hands, palms open outwards and declare, "I swear!" but there are no interlocutors that could explain their action. Three people sitting at a long table look outwards and say "We will think about it". Is this a business meeting? Has someone proposed something? One of the soldiers who is carrying the painting in the double-panel image says, "I don't like steak!" Can we link this one image to another man holding two steaks above an oil drum who says, "What beautiful steaks!"? Can we find an association among all the images where people move about or comment on paintings and drawings? Can we create a sort of dialogue between all the apparent businessmen and casually dressed people who are sitting on desks and tables and seem to be discussing something? Many of the images have no text, and at least four depict people saying "No!"

Do they belong to the same diegetic universe, apart from the fact they have been created within the same productive context? There is no comprehensible shared diegetic context for these characters, no unity of time and space, no linearity, no indisputably recurrent characters, no action-consequence relationships between each "panel" or "scene". But "the imperative to find narrative coherence is so embedded" (Luckhurst, 2008: 85) that we look for the links that would allow us to consider it as a coherent fictive universe. As we read in Edgar Allan Poe's short story "The Gold-Bug":

> This is the usual effect of such coincidences. The mind struggles to establish a connection - a sequence of cause and effect - and, being unable to do so, suffers a species of temporary paralysis (quoted in Ngai, 2005: 254).

This temporal slowing down is brought about, within *Post Shit*'s exhibition mode, by the variable spatial distribution of the post-it notes on the wall, which invites a virtual spatial commutability of sorts, and only through an effect of accumulation and multi-legibility, not a linear reading of the images, is it possible to access its phantasmatical narrative. From each crystalised image, the reader-spectator can proceed to a free montage with the next, a movement at once momentaneous and reversible, towards a signifying whole, even if fleeting. As Jill Bennett writes in *Empathic*

Vision, "micronarratives that constitute storytelling after postmodernism are not just discrete events, in this case, but events that overlap and envelop each other" (Bennett, 2005: 82). Whereas I do not believe that Bennett is using "micronarratives" in the same theoretical sense as the one outlined above, it is apt that the word appears here.

The minimalism of the situations and the repetition of gestures, contexts, facial expressions, and even the words of these characters turn each discrete note/panel into a unit that may or may not "overlap and envelop each other" but do create the phantasmatic idea of association that is hard to describe in more habitual narrative terms. As spectators of a wall filled with loose panels, we are forced to retrace our steps, or change the associations between different images, leading to "a drastic slowdown of language, a rhetorical enactment of its fatigue" (Ngai 2005: 255), which Sianne Ngai associates with works of art that deal with the survival of trauma.

Moreover, the slowing down and open-endedness of *Post Shit* - somewhat like Daniel Seabra Lopes's series of scenes of destruction - powerfully affects the reader-spectator. Many of the scenes seem to be fraught with some kind of tension, not only those where military personnel are present, but also those that portray the corporate world, teaching institutions, factory work, hospital scenes, and menial jobs, which together create a sort of middle- to working-class environment where the assuredness and the safety of narrative is denied.

It is this change in temporal organisation that in turn slows down the interpreter - as if the loss of strong links in the text paradoxically strengthens an affective link between text and reader, transferring the text's "stupor" to him or her (Ngai 2005: 256).

The reader may not be sure what to make of *Post Shit*, but an overall anxiety is bound to emerge, just as it does with Lopes's, Feitor's and Carneiro's work, especially because there is no definitive meaning that can be attributed to it.

It may seem that the events and happenings represented within these works by Carneiro, Figueiredo, Lopes, Pepedelrey and Borges are not associated with overwhelming shock, but as the insidiousness of these small economic, social and everyday pressures accumulate, they corrupt a "normal" quotidian life. In *Spectral Evidence. The Photography of Trauma*, Ulrich Baer refers to very specific historical contingencies, when he discusses how "one of the terrible effects of trauma is precisely the replacement of the normal lifeworld with a suffocatingly hermetic violent universe" (2002: 21), which seems a very apt description of *Post Shit*. But in the same breath he also opens up the possibility of "prolonged trauma" whose victims are "unable to envision a different universe or question their violent surroundings" (idem: 21-22). In the case of Joana Figueiredo's characters this is true, since the "lack" of coordination between each panel-unit does not allow even for the coalescence of a storyworld, which in turn would allow for a fictive beyond. Miguel Carneiro's permanent exploitations of style and format open up its fictional universe to a different configuration, however. Daniel Seabra Lopes's piece has a more coherent

Chapter Five

organisation, but it is still unclear whether we are witnessing a consequential, unitary action by the same characters, an issue that becomes even more complicated in the work of artists from *Buraco* and elsewhere. In fact, the way in which the characters from Carneiro's oeuvre, especially M. Pignon, directly address the reader, or question their own existence as characters, inflects Baer's words: it is as if Pignon is able to fathom a different universe, but only to fall back into it once again, fatally, inexorably. Pignon is like a "disobedient machine", which "behaves autonomously and *proves* its autonomy by misbehaving" (orig. emph.; Bukatman, 2012: 146). Like Töpffer's characters, Sammy Sneeze, Krazy Kat or Coyote, Pignon always suffers the slapstick, violent downfall that ends his stories.

The relationship of comics and the political (in both senses of the word, that is, the common meaning and the Rancière-influenced one) is never a result of pure circumstance. As in any other art form, there is always "a very clear consciousness of the social implications of artistic practices" (Baetens 1998: 124).

In *Formes et Politiques de la Bande Dessinée*, Jan Baetens zeroes in on the Belgian collective Fréon, which was a powerhouse in the comics avant-garde scene of the 1990s throughout Europe. The theoretician identifies four strategies that he calls "refusals" (1998: 131 and ff.), which set up a certain visual field that is conductive to the political positioning I have been addressing throughout this chapter, and that I believe to be still pertinent. The first refusal is that of "the homogeneity of material or of style" (131), that is to say, the refusal to found or be part of a "school", a recognisable common style (something discussed, albeit in a different fashion, in the first chapter). Indeed, many of the authors we are dealing with in this chapter not only do not share common traits with one another, even if often participating often in the same initiatives and publications, but sometimes try out different instruments, strategies and approaches that give the impression of multiple authorship. That is particularly true with authors such as Miguel Carneiro, Jucifer and José Feitor. Each new project has different aims, which underlines the flexibility of the artists' practice.

The second refusal is that of "the strait-jacket of genre". As I have explained in the contextualising chapter, Portugal does not offer most comics artists the possibility of publishing their work in common, commercial categories like those found in the stronger markets like the North American or the Franco-Belgian ones. And even though there are examples of people working in book format (which is slightly distinct from the "album format," and points to a process of legitimisation for contemporary comics), such as Miguel Rocha and Marco Mendes, of course, the authors of this chapter opt for other more atomised forms, from the classical black-and-white photocopied and stapled fanzine to an uncategorisable object (Miguel Carneiro's posters and silkscreened books or Jucifer's post-its).

The third refusal resides in the distancing from a narrative nature that, so often, is seen as an essential (essentialist?) trait of comics as a whole. Amanda Baeza's booklet was a narrative piece, to be sure. But many of the authors in this chapter try to come up with different strategies for the association of the multiple images they present, sometimes also at a material level. Lopes's shorter piece could also be read as narrative, despite the faintness of the narratological elements, but its placement in the *Futuro Primitivo* book renders it atomised, a part thrown into a larger, non- or anti-narrative sequence of heterogeneous works. Bruno Borges's one-pager seems to point to a certain *stasis. Post-Shit*, with its collection of narratively unrelated scenes drawn on individual post-it sheets, points to quite different regimes and protocols of reading. José Feitor, in the small booklet I will refer to further ahead, creates cumulative effects.

The final refusal identified by Baetens in relation to the Fréon collective is "the expulsion of a given material medium, that of the *book*" (132), which should in this particular context be understood less as a textual form than as the material means and driving force of introduction onto a market. Granted, we have referred to Rocha and Mendes's creation of volumes that entered the distribution and reception circles of the book world, but many of the artists have chosen as their first platform the web, the exhibition gallery, or even the street with their posters, not to mention fanzines and homemade booklets that are way off official, mainstream commercial outlets. And even in the case of books proper, these are independent projects devoid of the standardised decisions of the marketeers from big conglomerates. It is important to bear in mind how "the text-object has a distinctive physical presence which is constitutive of the modes of signification the form makes possible" (Poletti, 2008: 88).

The Mundane

One of ways in which these authors address small traumas is through a focus on the utter banality of everyday life. And this attention to the trivial, instead of "bigger themes", can be interpreted as a resistant act, contesting generalisations and sweeping statements about Portugal or the Portuguese.

Philosopher and literary theoretician Silvina Rodrigues Lopes vehemently criticises a certain fashion for philosophising about the so-called "Portuguese spirit" as practiced among many intellectuals (she mentions as her main examples Eduardo Lourenço and José Gil; Lopes 2010). In her essay "Portugal sem destino" [Fateless Portugal], Lopes quotes from a multitude of literary examples in which the Portuguese "personality" or "geist" is characterised in mystical terms, to the detriment of more grounded experiences in the everyday, from which it is disconnected, replaced by collective abstract units such as "the people". More often than not, this unifying notion inheres in a cluster of traits that become compulsory to any individual belonging to that collective. Anyone who does not share such a trait will not be a part of the said collective in the "proper" way. A typical sentence starts with, "He is not a good Portuguese who..." followed by things as diverse as "who does not love

Chapter Five

fado", "does not enjoy football", "does not defend bullfighting", and so on.

The *mundane* then, becomes a key political word in this immediate context. This is not simply an automatic, realist reflection and/or expression of a past experience. Quotidian life must be associated here with the daily, political effort of escaping the sovereign power, the control of society, in order to attain an independent subjectivity. Which becomes undoubtedly something to be fought against by power itself.

Without quoting Rancière at any point in this small text, Lopes seems to have in mind the French author's notion of the *partage du sensible* when she writes:

> Of course, governments will respond to the claims they do not satisfy by undermining the very force that sustains such claims: this undermining may characterize the claims as subversive or may even consider them non-existent. But this does not mean that they are turned into "non-actions", into "child's play" or into "non-performative actions". [This is] called propaganda, manipulation of information, and so on (2010: 234)[8].

Paying attention, then, to a grounded everydayness is a political act. Some authors may explore the quotidian within a historical modality, like Miguel Rocha, as we have seen in the chapter devoted to him, both solo, as in his *As pombinhas do Senhor Leitão*, extraordinary but devoid of salvific tones, and in collaboration, like *Salazar*, with João Paulo Cotrim, an exercise in exorcism. We have also addressed Marco Mendes, who, with his *Diário Rasgado*, responds to the current state of affairs through a naked realism mingled with derisory humour and fantasy, without however proposing "solutions" or entrepreneurship, which could integrate it into the normalising discourses of liberal capitalism.

Other authors, such as Marcos Farrajota, José Smith Vargas, Nuno Sousa, Carlos Pinheiro and Tiago Baptista, each in their own way, also use the quotidian as their prime subject matter. These are also acts of resistance, in the sense that they use seemingly banal episodes to comment upon systematic economic and social stresses in Portuguese society.

Tiago Baptista, from a younger generation, shapes his own subjectification through irony, addressing (his) life in the suburbs. This space is not seen as a dehumanising *non-place* but a heterotopic space of citizenship. Baptista is a visual artist, a painter, and has created a number of short comics stories in many fanzines, some of which he publishes himself, such as the collective titles *Cléopatra* and *Preto no Branco*. In 2012, he had an anthology published by Oficina do Cego and the association a9)))) entitled *Fábricas, baldios, fé e pedras atiradas à lama* [Factories, vacant lots, faith and stones thrown at the mud]. It collects many different pieces, from artist's statements in the shape of self-ironical deconstructions to cartoons appropriating popular forms of comics to comment on the state of contemporary art and artists in relation to the economic crisis in Portugal, and a series of autofictional dialogues, in which an avatar of the author watches Hollywood mainstream movies with world-class cinema directors (Manoel de Oliveira and *The Spy Next Door*, Truffaut and *Date Night*, Tarkovski and *Marmaduke*, and Bergman, who gives up going to the cinema, given the appalling offer). I want to focus on "Um dia no subúrbio" [A day in the suburbs], a five-page story in which the author himself reminisces about the way he spends his day in the suburbs, where he lived at the time (Fig. 5.11). As the "camera" pans over the many different vistas of the suburbs, the captions explain how interesting the diversity of architecture and life is in places like this. Even the "graffiti are very interesting and their messages have a deep emotive and dramatic charge". The "nice restaurants" refer to a McDonald's franchise, and horrible noises – that later we understand to be gun shots – are not interpreted as dangerous because the narrator feels safe within the walls of his comfortable room. The narrator also shows us the covers of vinyl records that he likes to listen to, from Brazilian singer-author Elis Regina, to Tchaikovsky's *Pathétique*, and Swans' *Greed*. On the one hand, the narrator seems to confirm that the suburban environment perpetuates a zombie-like life among disused premises, franchises and an utter lack of communality. But on the other hand, one can read it, perhaps, against the grain. The first images, almost four complete pages, show only disconnected scenes set in the suburbs with the narrator's captions, giving the story a very disenchanted, distant tone. When he enters the scene, he is always sitting on his sofa, somewhat akin to Spiegelman's character from the 1973 one-page story "I don't get around much anymore". Additionally, the presence of a Swans album, and their highly political lyrics, works as a sort of meta-comment. It points, in an somewhat oblique manner, to the possibility of reading "A day in the suburbs" as precisely a deconstruction of the current haughty attitude towards the uncategorisable experience of living in the suburbs: dependency upon lower rents, longer commuting hours, less cultural life, and so on.

Another short story, "A ribeira de carenque", seems to take us on a stroll to observe a small rivulet that separates the town limits of Amadora and Sintra, just outside Lisbon. A sort of no-man's-land between urban and rural settings, this stream is surrounded with very small agricultural plots, where people grow subsistence crops (cabbages, onions, green peas and so on). The narrator describes this landscape and the things found in it almost dispassionately. The last page (Fig. 5.12) shows a regular grid, listing the crops. The final text, which starts on the previous page, reads:

> Sometimes, I wonder why people use such a plot to take something from it? For food but also for emotional reasons, with no middlemen. Some feeling of resistance, disobedience even. (…) People need to believe in another system, to believe in what they sow, what they see growing from the ground. // They can believe in these peas. / These onions (…).

Chapter Five

Figure 5.11: Tiago Baptista (2012), "Um dia no subúrbio", *Fábricas, baldios, fé e pedras atiradas à lama*. Lisboa/Leiria: Oficina do Cego. n.p. Reproduced with the kind permission of the author.

Minor comics and atomised responses to small traumas

Chapter Five

Fig. 5.12: Tiago Baptista (2016), "A ribeira de carenque", *Gerador* # 6. Lisboa: O Gerador; n.p. Reproduced with the kind permission of the author.

Minor comics and atomised responses to small traumas

Figure 5.13: José Feitor (2014), *Uma perna maior que a outra*, and corresponding source photograph from António Gonçalves Pedro. Lisboa: Imprensa Canalha; n.p.

The last panel shows a plot where the plants are not sprouting yet, so that the caption reads, "Here, we don't know. But believe me, it's the future". Without referring directly to the everyday economic needs that lead people (perhaps even employed in an urban setting) to grow their own vegetables, Baptista underlines this reality as almost a literal illustration of Rancière's creation of a new space of expression, with the palpable fruits of the earth.

Another discussion that can be seen as a tension between an urban and a rural setting can be detected in José Feitor's project. This artist has also created an enigmatic oblique autobiography, called *Uma perna maior que a outra* [One leg bigger than the other]. The small self-published forty-plus page booklet was issued by Feitor's own self-imprint, Imprensa Canalha, through which he edits and publishes his own work or that of other artists who inhabit the *terrain vague* between comics, illustration, and graphzines. *Perna* is a book that presents a collection of 22 drawings printed on the right-hand page with a short titled paragraph on the left-side page, which acts as both a very short story and a commentary upon the image. The author states elsewhere in the book that these are "reflections on a point of departure and its respective reckoning" (n.p.).

Some of the images are "graphic appropriations" of a group of photographs by António Gonçalves Pedro, a landscape photographer from Mora who was discovered within artistic circles around the early 2000s (a compilation entitled *António Gonçalves Pedro Fotógrafo Mora* was published in 2003 by Dom Quixote) (Fig. 5.13).

Chapter Five

Feitor maintains, in the booklet, that when he saw Pedro's photographs, he "gazed once again into his shame as if in a mirror", which infuses the texts with Catholic overtones. The images by Feitor create a fantastical *ménagerie* of characters that recall a certain rustic Portuguese culture that only blasé urbanites may think is long gone (as they would judge the suburbs from the outside). This is a semi-rural world, outside the main city centres of the country, and which despite the social and economic developments afforded by the post-April 25 democratic regime, has not embraced the complexities of post-modernity. Rough language is used, rustic traditions are upheld, the hoe is preferred to the school satchel, and the traditional predetermined roles of men, women, of the *pater familias* and the village fool are secure. And as a permanent hovering shadow, the oppressive religious overtones of confession and sin, that the narrator's text tries to undermine.

Through literary labour and the transformation of the images, Feitor creates a fictionalisation that both reveals hidden meanings and brings to the fore a disquieting experience (Fig. 5.14). One image shows a man holding what seems to be a haloed child wrapped in cloth. The man's penis is exposed and smoke or a floating sperm escapes into the air. Two other men stand inside a circle, with a dog next to them, one of them holding a candle, and outside the circle lies the skinned corpse of a rabbit. A grieving woman, with a crucifix around her neck, looks at what seems to be a portrait of a devil. The caption reads, "«Manumission». And even so, at the very end, when those beasts croaked, the women still wept for them. That was the biggest mystery". Despite its elliptical nature, it is clear that by "beasts" the narrator is referring to the men, brutal and oppressive, who are able to elicit love from the women they have mistreated throughout an entire life, even after death.

Another picture shows a schoolboy, with a noticeable scar around his mouth. The text reminisces:

> «Master». We went without wanting to. There was almost nothing there. I don't remember anything, or barely. No wonder. I remember the rain and the slaps in the face. And the fucking smock. And the teacher. We grew up fast so that we could quickly escape.

The author is exposing himself and the culture he grew up in but also hiding it, by never using the common indicators that would allow the reader to infer the "autobiographical pact" or even the necessary elements for it to be perceived as an auto-fictional approach. Somewhat like Miguel Carneiro's *Pignon* stories, Feitor's work can also be read as a distorted autobiography. It is only after attentive reading in coordination with the extra-textual elements alluded to within the book that the possibility emerges that *Perna* may be a slightly autobiographic project, beyond its purported limits, touching its "constitutive ambivalence" (Gilmore, 2001: 7).

Minor comics and atomised responses to small traumas

Figure 5.14: José Feitor (2014), *Uma perna maior que a outra*, collage with two pages. Lisboa: Imprensa Canalha; n.p.

The poses of the characters, mimicking photographic sessions, the short paragraph inflecting its meaning and a small ink blot that expands as we turn the pages, suggest that *Perna* is a sort of votive booklet, an ex-voto, a disguised confession. We see the people involved in the narrated episodes, and some connection to a central life. Such a decentring of the autobiographical project through a religious context falls in line into a sub-category of autobiographical comics that finds its origin in Justin Green's *Binky Brown Meets the Holy Virgin Mary*, and is akin to some of the projects by Robert Crumb, Chester Brown, Marjane Satrapi, Joe Matt and a few others. Within autobiography more generally, this also opens up issues of the historical development and ontology of the literary genre, as discussed by Leigh Gilmore in *The Limits of Autobiography. Trauma and Testimony*:

> I invoke religious language here in part to recall Western autobiography's debt to the confession, a practice that institutionalizes penance and penalty as self-expression. The confession welds together an official and a spiritual discourse in a way that conflates a functional boundary between the public and the private. (…) In the imagined encounter with such judgments, many writers seek grounds

Chapter Five

other than the explicitly testimonial for self-representation. In swerving from the center of autobiography towards its outer limits, they convert constraint into opportunity (2001: 14).

Within that same book, Gilmore addresses the mode through which trauma-related autobiographical projects may further non-representative strategies, as when writers (or comics authors) use what Gayatri Spivak calls a "ghostly witness" (apud Gilmore 2001: 20). Gilmore refines it:

> Texts that are concerned with self-representation and trauma offer a strong case for seeing that in the very condition of autobiography (and not the obstacles it offers for us to overcome) there is no transparent language of identity despite the demand to produce one. As controversial as any evidence of shaping may be in a trauma text - and what text is not shaped? - part of what we must call healing lies in the assertion of creativity. The ability to write beyond the silencing meted out by trauma is an achievement I want to recognize here (24).

In the cases of Carneiro, Figueiredo and Feitor, the autobiographical project goes through a radical decentring, abstracting and fictionalising process that backs off from the purported "transparent language" of identity. In fact, the artistic work of figuration points toward just such a dissolution of identity. On the one hand, a contrast between styles seems apparent. Say, Miguel Rocha's sumptuous colours and textured collages, Marco Mendes' virtuoso intricacy, Tiago Baptista's filigree realism, and Miguel Carneiro's shifting excesses, against the slick, chiaroscuro approach of José Feitor and the simple line drawings of Joana Figueiredo. But more importantly than an appreciation of the superficial effects of style and drawing techniques is the understanding of common representational strategies that echo similar concerns about self-representation (even if the "self" is portrayed within non-autobiographical work). That is how we see some affinities between Feitor's oozing bodies, Carneiro's shifting styles and Figueiredo's interchangeable characters.

The body is always already a mediated and material thing. In fact, and to return to a quote used previously, it is "perhaps the most awkward materiality of all" (Highmore, 2010: 119). The affordances of comics, especially in these independent examples, are brought to the fore through the multitude of styles among the artists, the internal changes of each project, and its connection to a menagerie of characters touched by unsaid, unclear, small but pervasive traumas. I am always wary of the dangers of reading any work under the auspices of psychoanalytical tools. I take in account Susannah Radstone's caveats towards the dangers of a "dominant trend in memory research today, that is the extension and application of terms associated with personal memory to domains beyond the personal" (2005: 137). As Radstone particularises:

> Taken together, the terms *mediation* and *articulation* militate against any analysis of memory as reflective of or determined by the past, and against any notion that a text - a memoir, for instance - constitutes an unproblematic reflection of memory. More than that, though, these terms together remind us that texts and practices are complexly related to the broader social formation in which their meanings are forged (my emphasis, 134-135).

"Memory is always mediated" Radstone continues, and "...it is simply not possible to argue that certain modes of personal memory [i.e., written memoirs, a memorial statue, etc.] give more direct access to that past than others" (135, 136). Following literary scholar Isobel Armstrong, I consider the medium of comics to be a cultural medium, that is to say one that "provides a space of (serious) play, a transitional mode where knowledge and meaning can be constantly disarticulated and reassembled" (apud Luckhurst 2008: 79).

My use of "menagerie" for the depiction of the characters, especially in the specific visual and composition (and also publication) strategies of Carneiro, Figueiredo and Feitor is deliberate. Usually, the exhibition of any social or national group goes through a simultaneously political and aesthetic paradox, both implying, however, an "erasure". This phenomenon has been recently studied by art historian Georges Didi-Huberman, and presents itself either in the form of an *excessive* exposition, with spectacular and commercial ends, or as a *deficient* exposition, through censorship, which can be, according to the historian, economic or political (2012).

Excessive exposition often leads to the emergence of a stereotyped image of a group of people without documenting the historical processes that may have led to a specific situation (one could argue that this is what happens in Tiago Baptista's ironic take on suburban life). That's the way that circumstantial, partial or incomplete traits may appear as pure, ahistorical, essentialist, permanently fixed, characteristics: "The Portuguese are a people of gentle temperament" or "are brave and resistant" are some of the oft-repeated sentences, which Silvina Rodrigues Lopes discusses in her aforementioned essay (2010).

Deficient exposition is precisely what results from the current, ongoing, projected and ever-expanded extinction of spaces that Rancière would call "common" (the visible, sensible spaces of Es.Col.A, the Biblioteca Popular, but also the very capacity to discuss independent publications, and so on).

Rancière's "distribution of the sensible" is about forms of inclusion and exclusion that constitute the very participation in common life, whose roots are to be found in (daily) experience. It has to do with the political process of producing various and variegated images that, first of all, denounce inequalities affecting the the very condition of possibility of expression. To return to Rodrigues Lopes, it is a form of avoiding "political elision", which more often than not "raises the issue of identity" (236). This

Chapter Five

helps us rethink Deleuze's and Guattari's notion of the collectivity when considering minor practices. Instead of regarding any action as partaking solely of a symbolic economy that stands for the collective, each individual creates a particular, singular perspective upon a micro-experience. It is by looking to a certain quotidian, to the singular person, to other spaces where other sensibilities are to be found, other experiences, that one expands the notion of what can be said, of what can be seen, of what can be expressed. Like the vegetable patches of Baptista's story.

Despite the representation of seemingly violent episodes, social and economic tensions and an inheritance of oppressive religious and political principles that prevent people from struggling against or exposing domestic abuse, class difference and institutional tyrannies, we do not see the characters of these authors overcoming their "problems" or presenting clear-cut solutions or anything that may pass as a "happy ending". We remain within Ngai's "ugly feelings", "minor affects that are far less intentional or object-directed, and thus more likely to produce political and aesthetic ambiguities" (2005: 20). Such ambiguity is corroborated quite often by the very materiality of production of the pieces, within the so-called Portuguese "alternative" circles, that come up with "multiple and various ways of heaping and cohering" (idem: 291). From Daniel Seabra Lopes's series being reshuffled within an editorial project, Figueiredo's post-it notes scattered in disorderly fashion on the wall, or Carneiro's many episodes of *Pignon* that never coalesce into a coherent unit, these are works presented as "lumps", as "examples of an incapacity to organise discrete elements into a coherent form" (idem: 289).

A Return to Trauma

The fact that I have brought together many forms of fictive, experimental, unusual comics that do not offer clear representations of what may be considered "traumatic lives," and the elasticity that these texts seem to impose on an understanding of what constitutes trauma should not be taken as underplaying the factual importance of real-life trauma. Once again, I want to underline that we are discussing works of art, cultural productions, texts that mediate symbols and experiences into significant, analysable forms. I believe, however, that a consideration of these texts widens the scope of *what* we can discuss, and *how* we can discuss it, using the many tools developed within trauma studies. Indeed, the relationship of these deterritorialised forms to trauma may seem to go against the grain of one of the central tenets trauma studies', the unrepresentability of trauma.

Nevertheless, representation does not necessarily mean "identification", that is to say, a visual or narrative form that would have sufficient explanatory power in itself. When reading comics (or any other art form), critically and analytically, we have to remind ourselves that we are not discussing actual people. The characters are

210

fictional creations, even when there might be autobiographical connections (the clear case of Marco Mendes, the less clear ones of José Feitor or Miguel Carneiro). And the authors are an abstract entity, sufficiently detached from the empirical minds and bodies of the people who have created these texts and images.

Comics is an art form. As such, in its own act of emergence, it creates a sufficiently detached relationship with whatever trauma may have led its author to create it. Whatever situation it responds to, it is always already an act of mourning, a process of working through, even if the trauma is unnamed, unrepresented, invisible. The reading of comics through the lens of trauma studies, however, provides us not only with penetrating analytical tools but also with critical caveats. As Karyn Ball writes in her introduction to *Traumatizing Theory*:

> [p]sychoanalysis humbles our desire to attribute too much conscious intention to any art, literature, or theory, yet this recognition that not all elements in a work are intentional does not undermine our power to treat them as material to its meaning (Ball: 2007: xxxvii).

Contestation of the supposedly absolute unrepresentability of trauma has surfaced in the work of some authors, the most vocal being Ruth Leys and Susannah Radstone. The latter has presented very strong critiques of the work of Cathy Caruth, as well as of Shoshana Felman and Dori Laub, as for instance in "Trauma Theory: Contexts, Politics, Ethics". In this article, Radstone states the problem thus:

> In place of theories that emphasize the conventional, mediated, illusory, deferred or imaginary status of the relation between representation and "actuality" or "event," trauma theory suggests that the relation between representation and "actuality, might be reconceived as one constituted by the absence of traces (Radstone 2007: 12).

If, quoting Laub, we consider trauma to be "an event without a witness", the corollary to such position is that it "takes the traumatic *event* as its theoretical foundation" (original emphasis, idem). Radstone, like Ruth Leys, whom she quotes, is interested in a critique of the meeting of neuroscience and psychoanalysis, as in the case of Van der Kolk, whom Caruth quotes substantially, and who argues that: "the traumatic event is encoded in the brain in a different way from ordinary memory" (idem: 13). This has a powerful consequence. Radstone writes:

> According to this model [the anti-mimetic one], the production of memories is no longer understood to be linked to the unconscious, unbiddable, processes of the inner world. Instead, memories are understood to be the unmediated, though

Chapter Five

unassimilable records of traumatic events. These memories are understood to undergo "dissociation," meaning that they come to occupy a specially designated area of the mind that precludes their retrieval. Whereas in the mimetic theory, trauma produces psychical dissociation from the self, in the anti-mimetic theory, it is the record of an unassimilable event which is dissociated from memory (idem: 14).

This has two consequences. On the one hand, it leads to the idea that trauma is a "purely external event", where the subject's own individuality, personality, desires, have no part, and on the other hand to the idea that that very same subject is "fully constituted", again bringing to mind the problems we pointed out in the first chapter about who can be considered "traumatisable" and which are situations "traumatogenic". An alternative take on this stance allows for a negotiation between the unconscious and the event itself, a certain degree of mediation that is opened up to the specificities of the chosen medium, its history, and its context.

What is lost - to put this even more baldly - is that fundamental psychoanalytic assumption concerning the challenge to the subject's *sovereignty* posed by the unconscious and its wayward processes [the "radical ungovernability of the unconscious" (18)] (...) it is the unconscious production of associations to a memory, rather than qualities intrinsic to certain events, that is understood to render a memory traumatic (idem: 14).

To put it another way, and coming closer to media-related issues, if we are to believe that "trauma is a crisis in representation, then this generates narrative *possibility* just as much as *impossibility*, a compulsive outpouring of attempts to formulate narrative knowledge" (Luckhurst 2008: 83, original emphases).

The few examples that we have discussed in this chapter attempt to create narrative (and not so narrative) possibilities of addressing traumatogenic situations, especially the impediments in the way of finding a fair public space for political and personal expression.

Notes

1   This does not mean that there is no work being done on other vehicles, from magazine and newspaper comics to webcomics and beyond, of course. People like Ian Gordon, John Lent, José Alaniz, Mel Gibson, Mark McKinney and Bart Beaty, to name but a few, are scholars who have widened the scope of attention. Philippe Capart's *La Crypte Tonique* no. 12 (2015), for instance, is wholly dedicated to the French-speaking "petits formats", which can seen as "cheaper" forms of comics in every sense of that word.

Minor comics and atomised responses to small traumas

2 The word they use is "pasquim", which stands for 19th century forms of cheaply-produced, usually anonymous and satirical pamphlets, ultimately related to the *pasquinades*, with their origin in the Roman "Pasquino" statue.

3 President of the local PSD party, the one in power at the time at both City level and the national Government.

4 Such as a mix-and-match book with alternating pictures of public personalities and animals, creating variations on faces, names and descriptions.

5 http://lifeofpepe.blogspot.pt/2014/08/recuar-bd-censuradaproibida.html Acessed 2016, May the 23rd.

6 The name derives from Jacques Brel's character in Édouard Molinaro's film *L'Emmerdeur* (1973), but has no other connection to it (personal communication with the author).

7 *Tinta nos Nervos* (2011) and *SemConsenso* (2015-2016).

8 The expressions within inverted commas are quotes from José Gil, which Lopes is criticising.

Conclusion

This book has attempted a discussion of very different types of comics produced in the past two decades in Portugal. These works have acted out or worked through the pervasiveness of a number of problems that may be described as "small traumas". From unemployment to precarity, from economic and social strife to deep-seated melancholy, many are the traumatogenic subject matters addressed by the authors collected here. There is also the paradoxical presence of impotence, violent emotions, and clumsy reactions to an utterly foreign, abstract power exercised by distant, disembodied political bodies. Moreover, works manifesting such a wide diversity of stylistic, narrative and material choices, may appear to make up an almost anomic constellation.

All of them, I hope to have shown, allow for an approach to trauma that is rather different from the core tenet of "classical" or "non-mimetic" trauma theory: that of the impossibility of its being represented or even known. Indeed, G. H. Hartman considers "traumatic knowledge" to be a contradiction in terms (1995: 537). But the framework through which trauma is understood can be shifted to a framework within which "[t]raumatic and artistic kinds of knowledge conspire to produce their own mode of recognition" (idem: 545). Comics produce their own mode of recognition, as Dominick LaCapra observes, in relation to Spiegelman's *Maus*, through their unique "tensely interactive processes of acting-out and working-through" (LaCapra 1998: 149).

When we discuss trauma, we are always already discussing a negotiation with the past, the relationship between memory and visuality, remembrance and experience. Arguably, since their inception, comics have been addressing the many new modes of memory, visualisation and shock that have been afforded by modernity (Smolderen 2009; Bukatman 2012). Contemporary authors, by shifting their attention from genre and escapism to more complex and varied subject matter, have also found new ways of addressing the very possibility of representing the impressions of the past, even when brought into crisis by trauma, big or small.

Janet Walker, in her "Traumatic Paradox" essay, discusses a famous example in which an Auschwitz survivor misremembers the number of chimneys being blown up (the woman remembers four chimneys, instead of the actual one). Originally, this is something discussed by Felman and Laub (1992), on which Walker expands. Of course, this episode is not seen as something that undermines the act of

Visualising Small Traumas

witnessing itself, but rather shows how "[m]istaken memories also testify, here to the 'breakage of the frame'" (2006: 108). In the medium of comics, one such example in found in Emmanuel Guibert's *La Guerre d'Alan* (L'Association, 2000-2008). This is an outstanding example of a book that transforms the memories of an Other (Alan Cope, a World War II North-American veteran who was living in France before his death, and who became friends with the comics author) into a self-memory: although the book is created entirely by Guibert (who after Cope's death would go on to create *L'enfance d'Alan*, 2012 and *Martha & Alan*, 2006, both through L'Association), it is not only based on recordings of Cope's memoirs but is also written *in the first person*. It is an autobiography written by an Other. In the first volume of *La Guerre d'Alan*, there is an episode in which Alan cannot remember the name of a philosopher whom a friend of his had known personally (Vol 1, page 53). He declares textually that he does not remember who it was. Two pages later (page 55), Alan remembers: it was Bertrand Russell. It would be easy for Emmanuel Guibert simply to edit the story and insert the name, "correcting" the forgetfulness of the elderly Cope, just as he manipulates events and memories in order to create the particular text we are reading. But Guibert chooses to "make visible" that very forgetfulness, which "breaks" the flowing frame of the narrative, reminding us, the readers, that we are not witnessing the events themselves, but an artful recreation of them, a remembering via specific stylistic and structural devices (in this case, those of comics): "the original text, itself vulnerable, addresses us, reveals itself as a participant in a collective life, or life-in-death, one sign of which is tradition or intertextuality" (Hartman 1995: 549). Hartman also expounds this notion clearly when he shows that when thinking about texts - literary in his case, but extendable to other artistic creations - it "is hard to think of the real (in Lacan's sense) as being consciously experienced" (1995: 539). He adds:

> This leads toward literary theory, because the disjunction between experiencing (phenomenal or empirical) and understanding (thoughtful naming, in which words replace things, or their images), is what figurative language expresses and explores. The literary construction of memory is obviously not a literal retrieval but a statement of a different sort. It related to the negative moment in experience, to what in experience has not been, or cannot be, adequately experienced. That moment is now expressed, or made known, in its negativity; the artistic representation modifies that part of our desire for knowledge (epistemophilia) which is driven by images (scopophilia) (1995: 540)

Hartman leads us to the deployment of fantasy, when we take into account that "trauma can include a rupture of the symbolic order (...) Fantasy has entered to repair a breach. Not so much a breach *of* the symbolic as *between* the symbolic and the individual" (original emphases, 1995: 543).

Conclusion

In *Trauma Culture*, Ann E. Kaplan considers how a traumatic event can be seen as "open, fluid, specific" (Kaplan 2005: 17) and how it can elicit a "narration without narrativity" or how dreams, "[f]ragments, hallucinations, and flashbacks are modes trauma often adopts" (idem: 65), modes that the cultural theorist deems to belong to *visuality* (idem:69).

Whereas Kaplan is dealing with documentary film, my work is focusing on a completely different medium, one that is nonetheless able to express, expound, negotiate with and respond to "visually mediated trauma". That mediation opens up the possibility of finding texts that, while associated with real, contextualised, pervasive traumatogenic situations, opt either for fictive solutions or for modes of expression that involve a high degree of fantasy. In neither case, do they allow for simple closure in relationship to the "small traumas" that are addressed.

> I conclude that art that takes trauma for its topic but does not allow the spectator so easily to 'survive' the protagonist's death or wound [she is referring to Maya Deren's *Meshes Afternoon* and Tracey Moffatt's *Night Cries*, and to a sentence by Freud], refuses the safe closure that melodrama [such as Hitchcock's *Spellbound* or Kevin Costner's *Dances With Wolves*, also studied by Kaplan] perhaps vainly seeks. Art that leaves the wound open pulls the spectator into its sphere in ways other kinds of art may not (Kaplan 2005: 135).

Instead of viewing fantastical irruptions in the texture of reality, of autobiography or of responses to societal strife as a weakness of the reality principle, they must be understood as an intrinsic part of them all, a necessary structure that makes the discourse itself possible. Even if that structure seems not to be as solid as it "should" be, since "...by incorporating self-reflexive devices to call attention to the friability of the scaffolding for audiovisual historiography" (Walker 2005: 19), these texts become fragmentary. Marco Mendes's *Diário Rasgado* makes this visible both at a macro-level (the permutations among four-panel strips) and at micro-level (all the material traces that we have mentioned). Many of the works discussed in the last chapter also explore fragmentation, either at a level of narration or in the very material forms they assume (the editorial processes, the existence as separate folios and post-it notes, and so on).

Slavoj Žižek, in *The Plague of Fantasies*, expounding his Lacanian take on the relationship of desire and its impossible fulfilment, lest it (desire itself) would dissolve completely, writes:

> There is no connection whatsoever between the (phantamastic) real of the subject and his symbolic identity: the two are thoroughly *incommensurable*. Fantasy thus creates a multitude of 'subject positions' among which the (observing, fantasizing) subject is free to float, to shift his identification from one to another (2008: 7, nt 5).

Is this what allows, within a medium such as comics, for the authors to represent themselves, their avatars or their characters, in particular approaches (such as that of "trauma comics") as permanently shifting bodies? Carneiro's rendition of his characters, along with his drawing style, changed over the years but this may not be explicable solely as an "internal evolution" of the artist's skills. The evasion of self-representation in a slightly autobiographical project such as Feitor's *Uma perna maior que a outra* cannot be seen as a simple means of self-disguise. The negation of the centrality of a protagonist in Jucifer's or Daniel Seabra Lopes's work and the oblique manner in which Pepedelrey, Amanda Baeza and Bruno Borges address actual events are not simple fantasy or genre choices. They remain open to the "multitude of 'subject positions'" that Žižek refers to.

Let us not forget how the opening of *Diário Rasgado* presents multiple "body-pieces", which, diegetically, belong to the several men living in Marco's flat, but which can also be interpreted as one single, divided, broken man. The final strip is called "Férias" ("Vacations") (Fig. C.1). We see (probably) those same men sharing a room, sleeping. The final panels show a couple of joggers running past outside, contrasting with the sleepers. One of whom declares "today I won't get drunk". Note the beer cans and bottles on the window sill, both inside and out. Unlike the image of the healthy, proactive, entrepreneurial young people outside, Marco's friends seem to pay the price for inconsequent nights that lead only to these scenes. The words spoken by the unidentified friend seem hollow. They are quite probably empty promises, crushed already like the beer cans around them, a stand-in for their inaction and ineptitude in the face of the overwhelming odds of an indifferent society. Why is there no action?

Then again, perhaps the action is the very idle threat that has just been spoken out loud. It signals acknowledgement of the reality that has just dissipated. That in fact was constituted in the moment when it dissipated. Žižek continues:

> Consequently, the paradox to be fully accepted is that when a certain historical moment is (mis)perceived as the moment of loss of some quality, upon closer inspection it becomes clear that the lost quality emerged only at this very moment of its alleged loss... This coincidence of emergence and loss, of course, designates the fundamental of the Lacanian *objet petit a* which emerges as being-lost - narrativization occludes this paradox by describing the process in which the object is first given and then gets lost (2008: 14-15).

The acknowledgement of a loss is therefore a signalling, and even a celebration, of the very thing that is perceived as lost at that precise moment. It has less to do with an event proper than with its recognition, which is created and emerges within the very act of its expression (in comics, the scene itself). "Scale" here is of no importance, that is to say, the nature of this signalling comes across either in situations

Conclusion

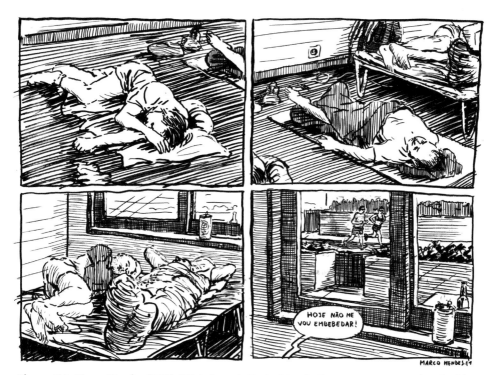

Figure C.1: Marco Mendes (2012), *Diário Rasgado*. Porto: Mundo Fantasma; n.p. Reproduced with the kind permission of the author.

that may be deemed as overwhelming traumas or in situations that, if seemingly banal, trivial, small, are nonetheless treated through the same mechanisms. One such example occurs when in *Diário Rasgado* the character Marco is leaving Barcelona, and Lígia verbally ends their relationship, just before he takes the bus to the airport back to Porto. What word does the author Mendes use as for the title of this strip? "Trauma". I will refer again to Žižek; he says:

> Here we can see clearly how fantasy is on the side of reality, how it sustains the subject's 'sense of reality': when the phantasmatic frame disintegrates, the subject undergoes a 'loss of reality' and starts to perceive reality as an 'unreal' nightmarish universe with no firm ontological foundation; this nightmarish universe is not 'pure fantasy' but, on the contrary, *that which remains of reality after reality is deprived of its support in fantasy* (2008: 84).

This "side of reality", this "nightmarish universe", is the material text itself. The very shape of these texts I have brought together in this book are witnesses to the changes operated by small traumas - the blog strips that are re-ordered, the post-it notes that act as a playful, re-combinable unity, the autobiography that uses pictures in order to create a nightmarish vision, the short story that is then interspersed with other people's work, the books that use collage and documents to complicate a unitary account. As Jill Bennett states, "trauma is not something immaterial that happens to the individual, leaving the world unchanged - rather, it has a palpable extension within the world" (2005: 49).

By giving material form to experiences of small traumas, the authors are not attempting to elicit sympathy from their readers, nor are they trying to "compete" with reports of other types of situation. They are however, and allow me to quote this again, "giving trauma extension in space or lived *place*, [and that] invites an awareness of different modes of inhabitation" (Bennett 2005: 12).

As non-melodramatic and unrealistic takes, sometimes even non-narrative or micro-narrative examples of comics, these small trauma comics fulfil the role of what Jill Bennett calls "non-affirmative forms of art", which "counter [a] kind of moralism and middlebrow humanism" (idem: 16), which is often expected from accounts of trauma and its (supposed) overcoming. Accounts that, dangerously, court "the tendency to overidentify with the victims of trauma" (idem: 21).

The political dimension of these texts is the agency they demand from their readers, an empathetic response that may find common ground or, conversely, may deny any close bond. No identification is sought, but instead an acknowledgement of the other's situation. Paying attention to what may seem "small" problems underlines the very importance of not judging the scale of such stories, but rather being prepared to listen to them.

Other examples could have come to the fore. A more concentrated focus on autobiography or auto-fiction, rather than the more diffuse approach of this book, could have yielded more concrete results. The consideration of other Portugal-based authors, such as Francisco Sousa Lobo, Cecil Silveira, Hetamoé (Ana Matilde Sousa), António Pedro Pinto Ribeiro, or a comparison with international artists whose projects are comparable, from Justin Green to Chester Brown, from Gabrielle Bell to Mattt Konture, could perhaps sharpen these ideas. What differences can we find in comics that address trauma (big or small) within a realistic/naturalistic framework and those that intercalate dreams and fantasies? What is the difference between comics that follow the now almost canonical principles of "literary graphic novels", which warrant almost immediate critical attention, and all those other forms that fall beyond the purview of the critical radar, such as blog, tumblr and instagram comics, or graphzines and small press material? It is not hyperbolic to observe that greater attention is lavished on "book comics" than anything else.

A focus on how the history of traumatic relationships can be rethought, rekindled, and even retaught could also provide us with a stimulating inquiry. Belgian and French comics are re-addressing their colonial past in innovative and engaging ways (McKinney 2011 and 2013), not only by looking at the past but by asking questions about how we, in the present, relate to that past. Portugal, has only recently begun to ask these questions within the medium of comics, not only about its own colonial history, but also about the 1828-1834 Civil War, the struggles of the Fall of the Monarchy and the emergence of the Republic in 1910, the 1926 military coup and the long dictatorship that lasted until 1974, the Colonial Wars of 1961-1974, fought against independence movements. Many of the ghosts of this past, including those that have survived in small things until today, are yet to be addressed by both society at large and by comics in particular, despite a few attempts at creating mainstream and even fantastical takes on that history.

Finally, a consideration of the ongoing struggles for alterglobalisation policies, as expressed in comics (say, the *World War III* anthology, or the political-economic essays by Philippe Squarzoni, the body-positive empowering comics by Tara Booth, or the dramatic shifts in subject matter in contemporary Brazilian comics by authors such as Pedro Franz, Aline Lemos, Aline Zouvi, Diego Gerlach and others), could also become a very productive field. By addressing the pervasive traumatic consequences brought about by neo-liberalism all over the world, and by providing counter-discourses to systemic disadvantages, social inequalities, a pervasive rape culture, victim-blaming and other sources of discrimination and prejudice, comics can be a powerful tool for the disfranchised and bridges towards the creation of empathy.

This book has attempted to identify the expressive possibilities of what I have called "small traumas" within the medium of comics. The point is not to evoke the possibility of the ultimate reparation and dissipation of trauma, a fundamentally unattainable goal, but to acknowledge both the traumas and the desire to make them known by the authors, as a proof of their agency and foundation of "modes or recognition", as Hartman called them.

And the comics medium is as capable as any other of engaging with the symbolisation of these realities, which, again following Hartman, "in this sense, is not a denial of literal or referential but its uncanny intensification" (Hartman 1995: 547).

References

Primary sources

AAVV. *Portrait/Lamb Haert.* Porto: A Mula 2005.

AAVV. *Estou careca e a minha cadela vai morrer!* Porto: A Mula 2005.

AAVV. *Hum, hum! Estou a ver...* Porto: A Mula 2005.

AAVV. *Cospe Aqui.* Porto: A Mula 2006.

AAVV. *Grande Prémio.* Porto: A Mula 2007.

AAVV. *Qu'Inferno.* Porto: A Mula 2009.

AAVV. *Buraco* no. 1. Porto: n.p. 2012.

AAVV. *Buraco* no. 2. Porto: n.p. 2012.

AAVV. *Buraco* no. 3. Porto: n.p. 2012.

AAVV. *Buraco* no. 4. Porto: n.p. 2012.

Baeza, Amanda. *Mini kus!* no 13, *Our Library/Mūsu bibliotēka.* Latvia: Biedriba Grafiskie stāsti n.d. [2013]

Baptista, Tiago. *Fábricas, Baldios, Fé e Pedras Atiradas à Lama.* Lisboa: Oficina do Cego/a9)))) 2011.

-- . "A Ribeira de Carenque". *Gerador* no. 67. Lisboa 2016.

Corradi, Alberto, ed. *Quadradinhos. Sguardi sul Fumetto Portoghese.* Treviso/Lisbon: Associzione Culturale Fumetti in Treviso/Chili Com Carne 2014.

Cotrim, João Paul and Miguel Rocha. *Salazar, Agora na Hora da sua Morte.* Lisbon: Parceria A. M. Pereira 2006.

Farrajota, Marcos, ed. *Futuro Primitivo.* n.p.: Chili Com Carne 2012.

-- , ed. *Mesinha de Cabeceira* no. 2, *Inverno.* n.p.: Chili Com Carne 2012.

Feitor, José. *Uma perna maior que a outra.* Lisbon: Imprensa Canalha 2014.

Jucifer. *Post Shit.* Lisbon: Crime Creme n.d. [2008]

-- . *Heavy Metal.* Lisbon: Crime Creme n.d. [2009]

-- . *A mãe de todos os agarrados.* Lisbon: Crime Creme n.d. [2009]

Mendes, Marco. *Tomorrow the Chinese Will Deliver the Pandas.* Porto: Plana 2008.

-- . *Diário Rasgado.* Porto: Mundo Fantasma/Turbina/A mula 2012.

-- . *Zombie.* Porto: Mundo Fantasma/Turbina 2014.

Rocha, Miguel. *As Pombinhas do sr. Leitão.* n.p.: BaleiAzul 1999.

Secondary sources

Alexandre-Bidon, Danièle. "La Bande Dessinée avant la Bande Dessinèe. Narration figurée et procédés d'animation dans les images du Moyen Âge". In *Le Collectionneur des Bandes Dessinées* Hors-série: *Les origines de la bande dessinée*. Paris/Angoulême: L'Association de la Revue Le Collectionneur des Bandes Dessinées/ Centre National de la bande Dessinée et de l'Image 1996; pp. 11-20.

Alferi, Pierre. *Brefs. Discours*. Paris: P.O.L. 2016.

Alphen, Ernst van. *Caught by History. Holocaust Effects in Contemporary Art, Literature, and Theory*. Stanford University Press: Stanford CA 1997.

Alphen, Ernst van. *Art in Mind. How Contemporary Images Shape Thought*. Chicago, IL: The University of Chicago Press 2005.

Araújo, Manuel António Teixeira. *A emancipação da literatura infantil*. Porto: Campo das Letras 2008.

Auerbach, Erich. *Mimésis. La représentation de la realité dans la littérature occidentale*. French translation of *Mimesis. Dargestellte Wirklichkeit in der abendländischen Literatur* (1946) by Cornélius Heim. Paris: Gallimard 1968.

Baer, Ulrich, *Spectral Evidence. The Photography of Trauma*. Cambridge, MA: Massachusetts Institute of Technology 2002.

Baetens, Jan. *Formes et Politiques de la Bande Dessinée*. Leuven: Peeters/Vrin 1998.

-- . "Revealing Traces: A New Theory of Graphic Enunciation". Robin Varnum and Christina T. Gibbons, eds. *The Language of Comics. Word and Image*. Jackson, MI: University Press of Mississipi 2001.

-- . "North and South in Belgian Comics." *European Comic Art*, 1.2 (2008a); pp. 111-122.

-- . "Of Graphic Novels and Minor Cultures: The Fréon Collective." *Yale French Studies* 114, *Writing and the Image Today* (2008b); pp. 95-115.

-- . "Bande dessinée et roman graphique: récits en images ou formes proprement littéraires?" *Esperienze Letterarie* no. 2 (2010); pp. 39-53.

-- . "Abstraction in Comics". *SubStance* 124, vol. 40, no. 1 (2011); pp. 94-113.

Bal, Mieke. *Narratology: Introduction to the Theory of Narrative*. Toronto: University of Toronto Press 1991.

Ball, Karyn, ed., *Traumatizing Theory. The Cultural Politics of Affect In and Beyond Psychoanalysis*. New York, NY: Other Press 2007.

Barsht, Konstantin A. "Defining the face: observations on Dostoevskii's creative process". In *Russian Literature, Modernism and the Visual Arts*. Kelly, Catrioma, and Stephen Lovell, eds. Cambridge, UK: Cambridge University Press 2000; pp. 23-57.

Beaty, Bart. *UnPopular Culture. Transforming the European Comic Book in the 1990s*. Toronto/Buffalo/London: University of Toronto Press 2007.

Belting, Hans. *Pour une Anthropologie des Images*. French trans. by Jean Torrent of *Bild-Anthropologie: Entwürfe für Eine Bildwissenschaft*. Paris: Gallimard 2004.

References

Benjamin, Walter. "The Storyteller: Reflections on the Works of Nicolai Leskov." Engl. transl. by Harry Zohn. *Illuminations.* New York, NY: Schocken Books 1969; pp. 83-109.

-- . *The Correspondence of Walter Benjamin.* Engl. transl. by Manfred R. Jacobson and Evelyn M. Jacobson of *Briefe 1, 1910-1928, Briefe 2, 1929-1940* (1978); Gershom Scholem e Theodor W. Adorno, eds. Chicago/London: The University of Chicago Press 1994.

-- . "Goethe's Elective Affinities". Marcus Bullock and Michael W. Jennings, eds. *Selected Writings. Volume 1, 1913-1926.* Cambridge, MA, London, UK: The Belknap Press of Harvard University Press 1996; pp. 297-360.

-- . *The Arcades Project.* Engl. transl. by Howard Eiland and Kevin McLaughlin of *Das Passagen-Werk.* Cambridge, MA/London: Belknap/Harvard University Press 2002.

-- . *Illuminations. Essays and Reflections.* Hannan Arendt, ed., Engl. transl. by Harry Zohn. Schocken Books: New York, NY 2007 [1st. ed. 1968].

Bennett, Jill. *Empathic Vision. Affect, Trauma, and Contemporary Art.* Stanford, CA: Stanford University Press 2005.

Berninger, Mark, Jochen Ecke and Gideon Haberkorn, eds. *Comics as a Nexus of Cultures. Essays on the Interplay of Media, Disciplines and International Perspectives.* Jefferson, NC and London: McFarland & Company Inc., Publishers 2010.

Bezanson, Kate and Meg Luxton, eds., *Social Reproduction: Feminist Political Economy Challenges Neo-Liberalism.* Montreal: McGill-Queen's University Press 2006.

Bhattacharya, Tithi. "What is social reproduction theory?". *SocialistWorker.org*; URL: http://socialistworker.org/2013/09/10/what-is-social-reproduction-theory (last accessed April the 10th 2014).

Blanchet, Evariste. "*Les revoltes ratees* [sic] de Guido Buzzelli". *Bananas:* n.p. 2003; pp. 44-45.

Blanchot, Maurice. *The Writing of the Disaster.* Engl. transl. by Ann Smock of *L'Écriture du désastre* [1980]. Lincoln/London: University of Nebraska Press 1986.

Boléo, João Paulo Paiva e Carlos Bandeiras Pinheiro. *A banda desenhada portuguesa 1914 – 1945.* Lisbon: Fundação Calouste Gulbenkian 1997.

-- . *A banda desenhada portuguesa: anos 40 - anos 80.* Lisbon: Fundação Calouste Gulbenkian 2000.

Borghi, Maurizio. "'The Public Use of Reason' A Philosophical Understanding of Knowledge Sharing". *The International Journal of the Humanities,* vol. 3, 2005-2006; pp. 179-186.

Breithaupt, Fritz. "The Invention of Trauma in German Romanticism". *Critical Inquiry,* vol. 32, no. 1 (2005); pp. 77-101.

Brown, Laura S. "Not Outside the Range: One Feminist Perspective on Psychic Trauma." Caruth, Cathy, *Trauma. Explorations in Memory.* Baltimore/London: The Johns Hopkins University Press 1995; pp. 100-112.

Bukatman, Scott. *The Poetics of Slumberland: Animated Spirits and the Animating Spirit.* Berkeley /Los Angeles, CA: University of California Press 2012.

Butler, Judith. "Gender is Burning. Questions of Appropriation and Subversion." *Bodies That Matter. On the Discursive Limits of Sex.* New York, NY/London: Routledge 1993.

Cabral, João de Pina. "A difusão do limiar: margens, hegemonias e contradições". *Análise Social*, Vol. Xxxiv (153) (2000); pp-. 865-892.

Capart, Philippe, dir. *La Crypte Tonique* no. 12, *Les Patrons de la bande dessinée*. Bruxelles: La Crypte Tonique 2015.

Carrier, David. *The Aesthetics of Comics*. University Park, PA: The Pennsylvania State University Press 2000.

Carroll, Noël. "The Specificity of Media." *Journal of Aesthetic Education*, vol. 19, no 4. Winter 1984; pp. 5-20.

-- . *A Philosophy of Mass Art*. Oxford: Oxford University Press 1998.

Caruth, Cathy. "Unclaimed Experience: Trauma and the Possibility of History." *Yale French Studies*, Vol. 79. *Literature and the Ethical Question* (1991); pp. 181-192.

-- , ed. *Trauma. Explorations in Memory*. Baltimore and London: The Johns Hopkins University Press 1995.

-- . *Unclaimed Experience. Trauma, Narrative, and History*. Baltimore/London: The Johns Hopkins University Press 1996.

Cerezales, Diego Palacios. A review of "Vítimas de Salazar". *Análise Social*. Vol. XLII, no. 4. 2007: pp. 1128-1135.

Chaney, Michael A., ed. *Graphic Subjects. Critical Essays on Autobiography and Graphic Novels*. Madison, WI: The University of Wisconsin Press 2011.

Chavanne, Renaud. "Le Complexe polonais, 1re partie". *Critix*. 7 (Fall 1998); pp. 61-64.

-- . *Composition de la bande dessinée*. Montrouge: PLG Éditeur 2010.

Cheah, Pheng. "Crises of Money." *Positions* 16: 1. 2008; pp. 189-219.

Chute, Hillary. *Graphic Women. Life Narrative & Contemporary Comics*. New York, NY: Columbia University Press 2010.

-- . *Disaster Drawn. Visual Witness, Comics, and Documentary Form*. Cambridge, MA/London: The Belknap Press of Harvard University Press 2016.

Clewell, Tammy. "Mourning Beyond Melancholia: Freud's Psychoanalysis of Loss". *Journal of the American Psychoanalytical Association* no. 52 (1), Winter 2004; pp. 43-67.

Confino, Alon. "Collective Memory and Cultural History: Problems of Method". *American Historical Review*, Vol. 102, # 5, AHR: Bloomington, IN Dec 1997; pp. 1386-1403.

Cotrim, João Paulo, ed. *Rafael Bordalo Pinheiro, Fotobiografia*. Lisboa: Assírio & Alvim 2005.

Cohn, Neil. "The Limits of Time and Transitions: Challenges to Theories of Sequential Image Composition". *Studies in Comics*. Vol. 1, no. 1. Intellect: 2010; pp. 127-147.

-- . *The Visual Language of Comics. Introduction to the Structure and Cognition of Sequential Images*. London/New York, NY: Bloomsbury 2013.

Costa, Sara Figueiredo. [Untitled text]. In Moura, Pedro, ed., *Tinta nos Nervos. Banda Desenhada Portuguesa*. Lisboa: Museu Colecção Berardo 2011; pp. 41-52.

Cour, Erin La. "Representation of Truth and Trauma in Personal Narrative: The Insight of Graphic Novels." *Frame. Tijdschrift voor Litteratuurwetenschap*, "Graphic Novel." 23.1. May 2010; pp. 41-55.

References

Crane, Susan. "Writing the Individual Back into Collective Memory". *The American Historical Review*, Vol. 102, no. 5 (Dec 1997); pp. 1372-1385.

Craps, Stef. *Postcolonial Witnessing. Trauma Out of Bounds.* Hampshire: Palgrave Macmillan 2013.

Crépin, Thierry and Thierry Groensteen. *"On tue à chaque page". La loi de 1949 sur les publications destinées à la jeunesse.* Paris: Éditions du Temps-Musée de la bande dessinée 1999.

Cunha, Luís. "A imagem do negro na b.d. do Estado Novo: algumas propostas exploratórias". *Cadernos do Noroeste*, vol. 8 (1) (1995); pp. 89-112.

-- and Rosa Cabecinhas. "A estética e o sentido: modos de representar o negro na banda desenhada contemporânea". In Silva, Manuel Carlos, org., *Nação e Estado. Entre o Global e o Local.* Porto: Edições Afrontamento 2006; pp. 73-91.

Cvetkovich, Anne. "Drawing the Archive in Alison Bechdel's *Fun Home*". *WSQ: Women's Studies Quarterly*, vol. 36, no. 1 & 2 (Spring & Summer 2008); pp. 111-128.

Deleuze, Gilles, and Félix Guattari. *Kafka, Para uma literatura menor.* Port. trans. by Rafael Godinho, of *Kafka, Pour Une Littèrature Mineur* (Éditions de Minuit 1975). Lisbon: Assírio & Alvim 2003.

Deus, António Dias de, e Leonardo De Sá. *Os Comics em Portugal. Uma História da Banda Desenhada.* Lisboa: Edições Cotovia e Bedeteca de Lisboa 1997.

D'Haen, Theo. "Why World Literature Now?" *University of Bucharest Review. A Journal of Literary and Cultural Studies*, no. 01: 2011; pp. 57-64.

-- . "Minor Literatures and Major Histories." *A World History of Literature*, Theo D'Haen, ed. Brussels: Koninklijke Vlaamse Akademie van België voor Wetenschappen en Kunsten 2012.

-- . "Major Languages, Minor Literatures, Multiple Legacies." (2013) URL: https://lirias.kuleuven.be/handle/123456789/411262. [last accessed April 2015].

Didi-Huberman, Georges. *L'Image Survivante. Histoire de l'Art et Temps de Fantômes selon Aby Warburg.* Paris: Éditions de Minuit 2002.

-- . *L'Image Ouverte. Motifs de l'incarnation dans les arts visuels.* Paris: Gallimard 2007.

-- . *L'Œil de l'histoire.* Tome 4: *Peuples exposés, peuples figurants.* Paris: Minuit 2012.

Dubois, Jacques. *L'instituition de la littérature.* Bruxelles: Éditions Labor 2005 [1st. ed. 1975].

Duncombe, Stephen. *Notes from the Underground. Zines and the Politics of Alternative Culture.* London: Verso 1997.

Eagleton, Terry, *The Function of Criticism.* London/New York, NY: Verso Books 2005 [1st ed. 1985].

Eakin, Paul John. "What Are We Reading When We Read Autobiography?". *Narrative*, Vol. 12, no. 2 (May 2004); pp. 121-132.

Eco, Umberto. *The Limits of Interpretation.* Blomington, IN: Indiana University Press 1994.

Edkins, Jenny. "Time, Personhood, Politics." In Beulens, Gert, Sam Durrant and Robert Eaglestone, eds. *The Future of Trauma Theory. Contemporary Literary and Cultural Criticism.* New York, NY/London: Routledge 2014; pp. 127-139.

Elsaesser, Thomas. "Postmodernism as mourning work". *Screen* 42:2 (Summer 2001); pp. 193-201.

-- , and Malte Hagener. *Film Theory. An introduction through the Senses.* New York, NY/London: Routledge 2010.

Fehrle, Johannes. Review of Martin Schüwer's *Wie Comics erzählen. Grundriss einer intermedialen Erzähltheorie der grafischen Literatur. Kritikon Litterarum* 37 (2010); pp. 290-298.

-- . "Unnatural Worlds and Unnatural Narration in Comics?". In Alber, Jan, and Rüdiger Heinze, *Unnatural narratives - Unnatural Narratology.* Berlin/Boston: De Gruyter 2011; pp. 210-245.

Felman, Shoshana, "Benjamin's Silence", in *Critical Inquiry* Vol. 25, no. 2, *"Angelus Novus": Perspectives on Walter Benjamin* (Winter 1999); pp. 201-234.

-- , and Dori Laub. *Testimony. Crises of Witnessing in Literature, Psychoanalysis and History.* New York, NY/London: Routledge 1992.

Ferro, João Pedro. *História da banda desenhada infantil portuguesa: das origens até ao ABCzinho.* Presença: Lisbon 1987.

Feuchtwang, Stephan. "Loss. Transmissions, recognitions, authorisations." In *Regimes of Memory.* Susannah Radstone and Katharine Hodgkin, eds. New York, NY/London: Routledge 2003; pp. 76-89.

Friedlander, Saul. "Trauma, Transference and 'Working through' in Writing the History of the Shoah". *History and Memory,* Vol. 4, No. 1 (Spring-Summer 1992); pp. 39-59.

Forter, Greg. "Freud, Faulkner, Caruth. Trauma and the Politics of Literary Form". *Narrative* Vol. 15, no. 3 (October 2007); pp. 259-285.

França, José Augusto. *Rafael Bordalo Pinheiro.* Lisbon: Bertand 1981.

Frey, Hugo. "History and memory in Franco-Belgian *Bande Dessinée* (BD)". *Rethinking History,* Vol. 6, no. 3 (Winter 2002); pp. 293-304.

Gabillet, Jean-Paul. *Des comics et des hommes. Histoire culturelle des comic-books aux États-Unis.* Nantes: Éditions du Temps 2005.

Gomes, Mário and Peuckert, Jan. "Memento Mori: A Portuguese Style of Melancholy". In Berninger, Mark and Jochen Ecke, Gideon Haberkorn, eds., *Comics as a Nexus of Cultures. Essays on the interplay of media, disciplines and international perspectives.* Jefferson, NC/London: McFarland 2010; pp. 116-126.

Giglioli, Daniele. *Senza Trauma. Scrittura dell'estremo e narrative del nuovo milenio.* Macerata: Quodlibet 2001.

Gil, José. *Portugal, Hoje. O medo de existir.* Lisbon: Relógio d'Água 2004.

Gilmore, Leigh. *The Limits of Autobiography. Trauma and Testimony.* Ithaca/London: Cornell University Press 2001.

Groensteen, Thierry. *Système de la bande dessinée*. Paris: Presses Universitaires de France 1999.

-- , ed. *Maîtres de la bande dessinée européenne*. Paris: Bibliothèque Nationale de France 2000.

-- . "L'enfance de l'art". *9e Art* no. 8. Angoulême/Paris: CNBDI-L'An 2 2003; pp. 72-83.

-- . *Un object culturel non identifié*. Paris: Éditions de l'An 2 2006.

-- . *Bande dessinée et narration. Système de la bande dessinée 2*. Paris: Presses Universitaires de France 2011.

-- . *M. Töpffer invente la bande dessinée*. Brussels: Les Impressions Nouvelles: 2014a.

-- . "L'hybridation graphique ou le patchwork des styles". In Gerbier, Laurent, dir., *Hybridations. Les rencontres entre du texte e de l'image*. Tours: Presses Universitaires François-Rabelais 2014b; pp. 167-175.

-- , and Benoît Peeters. *Töpffer. L'Invention de la bande dessinée*. Paris: Hermann 1994.

Grove, Laurent. "Autobiography in Early Bande Dessinée". *Bélphegor* Vol. 4, no. 1. (November 2004). URL: https://dalspace.library.dal.ca/handle/10222/47694 [last access 2013]

Hall, Stuart. "Whose heritage? Un-settling 'The Heritage'. Re-imagining the Post-nation". *Third Text*, Vol. 13, no. 49 (1999); pp. 3-13.

Harding, Jennifer, Pribram, E. Deidre, eds. *Emotions. A Cultural Studies Reader.* New York, NY/London: Routledge 2009.

Hartman, Geoffrey H. "On Traumatic Knowledge and Literary Studies." *New Literary History* Vol. 26, No. 3 (Summer, 1995), pp. 537-563.

Harvey, David C. "Heritage Pasts and Heritage Presents: temporality, meaning and the scope of heritage studies". In *International Journal of Heritage Studies*, vol. 7, no. 4 (2001); pp. 319-338.

Hatfield, Charles. *Alternative Comics. An Emerging Literature*. Jackson, MS: University press of Mississippi 2005.

Heesen, Anke te. "News, Paper, Scissors: Clippings in the Sciences and Arts Around 1920." In Daston, Lorraine, ed., *Things That Talk. Object lessons from Art and Science*. New York, NY: Zone Books 2004; pp. 297-327.

Heer, Jeet and Kent Worcester, eds. *A Comic Studies Reader*. Jackson, MI: University Press of Mississippi 2009.

Highmore, Ben. "Bitter After Taste. Affect, Food, and Social Aesthetics". Gregg, Melissa, and Gregory J. Seigworth, eds., *The Affect Theory Reader*. Durham/London: Duke University Press 2010; pgs. 118-137.

Hirsch, Marianne. "Family Pictures: *Maus*, Mourning, and Post-Memory". *Discourse* Vol. 15, No. 2, Special Issue: *The Emotions, Gender, and the Politics of Subjectivity* (Winter 1992-93), pp. 3-29.

-- . "Editor's Column: Collateral Damage". *PMLA* vol. 119. 5. October 2004; pp. 1209-1215.

-- . "Mourning and Postmemory". In Chaney, Michael A., ed. *Graphic Subjects. Critical Essays on Autobiography and Graphic Novels*. Madison, WI: The University of Wisconsin Press 2011; pp. 17-44.

-- . URL: http://www.postmemory.net/ [last access, March 9th 2013].

Huard, Pierre. "Question de méthode... 40 années de recherches sur la bande dessinée". *Critix*, nos. 8-10. Argenteuil: Bananas BD; pp. 1998-99.

Isabelinho, Domingos. "Comic's Expanded Field". In *The Crib Sheet* (2008). URL: http://thecribsheet-isabelinho.blogspot.pt/2008/10/comics-expanded-field.html [last access, February 2016]

-- . "Beyond Aliens, Mutants, and Heroes: The Hidden Face of Comics". In Moura, Pedro, ed., *Tinta nos Nervos. Banda Desenhada Portuguesa*. Lisbon: Museu Colecção Berardo 2011; pp. 73-83.

Kaplan, Ann E. *Trauma Culture. The Politics of Terror and Loss in Media and Literature*. New Brunswick, NJ/London: Rutgers University Press 2005.

Kardiner, Abram. *The Traumatic Neuroses of War*. Washington, DC: Committee on Problems of Neurotic Behavior Division of Anthropology and Psychology National Research Council 1941.

Klinkenberg, Jean-Marie, and Benoît Denis. *La littérature belge. Précis d'histoire sociale*. Brussels: Espace Nord 2005.

Krauss, Rosalind. "Sculpture in the Expanded Field". *October*, Vol. 8. (Spring, 1979); pp. 30-44.

Kukkonen, Karin. "Popular Cultural Memory. Comics, Communities and Context Knowledge". *Nordicom Review* no. 29 (2008) 2, pp. 261-273.

-- . *Contemporary Comics Storytelling*. Lincoln and London: University of Nebraska Press 2013.

Kunzle, David. *History of the Comic Strip. Volume I: The Early Comic Strip. Narrative Strips and Pictures Stories in the European Broadsheet from c. 1450 to 1825*. Berkeley, LA/London: University of California Press 1973.

-- . *History of the Comic Strip. Volume II: The Nineteenth Century*. Berkeley, LA/London: University of California Press 1990.

-- . *Father of the Comic Strip. Rodolphe Töpffer*. Jackson, MI: University Press of Mississippi 2007.

Labio, Catherine. "What's in a Name?: The Academic Study of Comics and the 'Graphic Novel'". *Cinema Journal* vol. 50, no. 3 (Spring 2011); pp. 123-126.

LaCapra, Dominick. *History and Memory After Auschwitz*. Ithaca and London: Cornell University Press 1998.

-- . *Writing History, Writing Trauma*. Baltimore and London: The Johns Hopkins University Press 2001.

Lefèvre, Pascal and Ch. Dierick, eds. *Forging a New Medium. The Comic Strip in the Nineteenth Century*. Brussels: VUB University Press, 1998.

Lejeune, Philippe. *Le pacte autobiographie*. Paris: Seuil 1975.

---- . *Je est un autre. L'Autobiographie, de la littérature aux médias.* Paris: Seuil 1980.

Lesage, Sylvain. "La bande dessinée en son miroir. Images et usages de l'album dans la bande dessinée française", in *Mémoires du livre / Studies in Book Culture*, volume 2, numéro 2, printemps 2011. URL: http://id.erudit.org/iderudit/1001764ar [last access, March 2016].

---- . "Mutation des supports, mutation des publics. La bande dessinée de la presse au livre", in *Belphégor. Littératures populaires et culture médiatique. 13-1 Distinctions That Matter/Fictions Économiques (2015)* URL: http://belphegor.revues.org/628. DOI: 10.4000/belphegor.628 [last access, November 2016].

Leventhal, Robert S. "Art Spiegelman's *Maus*: Working-Through The Trauma of the Holocaust", 1995. URL: http://www2.iath.virginia.edu/holocaust/spiegelman.html [last access, March 19th 2013].

Levinson, Jerrold. "Hybrid Art Forms." *Journal of Aesthetic Education*, vol. 18-4 (Winter 1984); pp. 5-13.

Leys, Ruth. "Traumatic Cures: Shell Shock, Janet, and the Question of Memory." In Antze, Paul, and Michael Lambek, eds., *Tense Past. Cultural Essays in Trauma and Memory.* New York, NY/London: Routledge 1996; pp. 103-145.

Lobo, Francisco Sousa. "Manta Banter - the openings of Portugal in the aftermath of the 1974 revolution". Presentation at The Carnation Revolution between African Anti-colonialism and European Rebellion, at the School of Arts of the University of London, May 22nd and 23rd 2014.

Lopes, Silvina Rodriges. "Portugal sem destino." *Como se faz um povo. Ensaios em História Contemporânea de Portugal.* José Neves, coord. Lisbon: Tinta-da-China 2010; pp. 227-239.

Lourenço, Eduardo, *Heterodoxia.* Assírio & Alvim: Lisbon 1987.

Luebke, Peter C. and Rachel DiNitto. "Maruo Suehiro's *Planet of the Jap.* Revanchist fantasy or war critique?". In Rosenbaum, Romanc, ed. *Manga and the Representation of Japanese History.* New York, NY/London: Routledge 2013; pp. 81-101.

Maigret, Éric. "Théorie des bandes débordées". In Maigret, Éric, and Stefanelli, Matteo (eds.), *La bande dessinée: une médiaculture.* Armand Colin/Ina Éditions: Paris 2012; pp. 50-70.

Mannheim, Karl. *Ideology and Utopia. Collected Works of Karl Mannheim.* Vol 1. New York, NY/London: Routledge 1997.

Marks, Laura U. *Touch. Sensuous Theory and Multisensory Media.* Minneapolis/London: University of Minnesota Press 2002.

Mao, Catherine. "L'artiste de bande dessinée et son miroir: l'autoportrait détourné". *Comicalités.* (September 2013). URL: http://comicalites.revues.org/1702. [last access, April the 5th 2014].

Matos, Álvaro Costa de. "Política e BD na I República". Communication at the 1st Conferências de Banda Desenhada em Portugal, 2011.

McCloud, Scott. *Understanding Comics. The Invisible Art.* Northhampton: Kitchen Sink Press 1993.

McKinney, Mark. "The Algerian War in *Road to America* (Baru, Thèvenet, and Ledran)". In McKinney, M. (ed.), *History and Politics in French-Language Comics and Graphic Novels.* Jackson, MI: University Press of Mississippi 2008; pp. 139-165.

— . *The Colonial Heritage of French Comics.* Liverpool: Liverpool University Press 2011.

-- . *Redrawing French Empire in Comics.* Columbus OH: The Ohio State University 2013.

Medina, J., ed. "Deus, pátria, família: ideologia e mentalidade do salazarismo". *História de Portugal dos tempos pré-históricos aos nossos dias,* vol. XII. Alfragide: Ediclube 1993.

Meskin, Aaron. "Comics as Literature?" *British Journal of Aesthetics,* vol 49-3 (2009); pp. 219-239.

Mikkonen, Kai. "Presenting Minds in Graphic Narratives". *Partial Answers* 6/2 (2008); pp. 301-321.

Miller, Ann. *Reading Bande Dessinée. Critical Approaches to French-Language Comic Strip.* Bristol, UK/Chicago, USA: Intellect 2007.

-- , and Bart Beaty, eds. *The French Comics Theory Reader.* Leuven: Leuven University Press 2014.

Miller, J. Hillis. "The Critic as Host." *Critical Inquiry,* Vol. 3, No. 3 (Spring, 1977); pp. 439-447.

Moretti, Franco. "Conjectures on World Literature." *New Left Review* no. 1. (February 2000); pp. 54-68.

Morla, Lucía Miranda. "Lisbonne en deuil, Portugal sans voix ou l'utopie de Salazar". In Alary, Viviane and Benoît Mitaine, *Lignes de front. Bande dessinée et totalitarisme.* Saint-Rémy-de-Provence: L'équinoxe 2012.

Morrison, Grant. *Supergods. What Masked Vigilantes, Miraculous Mutants, and a Sun God from Samallville can Teach Us about Being Human.* New York, NY: Spiegel & Grau 2011.

Moura, Pedro. "Bordalo leitor (e imitador) de Doré". *Jornal da Oficina do Cego* no. 1 (2010): n.p.

-- . "'To Find Places to Draw': Comics' Resistance to Insecurity". *Reconstruction* Vol. 12, No. 3 (2012a). URL: http://reconstruction.eserver.org/Issues/123/Moura.shtml

-- . "*A voz do oud*: Criação de espaços multiculturais e a assunção da voz ao "outro" na banda desenhada francófona contemporânea." *estrema. Revista Interdisciplinar de Humanidades.* (2012b.)

-- . "Ink Ghosts. Visual presence of haunted memories in comics." Presentation at *Traumatic and Haunting Images: Roles, Ethics, and Aesthetics.* Cultural Memory Studies Initiave of the Ghent University (October 2015).

Mowitt, John. "Trauma Envy". In, Bowman and Rochard Stampd, eds., The Truth of Žižek. London/New York, NY: Continuum 2007; p. 117-143.

Murray, Chris. "*Pop*aganda: Superhero Comics and Propaganda in World War Two". In Magnussen, Anne and Hans Christian Christiansen, eds., *Comics and Culture. Analytical and Theoretical Approaches to Comic.* Copenhagen: Museum Tusculanum Press 2000; pp. 141-155.

Ngai, Sianne. *Ugly Feelings*. Cambridge, MA/London: Harvard University Press 2005.

Nora, Pierre, dir. *Les lieux de mémoire*, tome 1, *La République*. Paris: Gallimard 1984.

Pagano, Ugo. "Cultural diversity, European integration and the walfare state". In Parijs, Philippe Van, ed. *Cultural Diversity Versus Economic Solidarity*. Brussels: De Boeck 2004; pp. 315-330.

Pedler, Martyn. "Suffering and Seriality: Memory, Continuity and Trauma in Monthly Superhero Adventures". URL: http://web.mit.edu/comm-forum/mit5/papers/Pedler_Suffering_and_Seriality.pdf [last accessed March 2012]

Pimentel, Irene Flunser and Luís Farinha. *Vítimas de Salazar. Estado Novo e violência política*. Lisbon: Esfera dos Livros 2007.

-- . *A História da Pide*. Lisbon: Temas e Debates 2011.

Pinto, António Costa. "O império do professor: Salazar e a elite ministerial do Estado Novo (1933-1945)". *Análise Social*, vol. xxxv., no 157, 2000; pp. 1-22.

Poletti, Anna. "Auto/Assemblage: Reading the Zine". *Biography* 31.1. 2008; pp. 85-102.

Precup, Mihaela. *Sites of Memory and Trauma in the American Graphic Memoir*. Doctoral dissertation. Under the direction of Prof. Rodica Mihăilă. Faculty of Foreign Languages and Literatures. University of Bucharest 2010.

Pulda, Molly. "Portrait of a Secret: J.R. Ackerley and Alison Bechdel". In Amihay, Ofra, and Lauren Walsh, eds., *The Future of Text and Image: Collected Essays on Literary and Visual Conjunctures*. Newcastle upon Tyne: Cambridge Scholars Publishing 2012; pp. 15-37.

Pylyser, Charlotte. "The Heirs of Frans Masereel". *Bangarang. Comics from Flanders*. Berchem: Flemish Literature Fund 2013.

Olkowski, Dorothea. "Catastrophe". In Ball, Karyn, ed., *Traumatizing Theory. The Cultural Politics of Affect In and Beyond Psychoanalysis*. New York, NY: Other Press 2007; pg. 41-65

O'Sullivan, Simon. "From Stuttering and Stammering to the Diagram: Towards a Minor Art Practice?". In Bleyen, Mieke, ed., *Minor Photography. Connecting Deleuze and Guattari to Photography Theory*. Leuven: Leuven University Press 2012; pp. 3-16.

Radstone, Susannah, "Reconceiving Binaries: the Limits of Memory", in *History Workshop Journal*, Issue 59, Spring 2005; pp. 134-150.

-- , "Trauma Theory: Contexts, Politics, Ethics", in *Paragraph*, Vol. 30, no. 1, (March 2007); pp. 9-29.

-- , "Social Bonds and Psychical Order: Testimonies". *Cultural Values*. Vol 5, no 1 (January 2001); pp. 59-78.

-- , and Katharine Hodgkin, eds. *Regimes of Memory*. New York, NY/London: Routledge 2003.

Rajagopal, Arvind. "Imperceptible Perceptions in our Technological Modernity." In Chun, Wendy Hui Kyong, and Keenan, Thomas, eds. *New Media/Old Media. A History and Theory Reader*. New York, NY/London: Routledge 2006; pp. 275-285.

Rancière, Jacques. *The Politics of Aesthetics. The Distribution of the Sensible*. Engl. trans.

by Gabriel Rockhill of *Le Partage du Sensible* (2000). London/New York, NY: Continuum 2004 (a).

-- . "Introducing Disagreement". Engl. trans. by Steve Corcoran. *Angelaki. Journal of the Theoretical Humanities*, vol. 9 no. 3, December 2004 (b); pp. 3-9.

-- . *The Emancipated Spectator*. Engl. trans. by Gregory Elliott of *Le spectateur émancipé*. London/Brooklyn, NY: Verso Books 2009.

-- . *Dissensus. On Politics and Aesthetics*. Engl. trans. and ed. Steven Corcoran. London/New York, NY: Continuum 2010.

Rappaport, Ernet A. "Beyond Traumatic Neurosis. A Psychoanalytic Study of Late Reactions to the Concentration Camp Trauma". *The International Journal of Psycho-Analysis*. Vol. 49; pp. 719-731 (1968). URL: http://www.ernestrappaport.com/traumatic%20neurosis.htm [last access, 12th November 2016].

Refaie, Elisabeth El. *Autobiographical Comics. Life Writing in Pictures*. Jackson MI: University Press of Mississippi 2013.

Rey, Jean-Michel. "Freud's Writing on Writing", Engl. trans. by G. W. Most and James Hulbert, in Felman, Shoshana, ed., *Literature and Psychoanalysis. The Question of Reading: Otherwise*. Baltimore and London: The Johns Hopkins University Press 1982; pp. 301-328.

Ribeiro, Gustavo Lins. "Economic Globalization from Below". *Etnográfica*, vol. X (2). Lisbon: Centro de Estudos de Antopologia Social/ISCTE 2006; pp. 233-249.

Ribeiro, Maria da Conceição. *A polícia política no Estado Novo*. Lisbon: Editorial Estampa 1996.

Richardson, Brian. "Time Is Out of Joint: Narrative Models and the Temporality of the Drama". *Poetics Today*, Vol. 8, No. 2 (1987); pp. 299-309.

Riegl, Aloïs. *El culto moderno a los monumentos*. Spanish transl. by Ana Pérez López of *Der moderne Denkmalkultus. Sein Wesen und seine Entstehung* (1903). Madrid: Visor 1999.

Rocha, Natércia. *Breve história da literatura para crianças em* Portugal. Lisbon: ICALP/Biblioteca Breve 1984.

Rosas, Fernando. *Salazar e o poder. A arte de saber durar*. Lisbon: Tinta-da-China 2012.

Samara, Maria Alice and Tiago Baptista. *Os cartazes na primeira república*. Tinta-da-China: Lisboa 2010.

Santos, Boaventura de Sousa. "Estado e Sociedade na Semiperiferia do Sistema Mundial: o Caso Português." *Análise Social*. No. 87/88/89 (1985); pp. 869-901.

-- . *Portugal. Ensaio contra a auto flagelação*. Coimbra: Almedina 2011.

Schlanger, Judith. *Trop dire ou trop peu. La densité littéraire*. Paris: Hermann 2016.

Schneider, Greice. *What Happens When Nothing Happens. Boredom and Everyday Life in Contemporary Comics*. Leuven: Leuven University Press 2016.

Schwab, Gabriele. *Haunting Legacies. Violent Histories and transgenerational trauma*. NY/Chichester, West Sussex: Columbia University Press 2010.

References

Silva, Marie Manuelle and Rui Malheiro. "A banda desenhada portuguesa: autores, temas e tendências". *Boletín Galego de Literatura* - "Olladas do Cómic Ibérico", no. 35 (2006); pp. 155-178.

Silverman, Kaja. *The Threshold of the Visible World*. New York, NY/London: Routledge 1996.

Smolderen, Thierry. *Naissances de la bande dessinée. De William Hogarth à Winsor McCay*. Bruxelles: Les Impressions Nouvelles 2009.

-- . "L'hybridation graphique, creuset de la bande dessinée". In Gerbier, Laurent, dir., *Hybridations. Les rencontres entre du texte e de l'image*. Tours: Presses Universitaires François-Rabelais 2014; pp. 148-165.

Sousa, Jorge Pais de. *O Fascismo Catedrático de Salazar*. Coimbra: Imprensa da Universidade de Coimbra 2011.

Stevens, Maurice. "From the Past Imperfect: Towards a Critical Trauma Theory." *Letters. The Semiannual Newsletter of the Robert Penn Warren Center for the Humanities* vol. 17, no. 2 (Spring 2009); pp. 1-5. URL: http://www.vanderbilt.edu/rpw_center/Letters/ls09a.htm [last access, May 9th 2014].

Tomlie, Jane. "Introduction", in Tolmie, J., ed. *Drawing From Life. Memory and Subjectivity in Comic Art*. Jackson, MI: University Press of Mississippi 2013; pp. vii-xxiii.

Tal, Kali. *Worlds of Hurt: Reading the Literatures of Trauma*. 3rd revision (1st editon Cambridge University Press: 1996). URL: http://kalital.com/Text/Worlds/index.html [last access, March 2013].

Töpffer, Rodolphe. *The Complete Comic Strips*. Kunzle, David, ed. Jackson, MI: University Press of Mississippi 2007.

Trondheim, Lewis. *Désoeuvré*. Paris: L'Association 2005.

Vann, J. Don. *Victorian Novels in Serial*. The Modern Language Association of American: New York, NY 1985.

Walker, Janet. *Trauma Cinema. Documenting Incest and the Holocaust*. Berkeley, Los Angeles, London: University of California Press 2005.

-- . "The Traumatic Paradox. Autobiographical documentary and the psychology of memory." In Hodgkin, Katharine, and Susannah Radstone, eds. *Memory, History, Nation. Contested Pasts*. Ew Brunswick and London: Transaction Publishers 2006; pp. 104-119.

Warhol, Robyn. "The Space Between: A Narrative Approach to Alison Bechdel's *Fun Home*". *College Literature*, vol. 38., no. 3 (Summer 2011); pp. 1-20.

Raymond, Williams. *The Long Revolution*. Orchard Park, NY/Hertfordshire: Broadview Press 2001 [1st. ed., 1961].

Zink, Rui. *O Humor de Bolso de José Vilhena*. Oeiras: Celta 2001.

Žižek, Slavoj. *The Plague of Fantasies*. London/New York, NY: Verso 2008.

Zunshine, Lisa. "What to Expect When You Pick Up a Graphic Novel". *SubStance* # 124, vol. 40, no. 1 (2011); pp. 114-134.